Management of Insurance Operations

institute of financial services

Management of Insurance Operations

Ian Bates
and
Derek Atkins

Institute of Financial Services
IFS House
4-9 Burgate Lane
Canterbury
Kent
CT1 2XJ
United Kingdom

T 01227 818649
F 01227 479641
E editorial@ifslearning.com
W www.ifslearning.com

Institute of Financial Services publications are published by The Chartered Institute of Bankers, a non-profit making registered educational charity.

Typeset by John Smith
Printed by Antony Rowe Ltd, Wiltshire

ISBN 0-85297-715-8

ifs institute of financial services

Preface

The objectives of this book are:

- to explain why property and casualty (P+C) insurance is different, in a management perspective, from other types of business;
- to look at the application of general management theory to a P+C insurance operation;
- to identify the management issues and challenges that the special nature of P+C insurance introduces and potential management approaches to them.

This book, by necessity of time and space, will not and cannot:

- attempt to teach the detailed theory underlying pricing, underwriting, risk assessment, claims management, reserving, or any other technical skill associated with P+C insurance or business service functions such as Finance or IT;
- provide an answer to all management problems and issues experienced in an insurance business;
- teach general management theory.

It is assumed that the reader of this book will already possess:

- a general understanding of current management theory;
- a general understanding of the nature of P+C insurance in a regulated environment.

What this book will do is:

- highlight where and how P+C insurance is different from other business types including:
  - the nature of the market
  - the nature of the products
  - the impact of law and regulation
  - the uncertainty of outcome at point of sale
  - the uncertainty presented by changes in the external environment;

- explain how general management theory and the high-level, theoretical concepts relating to underwriting, claims reserving, etc can be applied to the management of a generic P+C insurance operation;
- highlight a range of additional challenges and issues, both generic and specific to P+C insurance, that face management and propose approaches to how these can be addressed;
- provide a broad range of examples and illustrations to draw out the issues and challenges that management of a P+C business presents, how the theory can be applied in practice, and what can happen if the basic rules are ignored.

The reader will therefore gain key insights into the management of a P+C insurance operation in a complex and ever-changing environment, and be provided with a toolkit of theoretical and practical approaches and the questions necessary to determine how effectively a P+C business is being managed and is performing.

Ian Bates, Derek Atkins
2003

Acknowledgements

The authors wish to thank the large number of organizations and individuals that made important contributions to this book. They include Boston Consulting Group, McKinsey and Co, The Henley Centre, CREATE, Royal and Sun Alliance, Aon, Crawfords, London Business School, City University Business School, IBM, The Centre for Future Studies, Phil Bell and Kieran Flynn, and Julie Watts for doing most of the typing.

Contents

	Preface	v
	Acknowledgements	vii
	How to use this book	xi
	Additional reading	xii
1	Introduction and scene setting	1
2	Insurance: basic principles	15
3	The structure of the insurance market	27
4	An introduction to the legal and regulatory framework for insurance	41
5	Strategic planning in insurance operations	55
6	Commonly applied insurance strategies	79
7	Introduction to the value chain	99
8	Insurance products	109
9	The management of the front end – 1. Market analysis and segmentation	121
10	The management of the front end – 2. Practice	137
11	The management of underwriting – 1. Key concepts	153

12	The management of underwriting – 2. Reinsurance and ART	169
13	The management of underwriting – 3. Practice	175
14	The management of claims	191
15	The management of reserves	207
16	The management of business services	217
17	Cross-business challenges	235
18	Assessing the profitability and management effectiveness of an insurance operation	261
19	Conclusion	283
20	Glossary of terms	293
	Index	321

How to use this book

This book is designed to be read in support of other teaching, either college based or distance learning. It is laid out so that, over a 20-week semester, it will have taken you on a logical path through the subject and provided you with a good introduction to the challenges and issues associated with the management of insurance operations.

At the beginning of each chapter objectives are defined, which link back to the syllabus.

Also, at the end of each chapter, is a select bibliography. These include valuable references in their own right, and have been chosen to introduce you to useful books and journals.

Please do not attempt to read them all – it would take several years! However, you should try to read some of them, together with your own selections from a good business library. This will broaden your understanding of the subject, and may provide a very different perspective.

The references are a mixture of theory and practice, which very much reflects insurance as it is today. It is a practical profession which is underpinned by theories which, in some cases, are quite complex.

Sometimes, of course, real life does not follow what was expected in theory. In these circumstances you should heed the advice of the army officer teaching recruits to map read:

> 'If you should discover a discrepancy between the map and the terrain, you may safely assume that the terrain is correct.'

Additional reading

The reader should try and broaden his or her knowledge and understanding of the P+C insurance market by:

i) Reading the national press, in particular, but not limited to, the business pages.
ii) Reading insurance market and trade publications (in the UK market these include: *The Post, Insurance Times,* Datamonitor reports and Geneva Association papers).
iii) Monitoring trade associations' (eg ABI, ILU), regulators' (eg FSA) and market association (eg Lloyd's) web sites for new developments, proposals, announcements, special reports, analyses, etc.
iv) Gaining access to the output of investment analysts who periodically produce cross-industry analysis on key issues (liability, asbestos, reinsurance, capital, etc) in addition to their more specific individual company analysis.
    The authors have found the following UK market investment analysts' output to be of value: CSFB, SSSB, HSBC, DrKW.
    (If you are an employee of a financial services company it should be possible for you to gain access to the output of such analysts from within your company. If you are not an employee of a financial services company you may have to apply directly to the investment analyst to request access to such information.)
v) A very useful book covering the theory of insurance is:

    J Francois Outreville
    Theory and Practice of Insurance
    Kluwer Academic Publishers 1998
    ISBN 0-7923-9996-X

This book is recommended as a starting point for those wishing to delve more deeply into the detailed theory behind how insurance is conducted.

One

Introduction and scene setting

Objectives

On completion of this chapter, and wider personal research, the reader should be able to:

- understand the value of insurance to an economy;
- appreciate how some of the major changes in the business environment are impacting insurance, including: demographics, convergence, globalization, consolidation, technology and liability.

The modern insurance operation is an extremely complex organization, reflecting the multidisciplinary nature of insurance itself. Senior insurance managers, like their counterparts in banking, need to have a broad base of knowledge and experience, and an understanding of the business within which they work in order to understand the full implications of their decisions and actions.

Insurance operations employ a range of technical and professional specialists: actuaries, underwriters, technical claims managers, risk surveyors, marketeers, investment managers, economists, accountants, IT specialists, HR experts, etc. The senior managers themselves will, very likely, have come up through one or more of these disciplines, but at some stage they will become a manager of managers. Their need then for breadth does not mean that they must be an expert in all disciplines. They cannot be expected to be able to do the work of those below them, or in other parts of the organization, but they need to understand the core elements of what is done and why it is done, across the many disciplines, so that they are then able to apply appropriate and relevant challenges as part of their management role.

This book is designed to provide the foundation for this process.

1.1 An overview of P+C insurance

> **The value of insurance**
>
> 'Insurance: the services it provides are crucial to the running of a modern economy. Insurance allows both businesses and individuals to minimize the impact of financial loss resulting from the occurrence of future events and enables policyholders to organize a household budget or plan business activities with greater security. Without insurance many aspects of a free market economy would simply not function.'
>
> PricewaterhouseCoopers

While most people are aware of the P+C insurance market in general, through exposure to the more common products and household-name insurers for those products that most of us buy to protect our assets and lifestyle, very few actually understand either the nature of insurance itself or the complexities involved in managing a successful P+C insurer. In the rest of this book we shall look at the key issues and areas which insurance managers need to focus attention on to ensure the long-term viability of their business.

Firstly, let us consider the nature of insurance itself. Unlike other types of company a P+C insurer does not:

- manufacture a tangible product out of raw materials, as does an engineer
- sell tangible products produced by others, as does a supermarket
- provide a financial service that makes day-to-day activity in a developed economy easier, as does a retail bank or credit card issuer.

A P+C insurer's 'product' consists of a complex, conditional promise (generally on the following basis):

> In return for a premium from the insured – *if* within an agreed time period, an event of a specified (or not excluded) nature occurs, *and* the insured suffers loss or damage, *then* the insurer will take certain actions and/or make payments according to the detailed terms, conditions and limits set out in the insurance contract.

This is based on the general principle that, at the time of entering into the insurance contract, neither the insured nor the insurer knows with certainty whether an insured event will occur within the time period causing damage to the insured and, if it does, what the magnitude will be.

> **The challenge for the insurance marketeer**
>
> 'Insurance isn't soap, it isn't baked beans, it isn't Mars bars. It's a piece of paper with a promise to pay, valid for only one year, which can be rather costly. It offers no immediate consumer satisfaction – it isn't glamorous – at best it's a painful necessity.'
>
> Alan Everson 1985

The fundamental value proposition of a P+C insurer is therefore the transfer of risk from the insured to the insurer for an agreed price, the premium.

An insurer will make a profit if it knows how to assess the probability and magnitude of losses, is able to charge appropriate premiums, and can build up a large enough pool of separate risks to overcome the randomness of events. This process is fairly straightforward in a stable environment, as past experience can be used as a reasonably reliable indicator of future claims. The real problems arise when the environment becomes more volatile, risk patterns change and discontinuities occur.

Underwriting (the professional assessment of the probability and magnitude of losses and the calculation of premiums in respect of individual risks) never was an exact science, but recent years have certainly exposed its limitations. A survey conducted by the Centre for Future Studies in the aftermath of the World Trade Center disaster spelt this out. It concluded, 'insurance companies are failing to assess and model the complex risks and exposure they face'.

The mismatch between the quality of underwriting and the current volatile environment is, in general, fully accepted by insurers. At the time of writing there is a unprecedented effort by companies to build the core skills of risk assessment, underwriting and claims management going forward. But this does not stop the impact of any previous underwriting decisions and inadequacies (potentially going back decades) from impacting the insurer's results for many years to come.

1.2 Challenges

In addition to the complexity of the nature of risk and the insurance contracts themselves, insurers face challenges similar to other companies, but with particular variations specific to insurance. Many will be covered in detail later in the book, but at this point, by way of an introduction to P+C insurance operations as a whole, we should like to highlight the following selection.

1.2.1 Supply and demand

Supply

Barriers to entry in insurance are relatively low compared with those in some industries, eg motor car manufacturing. The main exceptions are:

- heavily state-controlled markets, eg China prior to its recent accession to the WTO, and agreement to deregulate its markets;
- niche markets requiring very specific competencies, eg professional indemnity.

In general terms there is therefore a tendency towards an excess of supply over demand. Prices are thus kept down and margins continually squeezed.

Demand

There has been growing demand for general insurance across the world. This is because the demand for insurance results from increasing economic activity and wealth, there being a steadily increasing number of cars, houses, factories, etc to be protected. There is a strong relationship between premium income and a country's Gross Domestic Product. Not surprisingly, the major economies of the USA, Japan, Germany, the UK and France dominate the sector and represent almost three-quarters of the $2,000bn total global P+C spend, but these represent relatively mature markets. More rapid growth has been experienced in the emerging economies of Latin America and Asia.

The split between personal and commercial insurance is approximately 50/50, although this is likely to move more towards 60/40 in the foreseeable future. The reason is that increasing personal wealth is driving demand in personal lines whereas commercial is subject to competition from other risk-handling mechanisms such as self-insurance, higher deductibles and alternative risk transfer. In the USA, for example, perhaps 20% of potential business from larger commercial customers has been lost to substitution from these alternative protection mechanisms.

Demographics also affect the demand for insurance. Although it is always dangerous to make extrapolations from demographic and sociological trends, factors such as ageing populations in the mature economies, the breakdown of the traditional family into more units, the increased fear of crime, all potentially increase demand. Perhaps the biggest factor is the view that state provision of welfare, health care and pensions in many countries is unsustainable in the long run and this provides opportunities for the private sector. This has had a profound influence on some insurers who are changing the balance of their product and geographical portfolios in anticipation (although the customers who most need cover as a result of the government's actions are often those least able to pay for it).

1.2.2 Convergence

Insurance can be regarded as one approach to meeting some of the financial needs of personal and commercial customers as shown in Figure 1.1.

Figure 1.1

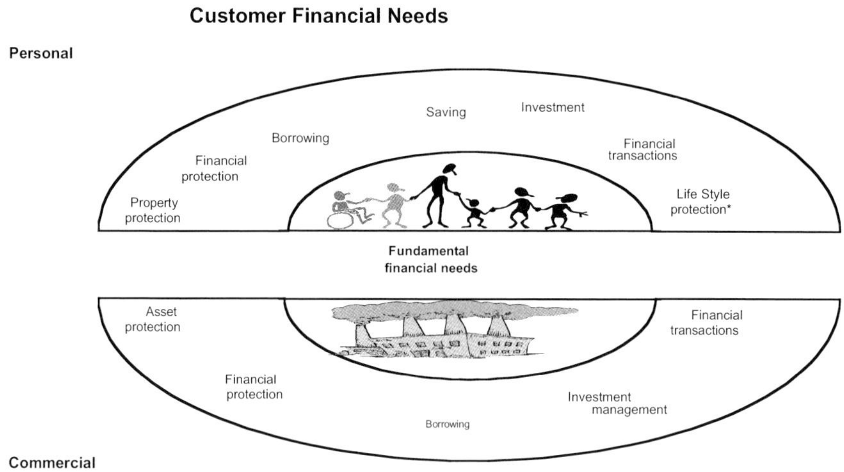

* Note: Lifestyle protection includes
- pension
- health
- long-term care

The other main suppliers of products to meet these needs have been the banks (including the building societies) and investment companies. In the past these three main sectors of the financial services industry tended to operate separately, kept apart by regulation and management choice. They provided their own product-focused solutions for the customer.

Figure 1.2

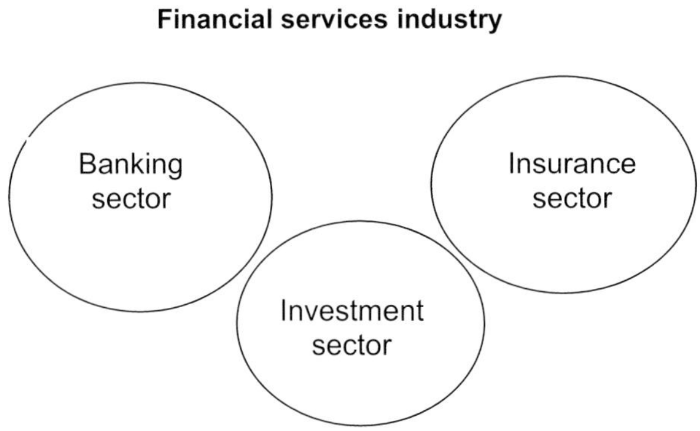

Where a company in one sector wished to provide complementary products from other sectors these were supplied via the agency mechanism, eg general insurers provided household cover via banks. However, since deregulation initiatives began in the late 1980s, the boundaries between insurance and other financial services have become increasingly blurred.

Figure 1.3

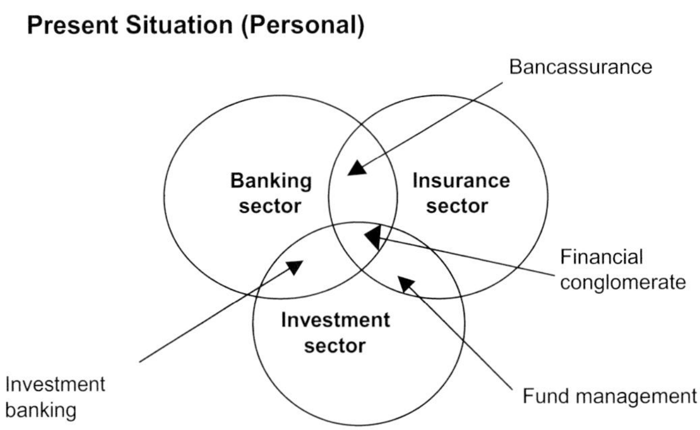

Professor Gerry Dickinson, City University

For personal customers there has been a movement towards greater convergence driven by a desire to build on customer relationships and lower the costs of delivery, both of which have been made possible by advances in information technology.

Some companies prefer to remain specialized. Others have moved into the domain of other segments. Bancassurance is one such interface where companies are providing both banking and insurance products.

For commercial customers there has been less change with banks tending to become more interested in providing insurance propositions to the small/medium enterprise (SME) sector and providing risk financing for the very biggest customers.

Convergence

'The distinction between an insurance company, a bank and an investment house is blurring. Frontiers between universal banks and insurance companies are dissolving as bancassurance expands in scope; banks and asset management houses are scrabbling to grow in businesses traditionally dominated by insurers. The distribution of life products through banks is already commonplace; the sale of property and casualty insurance through the same channel is starting to gather pace. Asset management is emerging as a business in its own right.'

McKinsey Quarterly 1998 No.3

How the convergence of financial services will develop in the future is not clear, although assembling product offerings from different sectors is becoming much easier using Internet technology.

1.2.3 Globalization

Insurance was one of the first of the international industries. Two centuries ago in the early 1800s, Phoenix Assurance already had business interests in Europe, North and South America, Asia and Africa.

Genuine globalization, on the other hand, is very different from trading in many countries. It is best defined as: responding to common customer needs using common delivery and support processes across a number of territories. The potential for globalization has become a reality only comparatively recently due to:

- improvements in communication technology
- deregulation and reduction of protectionism
- breakdown of the old communist empires
- creation of common trading areas, eg EU, ASEAN, NAFTA, Mercosur.

The degree to which globalization occurs varies considerably between industries. It is much easier to achieve in, say, manufactured goods or food and drink than in complex financial services propositions, where local business practice, distribution and law may differ.

Insurance companies are attracted to globalization in order to:

- service the local needs of their multinational customers
- derive profit streams from local economies
- spread risk (avoid overexposure to just a few national markets)

In practice, very few are likely to succeed. Many start from having a presence in many countries but adding value to local operations can be extremely elusive.

In insurance there appears to be a greater opportunity to have common, worldwide business models and propositions to offer the multinationals and larger commercial customers than to personal and SME customers where local differences are more marked. Nevertheless, all types of business potentially could benefit from activities such as knowledge sharing, common back office support, pooled purchasing leverage and consistent management processes.

Globalization in insurance

'Globalization is occurring in all industries, as companies implement organizational structures that cross borders. We, as a service industry, must follow our customers and so commercial insurance is well on the way to becoming a global business. On the other hand, personal lines, both life and general, is still very different for a variety of regulatory, legal, cultural and distribution reasons. Nevertheless, we are discovering that even here there is much that can be shared between national operations.'

Paul Spencer, RSA, CII Conference 2000

Technology and globalization

'The universal availability, access and ability to locate technology anywhere in the world has brought:

- universal availability and access to information; and
- the ability to locate production and service functions to optimum advantage at the organization's discretion.

This universal availability has however, so far failed to overcome:

- language barriers;
- cultural barriers; and
- the need to match hardware, software and human capability.

It is also necessary to understand that a global website presence does not mean that the organization itself is global.'

Richard Pettinger, *Global Organizations*, Capstone Publications 2002

1.2.4 Consolidation

The league table of the top ten UK general insurers at the beginning of the 1990s had changed considerably by the early part of the new millennium. Three have merged to form Aviva, another two to become Royal & Sun Alliance, and three of the remaining companies have been acquired by larger European insurers AXA, Zurich and Allianz. This pattern of consolidation has been repeated in many other countries.

Consolidation has not been restricted to insurance companies. Over the same period three brokers, Marsh, Aon and Willis Corroon, have taken over sixteen of their rivals and between them now control 40% of commercial insurance business in the English-speaking markets.

Consolidation occurs in a market when scale economies become highly attractive. The previous wave in financial services was in the 1960s when computerization was introduced and only the largest companies could afford and benefit from data processing. So what has driven the most recent wave? The key factors would appear to include:

- achieving the size and geographical spread necessary for globalization
- competitive pressures in the mature markets
- new technology helping to overcome diseconomies of scale
- corporate customers choosing to deal only with the stronger financial institutions.

The result of multiple mergers and acquisitions is complexity

Most large insurance operations are the end product of numerous mergers and acquisitions which have occurred over many years.

As a result, they tend to end up becoming unfocused and having increasing internal complexity, including duplication of systems, products, processes, etc. Eventually they reach a point where they cannot afford to carry this degree of complexity because it inhibits the ability to grow and develop the business, and produces diseconomies of scale. When this happens they are challenged to undergo the difficult and complex process of simplification, which involves concentrating on fewer products, systems, processes and channels, introducing more standardization and outsourcing non-core activities.

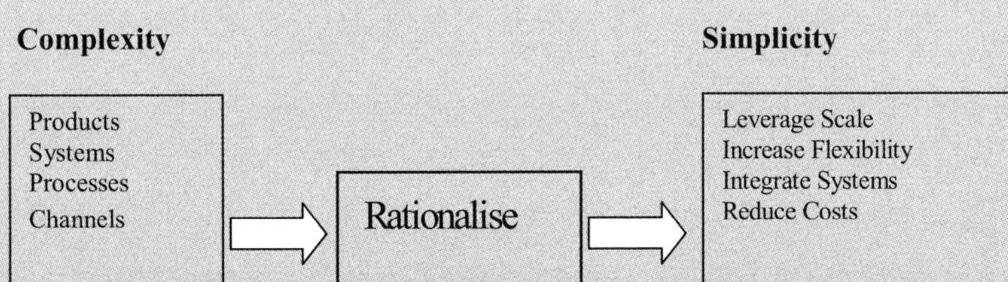

Diseconomies of scale

Large insurance companies 'can be hard to manage efficiently, particularly those that have grown up through a series of acquisitions and mergers. Often firms continue to operate multiple legacy systems, and face ongoing system integration problems, so production of consolidated management information is unreliable. This hampers the effective running of the group from the centre. The parts of the group may also have diverse types of business, structure, and culture, which again may make centralized control difficult and lead to poor financial and underwriting discipline.'

Managing Risks: Practical lessons from recent 'failures' of EU Insurers

William McDonnell, FSA 2002

1.2.5 Government/Regulatory action

As we have seen in the aftermath of recent corporate scandals, regulation, whether specific to insurers or more widespread, such as Corporate Governance or Sarbanes-Oxley, tends to increase as time passes, and very rarely decreases. By its very nature insurance tends to be more heavily regulated than many other industries.

Governments across the world frequently intervene in the insurance market, because it is a critical part of the nation's economy and an important way of protecting citizens and businesses from risk. They will normally require that all active insurers are formally authorized to trade within the country and are subject to local regulation and law. They may impose taxes, make certain types of insurance compulsory, prevent discrimination against high-risk individuals (eg so called 'red lining' in potential flood areas), increase bodily injury awards, or change the regulatory framework in response to the changing business environment or consumer pressures.

1.2.6 Technology

Along with all other industries, insurers must respond to the challenges presented by new technology such as the major advances in digital communications technology over the last few years, including the Internet, mobile phones, digital TV, etc. Insurers must look not only at the way they themselves use these new technologies, but also at how their customers, suppliers and business partners will use them and expect to be able to use them when communicating with the insurer.

An additional problem that insurers face is a result of history. As mass processors of monetary data, insurers have been leading users of IT since the early days of business computing. As a result, many long-established companies carry a 'legacy' of systems and processes that have evolved to support the core underwriting, claims and administration activities over decades. The problems have been compounded by successive waves of merger and acquisition activity, whereby new systems have been taken on and integrated without switching off/closing down other systems, so increasing the complexity. The industry is now in the situation where, despite the need to adapt to the new demands of the marketplace, over half the IT spend and most of the internal competencies are allocated to maintaining a creaking infrastructure.

The legacy not only adds cost but also makes insurers slow to react. The reason that the UK composites were unable to respond to the revolutionary tactics of Direct Line (introducing large-scale telesales) was not so much that they underestimated the threat, but that they were too cumbersome to change with the speed necessary to compete effectively. Unless the large, existing players are able to become more nimble they will be vulnerable to attack from new entrants who, to a great extent, are able to select where they compete and can adopt simpler business models and more up-to-date technology.

The challenge of technology developments

'Operationally, substantial problems and inefficiencies remain (in the P+C industry). New technologies present huge opportunities requiring huge investment, and present major transformational challenges.'

McKinsey 2002

And finally, having looked at some challenges that many other industries also face, we come to one of the big challenges facing the insurance industry in particular, and, increasingly, governments and national legal systems.

1.2.7 Liability

Rapid developments in consumerism have led to a 'compensation culture' developing in many countries, in particular the USA, whereby people are not prepared, as they used to be, to accept the consequences of accidents. As a result, liability claims have increased exponentially in both size and frequency.

The situation has been made more difficult for insurers through the advent of class actions (in commercial liability) and the contingent fee system (for both personal and commercial liability), whereby lawyers take a percentage of the court awards if successful.

Because of the long-term nature of many commercial liability policies, and historically vague wordings, claims are being made today against policies written perhaps decades ago for risks that could not have been envisaged at the time of underwriting. Improbable though it may seem, there is now a small, but active profession of 'insurance archaeologists' who research old liability policies in order to support potential claims.

The best known areas of large-scale liability claims are the industrial diseases (asbestosis, deafness, etc) but there are many emerging risks such as stress, abuse, electromagnetic radiation (mobile phones), passive smoking and genetically modified organisms. But there are also increasing numbers of 'injury' claims being made against the liability sections of more everyday insurance products such as motor and household. In the UK, both the number of claims and average amount of compensation for 'whiplash' injury has increased significantly in recent years.

The increase in both number and nature of liability claims, and the impact of the awards being given by the courts, is challenging many insurers to consider whether they can afford to continue to offer this type of cover, and has driven up premiums considerably in the last few years. The challenge, for both governments and society at large, is that liability insurance is often a legal requirement for businesses to operate, yet the premium increases necessary to meet the claims being faced by the insurance companies are threatening the viability of many businesses. Society needs either to rein back the 'compensation culture' in some way, or to accept the cost that such a culture transfers onto society as a whole through increased insurance costs or businesses having to close through not being able to afford the premiums for liability cover.

This will be a significant challenge to the P+C insurance industry as a whole over the coming years.

Select bibliography

L Van der Berghe, K Verweire *Convergence in the Financial Services Industry,* Geneva Papers in Risk and Insurance Vol 26, No 2, April 2001.

D Kessler *Anticipating and Managing Risks in the 21st Century*, Geneva Papers on Risk and Insurance Vol 26, No 1, Jan 2001.

G Taranto *The Contribution of Insurance to the UK Economy,* Insurance Trends, ABI April 2000.

Is there a Single European Insurance Market? Insurance Trends, ABI Jan 1999.

E Kist *Integrated Financial Services – A Framework for Success: Synergies in Insurance, Banking and Asset Management,* Geneva Papers on Risk and Insurance Vol 26, No 3, July 2001.

Richard Lynch *Corporate Strategies,* Pitman 1997, Chapter 4.

R Carter *The UK Insurance Industry – Retrospect and Prospect,* Journal of the Society of Fellows, Vol13, part 1, July 1998, CII.

Two

Insurance: basic principles

Objectives

On completion of this chapter, and wider personal research, the reader should be able to:

- understand the basic principles underlying P+C insurance;
- describe key aspects, including insurability of risk, how insurance works, utmost good faith, indemnity and insurable interest.

Having looked at an overview of insurance management issues in the previous chapter it is important, before we move on, to confirm some of the basic principles that govern the nature and conduct of insurance.

2.1 Why, what and how?

Why do we need insurance?

Risk in some form or other is always with us. Whatever we do, risk is always present, whether it be simply crossing the road, the risk that your house or other possessions might be damaged by fire, flood, lightning or earthquake, the risk of having an accident while driving, or any other chance of misfortune occurring to our person or our possessions.

Whether openly acknowledged or not, risk is an inseparable part of life and it determines the very way we live.

What can be done about risk?

We cannot stop things like lightning and earthquakes. So we must accept that they may occur. However, for other types of risk we can take action:

- We can take steps to reduce risk: cross the road at the crossing, build houses out of non-flammable materials.
- We can seek to avoid some risks: you can avoid your house being flooded by building it on a hilltop.
- We can share the risk with someone else and thereby share any loss.
- We can distribute or spread risk: one overloaded ship is more likely to sink than three ships carrying the same load between them (and also the risk of all three ships sinking is far less likely than any one ship sinking).
- Risk can be transferred: film actors transfer the risks in dangerous scenes to stunt men.

These are ways in which we can deal with risk, but few of them get rid of all risk completely.

When risks occur one or more of these is likely to result:

- Loss
- Damage
- Injury
- Liability (for loss, damage or injury to others)

Insurance protects people against losing financially when a risk occurs. Without insurance life would be entirely different – there would probably be fewer houseowners (who would want to buy a house knowing that he or she would be financially ruined if the house was destroyed by fire?). Similarly, there might be fewer businesses: there could possibly be less trade with other countries – few people would want to own ships, to import and export goods, knowing that they would lose hundreds of thousands of pounds whenever one of their ships sank; consequently, each country would have to try to grow most of its own food. In short, progress would be stifled. Our society without insurance is unimaginable, because insurance has grown out of one of the needs of an increasingly complex society such as ours – the need for protection.

The desire for protection in various forms has been with us since the beginning of civilization, eg the hiring of bodyguards for protection against robbers on a journey, because, once value has been created, men have always looked for ways to protect it. We could not get along without insurance: because as it protects us it encourages progress.

2.2 What is Insurance?

We have seen that there are a number of ways in which we can respond to risk. Insurance is a response to risk. Insurance cannot, for example, stop lightning from striking houses, but it can protect against the financial loss that an occurrence such as this entails.

It is at least 2000 years since merchants began to pool resources to protect themselves from the financial risks of hazardous trading voyages. A more scientific approach appeared in the UK around the turn of the 18th century with the emergence of Lloyd's and the early insurance companies such as the Sun Fire Office and the Royal Exchange Assurance. Such a long history has meant that what we now know as insurance is based on well-established market practice and an abundance of case law.

The basic principle underlying insurance is that of risk transfer. The insured exchanges the certainty of a premium for the uncertainty of a possible loss. The insurer creates a common pool from such premiums to meet losses and cover operating expenses and profit. As, in theory, the law of large numbers will apply, the insurer has a greater certainty in predicting the result and thus accurately setting the premiums. Pooling therefore lowers the risk and hence the average cost to those potentially exposed to loss. This is the main added value that an insurance company sells to its policyholders.

The law of large numbers

'Underlying the operation of an insurer is the law of large numbers (also known as the law of averages). The operation of the law of large numbers permits insurers to predict their ultimate losses more accurately, thereby enabling them to charge an adequate premium.'

American Institute for Chartered Casualty Underwriters

Looking at the five possible actions in response to risk noted above, what role can insurance/the insurer potentially play?

- Risk reduction
- Risk avoidance

} responsibility of the insured, but advice may be given by the insurer on how best to achieve this

- Risk sharing
- Risk spreading
- Risk transfer

} insurance can provide all of these

Selecting the risks to be insured and determining equitable premiums that reflect the probability and magnitude of potential loss to the pool forms the basis of the profession of underwriting.

Most risks can be insured, some even where financial loss does not always follow. The loss of, say, an eye, a limb, or a life, does not necessarily cause financial loss, but insurance companies will still pay money for such a loss, because this is the only means they have of trying to ease the burden.

Some risks cannot be insured. Broadly speaking, insurance gives protection only against loss resulting from risk occurrences whose likely incidence can be forecast by reliance on past statistical patterns. For example, the number of fires that are likely to occur in a given period can be forecast by analysing and projecting statistical trends; but losses caused by changes in fashion are not recorded and, therefore, cannot be forecast – in any case, forecasting the likelihood of such a risk occurring would be practically impossible, because of its inherent instability.

Note on Statistics

A significant amount of the theory and practice of insurance is based around statistics and statistical analysis. It is not within the scope of this book to examine statistical methods in any detail. However, there are several aspects of the subject that the manager of an insurance operation needs to be familiar with.

- The *least squares* method is commonly used in reserving to estimate the development of claims in future years.
- The *normal distribution,* with the attendant measures of standard deviation and confidence limits, and *Poisson* distribution are used in assessing average claims costs and frequency.
- Other probability distribution methods such as *binomial, log normal* and *Pareto* are also used, but more commonly by risk managers, analysing the risks of their own organizations.

Readers wishing to explore the subject further should read Chapter 5 of Outreville (see Additional Reading at the front of this book) and some of the many publications of the Institute and Faculty of Actuaries.

2.3 What risks are insurable?

In practice, almost anything is insurable at a price, but there are certain characteristics that an underwriter needs to bear in mind. Over the years there have been many instances where these have been forgotten and very often serious financial consequences have arisen. The main characteristics of an insurable risk are as follows.

a) Pure Risks

The risk should be a pure risk, ie one that results only in a loss to the insured person or company. Speculative or trading risks, which could result in a loss or gain as a result of normal trading activity, eg foreign exchange dealing, are not generally insurable. Other risk management methods such as hedging should be used.

The danger of insuring trading risks

There is a strong body of opinion against insuring trading risks such as those associated with fluctuations in market prices. The logic is that these risks form a core part of a company management's responsibilities, and are more properly retained within their business, or perhaps hedged within their industry. It is self-evident that an insurers' understanding of another industry's trading risks will be imperfect, so making risk assessment difficult and leaving it exposed to the vagaries of the business's trading policy.

This was amply illustrated in the case of domestic mortgage indemnity, DMI. UK insurers have traditionally provided this trading risk cover to mortgage lenders for losses incurred when selling-off repossessed houses when mortgagees have defaulted. This had been stable, profitable business for many years until an economic boom in the late 1980s triggered a rapid rise in house prices. Mortgage lenders advanced loans often in excess of their lending policies, assuming prices would continue to rise. In some cases mortgages in excess of 100% of the house price were granted. However, the optimism was short lived. In the sharp recession that followed, house prices collapsed, leaving millions of home owners in negative equity (their house value being less than the outstanding mortgage loan). Thousands defaulted, forcing the lenders to repossess the houses and sell them off at the bottom of the market. Where the sale price was lower than the outstanding mortgage, the DMI insurance made up the shortfall. The total loss to the insurers was eventually in excess of £2 bn, compared to total premiums received over the previous 10 years of around £100 million.

b) Determinable

The potential loss should be quantifiable in financial terms.

c) Fortuitous

There must be an element of randomness about the risk. For example, a deliberate act of the insured or something inevitable such as wear and tear is not fortuitous and so should not be the subject of insurance. One obvious exception is death. Life assurers take the view that death is inevitable but the timing is fortuitous.

d) Interest

The insured must have a legally recognized relationship with the loss, eg ownership of the property damaged. Before this concept of 'insurable interest' was introduced, 18th century gamblers used to be able to take out policies on the life of the king or other public figures.

e) Homogeneity

To enable an insurer to create a pool and calculate the probability of a loss there needs to be a large number of units exposed to similar risks. One-off risks such as the apocryphal film star's legs are extremely difficult to rate, although a market does exist for such contingency insurance.

f) Independence

Although an insurer requires homogeneity to create the pool, the individual units exposed should, as far as possible, be independent of each other, so that no single event may effect a large number of them at the same time and so create a catastrophe loss. Again, market practice does permit insurers to accept build-up of catastrophe exposure, which they then mitigate via reinsurance.

g) Public policy

Finally, it is clearly against public policy that someone should insure the benefits of a crime. The courts would undoubtedly declare such a contract to be illegal.

Insurance is therefore a means whereby the burden of risk can be transferred from the shoulders of individuals and organizations onto the broader shoulders of insurance companies.

2.4 How does insurance work?

A fundamental principle governing insurance is the concept of a fund or pool. The insurance fund or pool is the sum of money created by a collection of premiums, and is used to pay for insured losses and the insurer's expenses. Insurers rely on the expectation that the total value of the losses will be less than the total value of the premiums less expenses. The heart of this concept is that, while many people pay for protection against risks, only a few of them will be unfortunate enough to suffer loss and claim on the fund.

> '...the loss lighteth rather easily on the many than heavily on the few...'

These words, taken from an English Act of Parliament passed in 1601, provide an ideal summary of what insurance is, and from this viewpoint insurance may be seen as a way of spreading, or distributing risk. In other words, a large number of people make contributions to a common fund in order to make good the losses of the minority, who will receive compensation from the fund.

How do insurers know that only a relatively small proportion of the risks they undertake will materialize? How do they know that all the losses they insure against will not result in claims? The answer is simple – they don't; but over the years of experience they have accumulated statistics and knowledge, and using these they can make forecasts of how many losses are likely to occur in any given period of the immediate future. Once they have done this they can determine the size of the fund required in order to meet the losses; it follows, broadly speaking, that the size of premiums to be charged can be calculated from this.

Example

Imagine an isolated group of 2,000 factories. Each factory is worth £1m and each is insured for £1m. Based on previous experience, on average, **two** factories burn down accidentally every year. It is not known which two factories will be destroyed, but the historical statistics indicate the probability of two burning down.

1. If the losses are to be borne by all the factory-owners (2,000) through insurance, how much money is needed in the fund? (2 losses)		£2,000,000
How much must each factory-owner's contribution (premium) to the fund be?	$\frac{2,000,000}{2,000}$	£1,000
2. If each factory was worth £1.2m what would each premium need to be?	$\frac{2,400,000}{2,000}$	£1,200

The larger the risk, the more you pay in premium.

3. If each factory is worth £1m but it is likely that each year **three** will burn down, perhaps because they produce highly flammable goods and are, therefore, more likely to be destroyed by fire, then how much must be in the fund? (3 losses)	£3,000,000
How much is each premium?	£1,500

The greater the risk, the more you pay in premium

This very simple example shows that, while insurance is a sharing of risks and losses, it is also more than this. It is an attempt to share the risks and losses in a fair way. If you manufacture fireworks in your £1m factory, you will pay more premium than for a similar £1m factory in which concrete blocks are produced; and if you had a £1.2m factory you would pay more premium than someone with a similar factory worth £1m.

Premium calculations, however, are not based only on how much money is needed to pay for losses, but must also make an allowance for the insurance company's own expenses (such as staff salaries and telephone and electricity bills), payment of commission, and profit.

Another important element of the fund is investment and this also must be taken into account when deciding the size of the fund. The money in the fund is invested in such a way as to secure the maximum returns that can be gained with safety. The investments must also be convertible into cash as needed to meet the day-to-day requirements of claim payments, expenses, etc. There are numerous types of investment that can be held, such as mortgages, government securities, foreign government stocks, debentures, ordinary stocks and shares, and property. The return from investment (investment income) makes an important addition to the fund and can be used either to reduce the premiums charged or to boost the insurance company's profits.

Figure 2.1

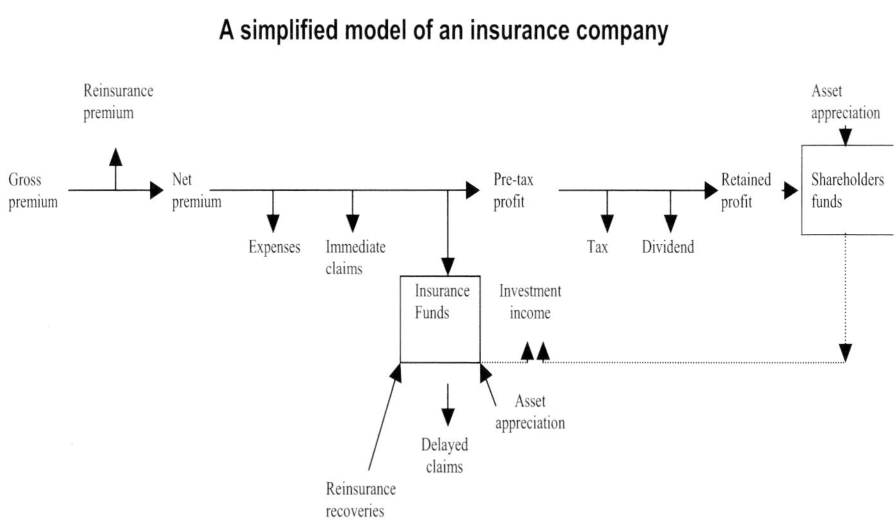

A simplified diagram of the flow of premium through an insurance company is shown in Figure 2.1.

Premium is received from the customer. This comprises a risk premium to cover the expected cost of claims, an expenses element to cover the cost of handling the business and a profit element. A proportion is then ceded to reinsurers to protect against excessive losses.

Expenses and immediate claims are subtracted from the premium and a further proportion placed into the insurance funds to reserve against future claims. Residual premium supplemented by any money released from prior year's reserves becomes pre-tax profit.

The insurance funds and the shareholder's funds are invested and any investment income is added to the pre-tax profit.

The value of the funds is hopefully rising as stock markets rise, increasing the net worth of the company.

Equilibrium conditions

Under equilibrium conditions the gross premium would be adequate to cover the claims, expenses and profit. Insurance funds are allocated enough money to pay the delayed claims. The investment of funds provides adequate income flow and asset appreciation and the right investment mix to provide liquidity when needed. After payment of an acceptable dividend, retained profit and asset appreciation swell the net worth of the company and the share price rises.

The shareholders are happy with their return on investment, the customers demand for good value products is satisfied, and the employees receive fair remuneration.

2.5 Some basic principles that govern the conduct of insurance

2.5.1 Utmost good faith

Until recently in the UK, when a man was selling his house he had to answer truthfully any questions asked him by the buyer and must not make any false representations. But if he was *not* asked a particular question about the property, he need not say anything. He did not have to disclose that the back garden is to be dug up soon to make way for a motorway, nor that a rubbish tip is about to be built next door. The buyer was expected to find these things out for himself. This is because most contracts of sale are based on the doctrine of *caveat emptor,* which means 'let the buyer beware', although this concept is becoming less prevalent as consumer protection/consumerism increases.

The insurance contract however is on a different basis completely, it is founded on the principle of utmost good faith – *uberrima fides*. This means that each party to a contract of insurance, instead of having to find out for himself the things that are relevant to the contract, is entitled to rely on the information provided by the other party, which must be disclosed in utmost good faith. The *proposer*, for instance, must disclose all the facts that would influence the underwriter's decision whether or not to accept the risk, and what premium to charge. These facts are called *material facts,* and facts that are not material facts need not be disclosed. This duty works both ways, so that the insurer must also disclose all the facts that would influence the proposer's decision whether or not to enter the contract.

Because the information disclosed in utmost good faith forms the basis of the insurance contract, if either party breaches his legal duty of utmost good faith, then the other party is entitled to avoid the contract. However, there is a trend for regulators to encourage insurers to take a more lenient view when the person who has not disclosed material facts is a private individual and the failure was unintentional.

2.5.2 Insurable interest

The most basic function of an insurer is to hand over money when a person, who has paid for insurance protection, suffers loss when the event insured against takes place. This leads to another important principle of insurance: insurable interest. This means that, before any contract of insurance can become legally binding, it is necessary for the person who wants to insure to have a legal interest in the person or thing to be insured. In other words, you can insure something, or someone, only if its preservation is beneficial to you, and if its loss would cause you to suffer, usually financially (eg an owner of a car has an insurable interest in his car; a mortgagor has an insurable interest in the house subject to the mortgage).

Without insurable interest, insurance would be merely gambling. In the early days of life assurance, ordinary people would insure the lives of public figures in the hope of profiting by their deaths – they were merely gambling. This does not happen nowadays because various Acts of Parliament (especially the Life Assurance Act, 1774, which came to be known as the Gambling Act) have provided that any insurance without insurable interest is unenforceable at law.

2.5.3 Indemnity

Insurable interest ensures that the money paid goes to the person who has suffered loss; but we must make sure also that the correct value is paid. It would quite clearly be wrong to pay the value of a new Rolls Royce to a man who has lost a new Mini, and equally wrong to pay the value of a new Mini to a man who has lost a new Rolls Royce. This is covered by the next principle of insurance – indemnity. When you suffer a loss the insurance company will try to place you in exactly the same financial position after the loss as you were in immediately before it, in other words, indemnify you. The principle of indemnity ensures that an insured cannot make a profit out of insurance.

Insurers may provide indemnity in several ways. The most common of these is by making a cash payment to the insured. Alternatively, the insurer may decide to repair the property (eg following a car crash), replace the property (eg buy another ring following a theft), or reinstate property (eg rebuild a house following a fire).

There are two important corollaries to the principle of indemnity: *contribution* and *subrogation*.

Contribution

The principle of contribution prevents people from making a profit by insuring one property with more than one insurance company, and claiming the full loss from each company when a loss occurs. Contribution means that, where more than one insurance covers the same property and the same interest against the same peril, any loss will be shared proportionately between all the insurers concerned – the insured is still indemnified, but only by receiving a proportionate contribution from each insurer. Thus, if a house worth £100,000 is insured with two insurance companies, each having granted an insurance for the full value of £100,000, the two companies will contribute £50,000 each in the event of a total loss.

Subrogation

According to common law, when an insurer pays an indemnity, it is allowed to take over the rights of the insured in order to try to recover the amount paid from any party who might be held liable for the loss. The insurer is said to be 'subrogated' to the insured's rights.

2.5.4 Contracts that are not contracts of indemnity

The value of a man's life to himself must be incapable of valuation by any objective assessment, so the principle of indemnity does not, in general, apply to life assurance or personal accident insurance. Contribution and subrogation, being corollaries of indemnity, also do not apply by the lame logic. But the tradition that someone may insure his or her own life for an unlimited amount is today no longer accepted. Constraints based to a large extent on common sense are applied to ensure that no proposer obtains an amount of life cover that is significantly more than he actually needs.

Additionally, many home contents policies these days provide 'new for old' cover, where items are replaced with brand new goods, even where those lost or damaged were not themselves brand new.

2.5.5 Average

Insurers calculate rates of premium according to the full value of the property they offer to insure. So, when they grant an insurance, they naturally expect the property to be covered for its full value, and they calculate a premium on this basis. To discourage people from 'underinsuring', ie insuring property for less than its full value, insurers make insurances 'subject to average'.

This means that when property is underinsured, the insured is considered to be his own 'insurer' for the difference between the sum insured and the true full value of the property. The insured himself must bear a proportionate share of any loss. If, for example, a £1m factory is insured for only £600,000, the insurance company will be liable to pay only three-fifths of any loss, and the insured must bear the other two-fifths himself, even if the loss incurred is less than the sum insured. For example, if a fire caused a partial loss of £100,000 to the property, the insurance company would pay only £60,000 and the insured would have to pay £40,000 himself.

Select bibliography

E Vaughan, T Vaughan, *Essentials of Risk Management and Insurance 2nd Ed*, John Wiley & Sons 2001.

A Couchman, R Litton (Ed) *Kluwer's Handbook of Insurance,* Kluwer 2003.

D Hansell, *Introduction to Insurance 2nd Ed*, LLP 1999.

Three

The structure of the insurance market

Objectives

On completion of this chapter, and wider personal research, the reader should be able to:

- describe the insurance marketplace and the different players;
- explain ways in which insurance may differ from other industries;
- appreciate the need for capital;
- distinguish between the main types of operating structure: shareholder based limited companies, mutuals and Lloyd's-type associations;
- discuss the influence of key socio-economic drivers on the supply of, demand for, and profitability of, insurance.

3.1 The players

The formalized insurance market has grown up over a period of 300 years although, as previously mentioned, it existed in an informal sense through risk-sharing ventures for centuries before that.

A simplistic diagram of the different types of players in the market is shown in Figure 3.1.

Figure 3.1

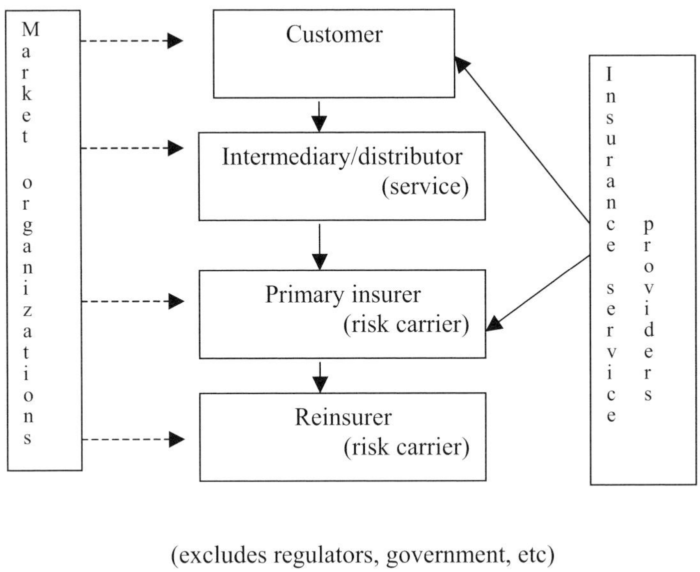

3.1.1 The primary insurer

The primary insurer is the cornerstone around which the entire insurance market fits. This is the organization that accepts the transfer of risk from the customer/purchaser of insurance and contracts to pay out valid claims within the policy provisions.

Just under 70% of the world's 13,000 insurers concentrate on P+C, another 25% concentrate on life, and the remainder are composites undertaking both. There is also a spread between generalists (offering a wide range of products/serving a wide range of customers) and niche operators (focusing on a much smaller range of specialist products and customers). The majority of insurers operate solely within a single market/country, a relatively small number operate internationally across a number of countries, and only a few can be said to be truly global in reach/scope.

Some large corporations (or groups of corporations), where it is tax efficient to do so, set up their own insurance companies to carry the primary risk for the owning company(s). This is called a 'captive' insurer. The captives in some cases then reinsure most of the risk, retaining little for themselves. Captives are discussed in more detail in Chapter 12.

As a norm, most risks will have one primary insurer who accepts the entire risk. However, in certain specialist types of business, or for particularly large or complex risks, a risk may be shared between a number of primary insurers, each accepting the transfer of only a defined element of the total risk. The most common examples of such insurance business are:

- *coinsurance*/London Market 'slip' business for large risks: in this situation a number of primary insurers each accept a proportion of the total risk in return for a proportion of the premium. Each insurer as a primary insurer has responsibility only for meeting its share of any claims, and is not responsible should one of the other coinsurers be unable to pay its share. There would normally be a 'lead insurer' who performs the administration processes and determines the rate of premium, the others 'follow' the lead insurer and take a share of the premium, adjusted for the administration costs of the lead insurer if they believe the risk is acceptable and appropriately priced.
- insurance *pools* (eg atomic energy, aviation): as a rule, the pool, which operates as a de facto separate business, would employ its own underwriters and administration staff. Member insurers share the results of the pool as a whole (ie do not get involved at individual risk level) in agreed proportions, and are responsible for overseeing the management and underwiting of the pool.

3.1.2 Intermediaries/distributors

Although some primary insurers (eg Direct Line in the UK) offer their products (primarily) direct to the customer, the majority of insurance product is sold via distributors, who take a commission from the insurance premium charged to the customer for the service performed.

Confusingly, under UK law distributors can, at different times, act as both an agent (in contract law) for both the primary insurer and the customer (insured); more detail is provided later in the book.

Distributors vary in size from very small one-man operations to large multi-billion turnover international operations such as Aon. In recent times the range of distributors has also increased dramatically with banks, supermarkets, motor vehicle manufacturers, etc taking active positions in distributing insurance products to their customers, taking advantage of existing distribution networks and widening their sales franchises. Affinity groups (organizations where people are linked together by a common interest/cause, eg disability groups, car ownership clubs, etc) are also increasingly acting as insurance distributors to their members.

3.1.3 Reinsurers

These are companies that accept a transfer of the insurance risk taken on by the primary insurers, and so take on risk themselves. This allows the primary insurer to both spread the risk and take on a greater level of business than their capital base would normally allow.

The reinsurer has no contract with the customer, only with the primary insurer, thus the primary insurer remains fully liable to the customer for all valid claims, even if the reinsurer should default or in any other way fail to pay the primary insurer under the reinsurance contract.

3.1.4 Insurance service providers

There are a whole range of non-risk bearing insurance service providers operating in the insurance market, paid by either the customer or the insurer, depending on the service performed. These include but are not limited to:

- Risk assessors/surveyors/inspectors
- Loss adjusters
- Loss assessors
- Damage/loss control services/salvors/etc
- Assistance services, eg medical repatriation from overseas
- Third party policy and/or claims administration service providers.

3.1.5 Market representation and market management organizations

Most insurance markets have their own market organizations to maintain market stability, to act as a focus for lobbying government or presenting the industry to the public. These organizations and associations may also set industry/market standards or operate market-wide activities (eg uninsured motorist compensation schemes, fraud prevention databases, policyholder compensation schemes (in the event of an insurer's insolvency), etc).

3.1.6 The role of rating agencies

Rating agencies such as Standard & Poors, AM Best, and Moodys give ratings assessing the strength of insurers in a similar way to the way in which they rate corporate debt. Such ratings can and do influence the way that insurance business is carried out, eg brokers may deal only with primary insurers with a certain level of rating or better, similarly, primary insurers may choose to transact business only with reinsurers with high ratings. The need to maintain a high rating may be a significant factor influencing a company's management.

3.2 Operating structures

The remainder of this book will focus mainly on the management of insurance operations from the perspective of the primary insurer.

3.2.1 The need for capital

A key requirement for any primary insurance risk carrier is the availability of capital to support the insurance business transacted. The regulatory authorities will require adequate capital to be in place before any insurance policies can be written, and customers will want comfort from the existence of a solid capital base that their claims will be met in the future. Credit rating agencies and investment analysts will also look at the level of capital in their assessments of the organization.

3.2.2 Company organization types

The most common organization types for an insurance company are:

- Shareholder-based limited companies – owned by independent shareholders who invest capital in the business with the aim of making a profit for themselves. These can be private limited companies, where shares are difficult to trade, or publicly quoted companies where there is a free market in the shares.
  Shareholder-based limited companies have the power to raise additional capital by issuing new shares.
  The liability of the company is limited to the capital subscribed, and on a normal basis shareholders are not liable for any unpaid debts of the company should its capital be exhausted.
- Mutuals – companies owned by their customers/members for mutual benefit. There are no separate shareholders who expect to make a profit from the company. Most mutual companies are established with limited liability but, because they do not have shareholders, have much more restricted opportunities to raise capital should it be needed. Although, in practice, if they are in a healthy financial position and have a convincing future strategy, raising loan capital in the market may not be a problem, eg Standard Life in the UK. The capital of the company tends to be that which has built up over many years of business activity (retained profits) plus any loan capital.
- Unlimited liability vehicles – a third, though much less common, organization type is an association or partnership with unlimited liability for some or all of its members, the best known of which is Lloyd's of London. Such associations have their own rules and rely on their members to provide

capital as and when it is needed. However, even at Lloyd's, the unlimited liability concept is in decline, with the growing influence of corporate, rather than personal, capital in the market. Such corporate capital is made available to the market via a limited liability company and thus is finite, not unlimited.

Case study – Lloyd's of London

Lloyd's is a unique insurance market that has evolved out of the activities of a City of London coffee house of that name in 1688. Today's massive organization enables its members to write P+C insurance business in over 60 countries. It is probably the world's strongest insurance brand, and has a reputation for innovation and, despite recent troubles, for security. Individual members (Names), who provide the capital to support the insurance business, act through associations called syndicates, using managing agents to conduct the business on their behalf. The managing agents employ underwriters to accept risks, pay claims, obtain reinsurance, etc. Lloyd's provides a supporting infrastructure to enable policies, claims and account settlements to be processed centrally. It is a very early example of value chain disaggregation.

One special characteristic of Lloyd's is that the Names put their entire personal wealth at risk with unlimited liability. Although this caused relatively few problems for three centuries, in the period 1988 – 1992 Lloyd's made a pre-tax loss of almost £8 bn. This was due to a catalogue of disasters: asbestos and pollution in the USA, the Piper Alpha rig fire, Exxon Valdez oil spillage, Hurricanes Hugo and Andrew, etc. These were compounded by the LMX reinsurance spirals that concentrated huge losses onto a number of syndicates. As a result, great hardship was suffered by thousands of Names, many of whom were financially ruined.

In the following period, Lloyd's undertook a radical restructuring. This included:

- a settlement with Names for past losses to alleviate distress,
- a reduction in the number of syndicates and brokers, and
- pre-1992 liabilities were reinsured in a new corporate run-off entity called Equitas.

Perhaps the most far-reaching reform was the introduction of corporate capital. This has meant that companies are allowed to join syndicates. As a consequence, capacity has been maintained and half of all Lloyds's capital now comes from this limited-liability source.

3.3 Capital

Why is capital critical to a primary insurer?

As in all companies, capital (the residue of the organization's funds not allocated to meet its short-term liabilities) is required to fund working capital (the difference between amounts owing to the company and amounts owed by it) and fund day-to-day operating costs and the development/growth of the business.

However, a primary insurer, unless it reinsures 100% of the risks it writes, must be able to withstand a loss on the insurance book of business. On occasion, the out-turn will be worse than expected/priced for, and the company may need to pay out more in claims and expenses than it has available from its income stream. Sufficient capital needs to be available to cope with such events to prevent the company becoming insolvent.

To maintain a stable market of insurance companies that are in business for many years, and are not put at risk by one-off events such as bad weather, a set of large claims or investment value fluctuations, insurance regulators specify minimum capital requirements for a company to be authorized to transact insurance. Typically this is in the range of 15-20% of net premiums written. In practice, most reputable insurers operate at a substantially higher level than this – typically 40% of premiums or greater, to provide greater resilience to external shocks and events.

In essence a P+C insurance company 'rents out its capital' to its customers. In exchange for an insurance premium (rent) the insurer's capital is made available to the insured in the event of specified loss or damage to the insured's own capital position. As a result, the primary insurer's capital position is critical to its ability to generate income.

The way in which an insurer manages its capital is therefore vital to its long-term success and profitability and is a core indicator to the outside world of its strength and reliability. This is part of what the rating agencies seek to assess when rating insurers and reinsurers.

3.4 Insurance is different from other industries

What makes the insurance industry, and therefore the way it needs to be managed, different from other industries, including other financial services providers?

3.4.1 Maximum loss

In most businesses the maximum loss on any one sale is limited to the cost of producing/buying the product sold plus any allocation of general overheads. In normal practice this would be expected to be less than the selling price, as most businesses would expect to make a profit on most sales. In lending, the maximum potential loss would be the value of the loan advanced, plus any rolled-up interest, less the value of any security held.

However, in most forms of P+C insurance, the maximum possible loss on any one product sale is many times the invoice price. For instance, personal injury awards are now running into the millions of pounds for permanent disability (eg quadriplegia) in the UK, yet the average private motor car premium is in the range of £300-400. This implies a maximum loss potential of around 10,000 times the sale price on any one policy sold, before allocation of expenses, etc, and the maximum is not known at the outset.

3.4.2 Investment income

On the basis that insurance premiums are received in advance of claims being paid, and some large and complex claims can take many years to resolve and settle (a cash-flow opportunity that attracted the likes of Warren Buffett into the insurance market,) the insurance company invests its capital plus money received in excess of its operating expenses and immediate claim payment requirements.

In the latter part of the 20th century the substantial investment earnings generated on these funds were able to subsidise losses on the pure insurance activities, and companies were able to declare reasonable profits over time. However, this made it difficult to price the insurance products appropriately to make a profit in their own right. An observation at the time was that, in general, a P+C insurance company was basically an investment trust with an expensive hobby (its insurance activities).

In the last few years, with low interest rates and falling stock markets, P+C insurers can no longer rely on investment income to subsidize losses on the insurance activities to anything like the same extent. Increasingly, insurance products have to be priced to make an overall profit in their own right before investment income is taken into account.

3.4.3 Certainty of outcome/exposure

In most businesses, you are reasonably certain of the outcome of the transaction at the time of completion. Insurance by its nature, and the nature of the society we live in, is far less certain.

- It can take a long time for the exact extent and cost of a claim to be finalized, eg pollution, long-term injury, complex liability issues.
- There can be substantial argument as to whether, and to what extent, an event is covered by the insurance policy. Such disputes can take a long time to resolve before certainty as to final liability/cost is known.
- Developments in national law and case law (and the impact of regulatory regimes applying 20:20 hindsight) can dramatically impact the cost not just of future claims, but for all claims that are not fully settled, eg increases in liability/injury awards.
- An increasingly litigious society, and a belief that there is always someone to blame for any unfortunate event/loss, means that insurers are continually being looked on to compensate claimants for damage resulting from risks that were not envisaged at the time the policy was sold.

As a result, the insurer is exposed to constant uncertainty regarding its exposures and the quantum of current and future claims. This is a key reason for having a substantial capital base to absorb the impact of negative out-turns/developments, but also a reason for shareholders expecting a higher return on the capital invested in insurance companies than from other investments because of the uncertainty/risk involved.

3.5 Socio-economic drivers for insurance

In the current marketplace there are many different drivers affecting the demand for and profitability of insurance products.

As a general rule P+C insurance spend, by both individuals and companies, grows at a faster rate than GDP growth, once economies reach a certain stage of development, as individuals seek protection for their increasingly valuable possessions (houses, cars, etc), companies seek to protect their factories and other assets, and governments make certain types of cover (eg employers liability or motor third party) compulsory for the protection of society as a whole.

The range of personal P+C insurance products to meet different needs

As a society becomes more complex, personal assets are both more valuable and complex and as people's behaviour, lifestyle and expectations change so their insurance needs change.

Also the impact of the end of 'jobs for life' and the trend to less paternalistic employers effectively pushes more risk onto the individual consumer.

Buildings – fire	↑	Simple needs
Buildings – other perils	│	
Contents/personal possessions	│	
Car (third party)	│	
Car (comprehensive)	│	
Travel	│	
Car breakdown/recovery	│	
Legal expenses	│	
Health	│	
Credit/unemployment protection	│	
Extended warranty/domestic appliance breakdown	↓	Complex/ sophisticated needs

And in the same way as customers' needs change as markets develop, the products offered become more complex. For example:

- the addition of liability and other perils covers to buildings cover;
- 'new for old' covers for personal possessions.

Governments and regulators also play a key role in creating a market requirement for insurance, by making it a legal requirement to purchase certain types of insurance for the protection of society at large. Typical examples would be:

- compulsory third party motor insurance for all motor vehicles;
- compulsory employers' liability insurance for all companies/employers;
- compulsory professional indemnity insurance for certain types of professional services companies (eg accountants).

Any such legal requirement creates a defined market for insurance companies to service.

In the same way as demand increases with economic growth and sophistication, economic downturns also have a significant impact on the insurance market:

- when money is tight more people will decide to do without insurance, even compulsory insurances (there are estimated to be up to 2 million uninsured drivers on UK roads at any time);
- in economic recession there is a greater tendency for fraudulent claims, whether from fires at badly performing businesses, or for household goods, supposedly stolen, which have either been sold or never existed in the first place.

3.6 Investment markets and interest rates

As previously noted, insurance companies invest all funds not required to service day-to-day operations to obtain investment income and, potentially, capital gains. High interest rates and strong investment markets will generate significant investment returns, which are then added to (or offset against) the insurance business result (underwriting result).

Strong investment returns reduce the pressure on companies to make underwriting profits, and may even allow them to make underwriting losses for a period and still achieve acceptable overall returns. However, weak investment markets and low interest rates emphasize the need to make underwriting profits. The significant worldwide stock market and interest rate falls in 2000-2002 brought to an end a 20+ year period of investment returns being used to support substantial underwriting losses in many P+C businesses.

3.7 The supply of insurance

While most insurance markets are regulated, ie participants must be authorized by the local regulator and comply with the rules established by the regulator, it is not particularly difficult for new entrants to set up as insurers or reinsurers in most markets, given sufficient capital and the ability to convince the local regulator that the business will be conducted in accordance with market rules.

Similarly, it is relatively easy for existing market operators to grow volume (capacity) if they have sufficient capital to support the increased volume; such growth typically is achieved by offering lower retail prices than competitors.

As a result, and unlike many other industry sectors, insurance markets tend to suffer from clear cycles in profitability; this can be at both individual product line level and overall market level. The typical cycle consists of:

- Either a shortage of capacity or a significant event (eg September 11, a major storm) allows existing market operators to increase significantly the premium charged for the same risk, creating the potential for above-average profits in the future.

- New capacity (either from existing operators or new entrants) comes into the market attracted by the opportunity for high profits.
- Increased competition pushes down prices and profits until most of the market is making underwriting losses.
- Capacity withdraws from the market, either in response to a significant loss event, or the continuing losses being incurred.
- Which allows remaining participants to put up premiums due to a shortage of capacity... etc.

Typically such cycles run for about 5-7 years, but vary by product and market and can be significantly affected by major loss events that affect the market as a whole.

Figure 3.2

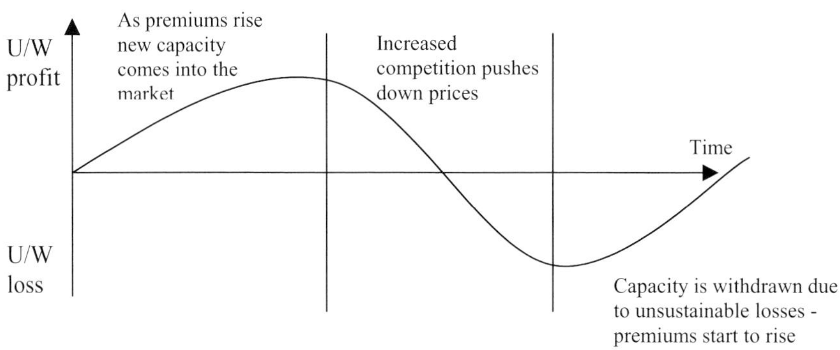

Simplified underwriting 'cycle'

Given such cycles, it would seem optimal for a long-term P+C player to seek to maximize returns by putting on volume as the pricing cycle moves upward, and then reducing volume and being more selective in risks accepted as the pricing cycle turns down. In practice, few companies have so far managed to implement such a strategy effectively. A significant issue is the flexibility and variability of the administrative cost base, such that costs can be adjusted quickly in line with the volume of business written.

The UK underwriting cycle is discussed in more detail in Chapter 13.

3.8 Insurance markets

Insurance markets tend to split into two distinct types on a worldwide basis.

Domestic

Most personal customers, small businesses and large national companies tend to require protection solely within their domestic markets, and as a result, over time, each country has developed its own domestic insurance market with its own customs, product variations/structures, regulation and law, etc that can satisfy the needs of these customers. There is little pressure to have worldwide standard car insurance products, applicable to multiple legal jurisdictions, because most people do not drive their own vehicle outside their own country on a regular basis. Any occasional need for cross-border cover can usually be acquired as additional, one-off covers as required (eg travel insurance, Green Cards, etc).

Multinational/worldwide

Multinational corporations frequently operate on a worldwide basis and many want to purchase their core insurance covers on a similar basis. Insurers who wish to supply these customers must therefore be able to offer global, or at least multinational, solutions that operate across multiple legal/regulatory jurisdictions.

Some types of insurance covers (international marine, aviation, oil rig) operate almost entirely on a worldwide basis because of the nature of the risks.

As a result of this, and even though insurance – like most other industrial sectors – has gone through substantial consolidation over the last half century, the insurance operators tend to operate either within a single domestic market (or multi-domestically, ie entirely separate domestic operations in a number of different countries) or in a worldwide market for the products they choose to offer to large corporate customers. The drivers are the lack of demand for the multi-territory products from most customers and the complexities created by the different customs, law and regulation requiring different policy structures, wordings, and conditions for the same basic type of insurance in different countries.

Even following the creation of the 'single market in financial services' in the EU, and the introduction of a common currency, the euro, no-one has yet been able to offer a single motor or household product that is saleable/attractive to customers and valid across multiple EU countries, let alone more sophisticated or complex products.

Select bibliography

W Clarke, *How the City of London Works 5th Ed,* Sweet & Maxwell 1999, Chapter 3.

Insurance Pocket Book, Tillinghast-Towers Perrin, 2003.

B Webb, C Harrison, J Markam, *Insurance Operations and Regulation,* Insurance Institute of America 2002, Chapter 1.

G Dionne, *Handbook of Insurance,* Kluwer 2000, Chapter 21.

J Outreville *Theory and Practice of Insurance,* Kluwer 1998, Chapter 2 and Chapter 11.

Diacon (Ed), *A Guide to Insurance Management,* Macmillan 1990, Chapter 6.

Four

An introduction to the legal and regulatory framework for insurance

Objectives

On completion of this chapter, and wider personal research, the reader should be able to:

- outline the regulatory, legal, fiscal and accounting frameworks within which P+C insurance is conducted;
- analyse their influence on the management of insurance operations and the conduct of business.

> 'There are also substantial variations in the legal system under which insurers operate. In all countries there is at least some form of government supervision, but ... the control differs widely in form and substance. The extent to which insurers may form agreements, tariffs or cartels to control the market also depends on any anti-trust legislation in force.'
>
> Hans van Gelder, Consultant

4.1 Introduction

Insurers in most countries, as well as being bound by the laws and regulations that cover most other corporate entities, are also impacted by substantial additional legislation and regulation. This chapter provides a high-level overview of the broad regulatory and legal framework and types of issues that this presents to the management of insurance operations, covering a UK-registered insurer. It cannot, for obvious reasons, be either complete or detailed in the space available or attempt to cover the detail of regulation across a range of countries.

Examples of legislation and regulation affecting a UK-authorized P+C insurer:

Affecting all corporate entities, not just insurers:

- Employment Law
- Health & Safety regulations
- Contract Law
- The Law of Agency
- Property Law and regulations (eg construction, planning)
- Generally accepted accounting principles (GAAP)
- Company Law
- Stock Exchange rules
- Corporate Governance regulations
- Taxation regulations in respect of:
  - employees' remuneration
  - corporate earnings
  - VAT
- Data Protection and privacy law
- Competition Law and regulations
- Human Rights law
- EU Directives
- Environmental reporting regulations

Specific to insurers:

- Numerous Insurance Acts
- EU Insurance Directives
- Financial Services and Markets law/regulation including:
  - Solvency requirements
  - Governance and prudential management
  - Conduct of Business
  - Statistical reporting
- ABI/industry/market (eg Lloyd's) standards/rules
- Insurance-specific accounting standards
- Insurance-specific taxation rules (IPT, catastrophe reserves, discounting of reserves, etc).

A wide range of other law and regulation specifies that certain insurance is compulsory, eg:

- third party cover for all motor vehicles
- employers' liability cover for all businesses
- professional indemnity cover to trade in a specific profession.

or affects the nature of insurance covers, the nature of the risks subject to cover, or the value of existing risks, eg:

- The proposal to exclude terrorism cover from standard commercial covers in the UK led to the establishment of a market-wide 'pool' for such covers under government pressure (Pool Re) and the Terrorism Act definition of what constitutes terrorism for insurance purposes.
- Case law, particularly in liability cases, frequently amends the extent and nature of past covers and the monetary value of liability.
- Government and regulators, in response to public opinion, have been known to introduce new law/regulation that has a retrospective effect that affects the nature of cover and/or risk or, the way in which insurance business is conducted. To date, in the UK, this has largely been in the life arena, (eg pensions mis-selling, endowment policy review) but this can also occur in P+C areas, particularly in respect of liability covers.

4.2 Other influences

In addition to law and regulation, the insurance industry will also come under general pressure from the government, regulators or consumer groups to act in ways that are not in the interests of the insurance companies themselves. Examples include:

- The availability and pricing of flood cover for property that is regularly subject to inundation;
- The availability and pricing of motor or property covers in high crime, inner city areas;
- The availability and pricing of liability cover in the post Enron/Worldcom environment.

In such instances 'social good' pressure, to make sure that covers are available to all, at an affordable price, conflicts with the insurers' risk assessment and pricing for such risks.

Financial Ombudsman: dispute resolution

The UK Financial Ombudsman handles retail consumer complaints about most financial products, including insurance, pensions, banking and investment. The procedure is as follows:

- the firm must be given the opportunity to deal with the complaint first;
- the Ombudsman may step in if the customer is not happy with the final response letter;
- the Ombudsman will take a fresh view of the facts and help to reach an agreement by mediation;
- if the complaint cannot be resolved by mediation an adjudicator will make a full investigation and inform the customer and the firm how it should be resolved;
- if a formal decision is made the firm has no appeal but the customer is still free to use the courts.

The UK Financial Ombudsman scheme is now compulsory for all financial services companies that deal with the public.

International insurance regulation and the role of the IAIS

In the face of the greater internationalization of insurance operations, and more cross-border insurance and reinsurance transactions, insurance regulation and supervision have had to adapt. Regulation is essentially national in character; the licensing of insurance companies, prudential supervision and market conduct standards are the prerogative of national governments. The European Union is an example of an attempt to harmonize national regulation between a group of countries in order to protect consumers more effectively and to ensure that regulations do not distort competition within an integrating market. But there is need for wider coordination between national regulatory and supervisory systems at the international level. Moreover, in a number of emerging markets, insurance regulatory systems have to be brought up to an acceptable international standard to ensure that national insurance markets develop soundly, by minimising the company failures and malpractice that undermine consumer confidence, and ensuring that there are no weak links in the international insurance mechanism for the spreading of large-risk exposures, such as from natural or man-made disasters.

The **International Association of Insurance Supervisors** (IAIS) is a voluntary organization of insurance supervisors, set up in 1994, and over 100 national jurisdictions are now members. Its secretariat is located in Basel within the Bank of International Settlements, and it maintains close links with the Basel Committee on Banking Supervision, which sets international regulatory standards for commercial banks, and with the International Organization of Securities Commissions (IOSCO), which is responsible for setting the regulatory standards for the securities industry. Since 2000, the Basel Committee, IAIS and IOSCO have worked closely together to ensure that the regulation and supervision of all financial services enterprises operates under similar principles, in part, because of the greater convergence within the financial services industry.

The IAIS has three main aims:

a) to promote cooperation among insurance regulators;
b) to set international standards for insurance supervision; and
c) to coordinate work with regulators in the other parts of the financial system. It has developed a set of core principles which it considers should be embodied within all national insurance regulatory and supervisory systems.

These core principles have been endorsed by the IMF and the World Bank and are seen as helping to ensure that insurance regulatory systems around the world are robust enough to reduce the systemic risk that could undermine stability within the global financial system.

The website for the IAIS (www.iaisweb.org) provides information on its activities and on various aspects of international insurance regulation and supervision.

Professor Gerry Dickinson

An insurance company fraud that was influential in the development of the scope and role of regulation in the UK insurance market is detailed below.

Case study – Fire, Auto and Marine 1963-1966

Dr Emil Savundra had a history of fraudulent business dealings in Colombo, Ghana and Goa, culminating in a 5-year prison sentence. His record did not prevent him from starting an insurance business, Fire, Auto and Marine, in 1963 from a small office in the West End of London. Charging motor premiums averaging half of those of existing companies, and offering an above average commission of 20%, he quickly attracted large numbers of brokers. In the first year he wrote more new business than any other insurer. All went well for the first two years, but inevitably claims began to catch up. Savundra explained this away as teething troubles and was able to convince the public that his strong investment portfolio and low expense ratio would ensure long-term success.

However, by 1966 it was clear that massive reserve strengthening was necessary. Savundra tried to sell the company but refused to show the accounts to potential buyers. The auditors were suspicious and asked to see evidence of the investments. Unfortunately for the 230,000 policyholders, many of the share certificates proved to be forgeries and a sum of money equivalent to 20% of the total NWP had disappeared forever.

Savundra was subsequently convicted of fraud and false accounting and was sentenced to 8 years imprisonment.

4.3 Compliance

In a P+C insurer, as in most companies, responsibility for compliance with most laws and regulation will generally be split up to the relevant parts of the business to look after specific elements, eg HR to look after Employment Law compliance, Finance to ensure compliance with financial regulations and reporting requirements. However, with the increasingly detailed requirements of the Financial Services Authority (FSA) in the UK, many UK P+C insurers are establishing specialist functions to manage and monitor compliance with FSA rules and regulations. Such functions have been common for some time in life insurance, but are now felt necessary for P+C, particularly following the Financial Services and Markets Act 2000 and the subsequently published FSA requirements and rule books.

4.4 The interests of government

Most governments acknowledge that an effective and efficient P+C insurance market will support the economic growth of the country. People will be able to acquire valuable assets and engage in profitable trade, safe in the knowledge that they are protected from the impact of certain (but not all) risks. For an effective market to exist, governments must look to create an insurance market where:

- customers can buy appropriate products at an affordable price;
- customers are protected (as far as possible) from malpractice or mismanagement of insurance companies;
- as a general rule, there is confidence that the insurer will pay the amount due, should there be a claim;
- insurers are allowed to generate (for their owners) sufficient returns on the capital invested to make it worthwhile continuing to participate in the market (and these profits generate taxation income for the government);
- as far as possible, the market is seen to operate in an environment of openness, confidence and trust.

Governments can facilitate this kind of market in many ways, either overtly or covertly, and through many types of legislation or regulation. However, in most countries, the government establishes a formal regulatory body to oversee the insurance industry and to authorize and monitor the market participants. In some cases this regulator covers only the insurance market, in others it covers the broader financial services industry including banking, investment management, etc.

Types of regulation

There are basically three types of insurance market regulation that can be employed:

- Solvency of participants: Seeks to protect society from the risk of insurance company insolvency.
- Market confidence: Seeks to ensure an efficient market; all parties have adequate information, the market adjusts appropriately to changes in supply and demand, there is adequate competition, etc.
- Consumer protection: Retail consumers are able to buy the most appropriate products for their needs, at an affordable price, and have recourse if insurers act improperly. (Commercial insurance buyers are generally less well looked after by regulation because they are deemed to be 'knowledgeable purchasers' and therefore less in need of protection.)

4.5 The role of the Regulator

The Regulator's duties/obligations/powers will be established (and amended as necessary) by the Government of the country. Typically, a regulator of insurance will cover some or all of the following:

- authorization/licensing of market participants – ensuring that all market participants are likely to be reliable, properly managed, have adequate capital, and have the skills to transact business without destabilizing the market.
- regular financial and statistical monitoring of authorized market participants, including obtaining detailed statistical returns from insurers that analyse the business written, reserves, capital, etc in a standard format for the regulator to analyse and compare with regulatory limits (eg solvency) or other market participants, and to create industry-wide statistics and analysis on a common basis.
- establishing rules for the way that an insurance company should be operated or managed. This could include:
    - Corporate Governance structures and processes
    - Risk Management processes
    - Licensing of executives to perform their specific roles
    - Conduct of business (sales process, relevance of product to customer needs, disclosure of commission, competence of intermediaries, etc)
    - A process for inspection/review of authorized companies to assess the competence of management, the adequacy of processes, the compliance with regulations, or investigate specific issues or concerns.

Regulators are generally funded by way of annual licence fees from the authorized companies they regulate, or by direct government funding.

The UK Financial Services Authority (FSA)

Statutory objectives:

- to maintain confidence in the UK financial system
- to promote public understanding of the financial system
- to secure the appropriate degree of protection for consumers
- to reduce the scope for financial crime.

Scope:

- Banking, investment management, insurance.

Stated approach to regulation:

Risk-based within the following principles of good regulation:

- maintaining the UK's international competitive position
- seeking to ensure the most efficient and economic use of resources
- encouraging competition
- facilitating innovation
- emphasizing the responsibility of firms' own management
- being proportionate (in how it deals with issues).

4.6 Corporate governance

Following the corporate scandals across the world over the last decade or so, there has been an increasing focus on the need for improved standards of what is now called corporate governance (the process by which companies are managed at the highest level) from governments, stock exchanges and regulators. Insurers are bound by the same corporate governance rules as the other companies but must also comply with any additional rules established by the regulator.

Typical corporate governance rules cover:

- The composition of the board and allocated powers and responsibilities including the roles of chairman and chief executive and the responsibilities and competencies of non-executive directors.
- The role of specific board committees (audit, risk, finance, remuneration, etc).
- Structures and processes for risk management and internal control assessment and monitoring.
- Reporting on corporate governance activity and compliance with relevant corporate governance rules and standards.

As in most public responses to high-profile problems, not all the recommendations and regulation that are produced actually improve the overall management of companies, or make sense in the commercial world.

- The Sarbanes-Oxley act in the USA, while placing additional responsibility on executives and directors to take responsibility for the published financial results of their companies, is unlikely to prevent another Enron or World Com from occurring.
- The Higgs Report (UK) on the role of non-executive directors has received significant criticism for being unworkable in practice.

The challenges that insurers face, in addition to other industries, are primarily:

- the additional regulatory requirements; in the UK, the FSA has produced significant guidance on the expected structure and operation of corporate governance processes; and
- the inherent uncertainties attaching to a business that is solely based on the acceptance of other parties' risks with no certainty of how events will develop over time. If an insurer is too risk averse it will never take on any business.

As with all such obligations, which have been imposed by the government/ regulators based on the best possible motive, but which are onerous and expensive to implement thoroughly, there is a risk that companies reduce the whole corporate governance process to a 'box ticking' exercise, rather than seek to gain value from it.

Wherever practical, compliance with all regulation should be done in a way that addresses the issue positively and maximizes the value of the process to the company, and not in a way that treats it as an unnecessary chore that adds no value. Treating such activity as a chore makes it far more likely that compliance will fail to be achieved due to lack of true commitment, potentially leading to substantial penalties, bad publicity, etc.

4.7 Areas of specific emphasis for Insurers

4.7.1 The law of Contract

Each insurance policy is a contract between the insurer and the insured. As such, it is clearly bound by the laws of contract relevant to the policy. Key issues that need to be specified in any insurance policy:

- The jurisdiction/country in which any disputes regarding the contract will be resolved (ie the law applicable to the contract).
- The specific rights, duties and obligations of all parties to the contract, specified as clearly and unambiguously as possible.
- In relation particularly to contracts with retail consumers, compliance with all rules regarding clarity, fairness of terms, etc that are appropriate to the jurisdiction of the contract.

4.7.2 The law of Agency

As specified in more detail in a later chapter, the role of the intermediary (agent, broker, etc) who brings a customer's business to an insurer, is quite complex. In UK law the intermediary can, in dealing with the same insurance policy and customer, be an agent for the insurer or the insured at different times. This is a fairly unusual situation; normally an intermediary is an agent for only one party to a transaction.

In addition to the role the intermediary plays, it is also important to understand on whose behalf any other third parties involved in the contract are acting (risk surveyors, loss adjusters, loss assessors, replacement goods providers, etc). Whom they are acting for will make a substantial difference in the role performed and the responsibilities of the party on whose behalf they are acting.

4.7.3 Taxation

In addition to having to comply with normal tax rules regarding employees' remuneration, corporate earnings and VAT (sales tax for non-insurance activities and purchases), insurers also have two other areas for focus.

- In many countries a tax is levied on insurance premiums similar to general sales tax (VAT). In the UK, Insurance Premium Tax (IPT) has completely different rules to VAT and is collected by a different process. Insurers' systems must be capable of identifying, separating out and paying over any such sales-based taxes in compliance with local rules.
- Because of the basic uncertainty regarding the eventual cost of claims (particularly for long-tail liability/injury claims) insurers need to make substantial judgments in establishing claims reserves, not just for known claims, but for claims not yet reported and for large events that occur only occasionally but have a big impact when they do. Having made a judgment on the value of future claims, there is then the decision as to whether to reserve for the total amount now, or to discount the reserves to a current value (allowing for the investment income to grow the reserves to the amount required at a future date). The tax authorities will have their own rules as to whether full reserving or discounting is allowed/required for determining taxable income, and whether catastrophe reserve provisions can be charged against taxable income.

4.7.4 Three-year accounting

Lloyd's of London and some commercial classes of business have historically adopted three-year accounting. This was due to the fact that, because of delays in claims notification, the time required for the assessment and full quantification of many complex commercial cases, and the need to manage complex reinsurance positions, it is inappropriate to try to accurately estimate the results of a single financial year in the few months immediately following the financial year end.

Under three-year accounting, a financial year is kept 'open' for two years after the actual year end, to enable a full assessment of all claims to be made, and is only closed, and a final profit or loss calculated, after this further two-year period. So at any point in time, a company operating three-year accounting will have 'open' the current financial year plus the two preceding open years, against which adjustments to claims, etc continue to be made.

Under current accounting standards however, non-Lloyd's entities operating three-year accounting must, if they expect a significant loss to result in any of the open years, provide for this at the next year end, rather than wait for the year(s) to be closed. Anticipated profits, however, do not have to be taken until the year is closed.

Whilst still allowed by accounting standards, there is currently a general move away from three year accounting, except for the most complex books of business, in both the Lloyds' and company markets.

4.7.5 The interpretation and value ascribed to tort

The law of tort (civil wrong or injury arising out of an act or failure to act, independent of a contract) exists in some shape in most legal systems. Consumer-driven developments over the last 20 or so years have dramatically changed what is considered to be a valid basis for a claim under tort, and over the same period, the value placed by courts on the 'injuries' claimed for has also increased substantially. As both the number of successful claims (eg actions against tobacco companies) has increased substantially alongside the average cost of such claims, the total value of tort litigation has climbed exponentially. Successful tort claims will eventually fall, at least to some extent, on the defendant's insurers.

4.8 Other influences

In addition to formal law and regulation, there are many other organizations and pressure groups seeking to influence both the thinking and the conduct of the insurance industry itself; governments in respect of insurance/risk-related issues, or the public in terms of their understanding of insurance and insurance products. These range from consumer champions (such as the Consumers' Association in the UK) through industry lobbying (eg via the ABI) and academic research groups, to special interest groups seeking to promote a specific issue (eg tort reform, industrial disease compensation, etc).

A significant thought leader in insurance and insurance-related matters, on an international level, is The Geneva Association.

The role and activities of The Geneva Association

The International Association for the Study of Insurance Economics (The Geneva Association) is the leading organization for the study of economics of risk and insurance worldwide. Its membership consists of the chief executive officers of 80 of the world's leading insurance companies. Its aim is to encourage a better public understanding of insurance and risk, and to ensure that there is an informed dialogue between the insurance industry and government policymakers.

The Association organizes a range of annual seminars for academics, insurance executives and senior government officials. It also funds research projects at universities and research institutes around the world. It sponsors two of the most highly regarded academic journals in the field: *The Geneva Papers on Risk and Insurance: Issues and Practice*; and *The Geneva Papers on Risk and Insurance Theory.*

The Annual Lecture of the Geneva Association is given by a leading economist on an insurance or risk theme. Past lecturers have included five Nobel prizewinners in economics, including Kenneth Arrow, Robert Merton and Joseph Stiglitz. These lectures are published in *The Geneva Papers on Risk and Insurance: Issues and Practice.*

The research of The Geneva Association has made important, original contributions in a number of areas including: the reform of social security systems; the social and economic impact of ageing (the concept of the 'Four Pillars' was developed by the Association); the strategic links between insurance and banking; the holistic approach to risk management (including what is now known as 'enterprise risk management'); the growing role of services in the modern economy; the liberalization of trade and investment in the financial services sector; and frameworks that seek to integrate aspects of law and economics. Apart from its journals, it has a useful website (www.genevaassociation.org).

Professor Gerry Dickinson
Honorary Vice Secretary General
The Geneva Association

Select bibilography

J Young, *A Practitioner's Guide to the FSA Regulation of Insurance,* City & Financial Publishing 2002.

J Birds, N Hird, *Bird's Modern Insurance Law 5th Ed,* Sweet & Maxwell 2001.

A Coughman, R Litton (Ed), *Kluwer's Handbook of Insurance,* Kluwer 2003.

Policy Issues in Insurance, Insurance Regulation, Liberalisation and Financial Convergence, OECD 2001.

J MacLeod, M Newstead, *Taxation of Insurance Business,* Butterworths 1999.

J MacLeod, J Sharp, *Insurance Premium Taxes: A Guide to Indirect Taxes on Insurance Products in 90 countries,* Ernst & Young 1996.

J Outreville, *Theory and Practice of Insurance,* Kluwer 1998, Chapter 16.

Claude Bébéar *Remarks on the Development of Global Regulation for Financial Services Industries and its impact on Insurance, Geneva Papers on Risk and Insurance, Vol 27,* No 1/2, Jan 2002.

C Sergeant, *Risk based regulation in the Financial Services Authority,* Journal of Financial Regulation and Compliance Vol 10, No 4, Nov 2002.

A Carey, N Turnbull, *The Boardroom Imperative on Internal Control in Mastering Risk, Vol 1: Concepts,* Prentice Hall 2001.

S Diacon (Ed), *A Guide to Insurance Management,* Macmillan 1990, Chapter 17.

Five

Strategic planning in insurance operations

Objectives

On completion of this chapter, and wider personal research, the reader should be able to:

- understand how strategy is developed, implemented and monitored in an insurance operation;
- describe the process;
- outline some of the common strategic tools used by insurance management;
- describe some of the insurance-specific challenges of strategy development in an insurance operation.

> 'Strategic Planning is the process of reaching and implementing those decisions which significantly affect the company's ability to achieve its objectives and sets the pattern for resource allocation within the company in the context of the opportunities and threats in the external environment.'
>
> Samuel Msheliza, University of Nottingham

What makes an outstanding company?

Jules Goddard has identified the following characteristics of 'outstanding' companies:

- they find their path to greatness by first confronting the brutal fact of their current reality
- they set their goals and strategies based on understanding, not on bravado
- sustained results depend on self-disciplined people who take disciplined actions: 'stop-doing' lists are more important than 'to-do' lists
- they use technology as an accelerator of momentum, not a creator of it.

Dr Jules Goddard, London Business School

5.1 The importance of recognizing and working with the organization's culture

Any strategic planning or significant planned change to the organization must acknowledge the current culture of the organization.

'Culture – The way things are done around here.' Charles Handy

The influences on an organization's 'culture'

'Culture is the set of beliefs, values and learned ways of managing the organization. Each organization has a culture that is unique.

Factors within an organization influencing culture include: history and ownership, size, technology, and leadership.'

Richard Lynch, Corporate Strategy

Culture can be very deep-seated within an organization and can be difficult to change. As a result, any strategic planning or significant change must either seek to work within what is possible within the current culture, or incorporate within it specific approaches as to how the culture of the organization will be changed to that required for the future.

5.2 The need for strategic planning

Strategic planning, in one form or another, will have been practised in every prudent business since time immemorial. Managers would undoubtedly have tried to look ahead and organize themselves in the light of possible future circumstances and developments. Nowadays, particularly in higher-risk ventures such as insurance operations, the need for a well thought out, implementable strategy is more than ever necessary. This is because:

- companies must respond to the pace and magnitude of change in the business environment. The response often involves long lead times, cooperation between business units, reallocation of resources and considerable advance investment.
- the increased size and complexity of companies creates demands for better coordination, communication and clarification of objectives.
- a well thought out strategy can help to avoid many of the day-to-day crises that occupy so much management time.
- analysts and investors expect to see a credible story – how a company will produce returns in the future.
- a strategy provides a focus for motivating staff.
- regulators are increasingly demanding it.

What institutional investors are seeking

From all companies

- A leading position in its sector
- A record of delivering shareholder value
  - dividend growth
  - market capitalization v the market
- A record of business performance
  - return
  - growth
- A convincing strategy, showing how performance will be maintained/improved in the future
- Credible management
- No surprises

And additionally from insurance companies

- Capital adequacy
- Reserving adequacy

Sources: Ernst & Young, PwC and others

5.3 The importance of being realistic

The development of strategy is a difficult and complex process that places demands on skill, intellect and judgment. It is an imprecise science and is prone to attract criticism from managers of insurance operations. Some consider it a waste of time, because it may miss the sudden discontinuities we sometimes encounter in the insurance market. Others may want to turn it into an over-bureaucratic and analytical process in the hope that 'we might get it right if only we were more thorough'.

The answer to such criticisms is that managers have a duty of care to look after the shareholders' interest to the best of their ability. This means they must make plans for the most likely scenario, give due consideration to alternative outcomes, and build in some flexibility. To do this they will need to display both insight and leadership, and above all they must remain realistic.

5.4 What does a strategic plan do?

A strategic plan for an insurance operation sets out how the senior management intends to deal with the challenges that faces it. To arrive at these decisions they will have had to think of the operation as a totality. This involves identifying the key factors for the success and growth of the enterprise and devising a framework of objectives, policies, plans and actions for addressing them.

The emphasis of the strategy may differ depending on whether it is created for, say, a holding company, a major national subsidiary, or an individual business. Nevertheless, when a management team begins the process it should be looking to find answers to questions such as the following:

Strategic questions

a. What position does the operation seek in the market?
   - What is its value proposition?
   - What size?
   - What is the portfolio balance and spread?
   - Where in the value chain will it operate?
   - What returns are required?

b. What is its disposition to change:
   - Radical or stable?
   - Willingness to take risks?

c. What sort of corporate citizen does it want to be?
   - Responsibilities towards each stakeholder group?

d. What is the preferred management style?
  - Centralization v decentralization?
  - Core competencies?
  - Value added to the businesses?
  - Control structure?

e. What are the major priorities?

f. How will the strategy be delivered?
  - What, why, where, when, who, how?

g. How will progress be measured?
  - What metrics will be used?

Insurance operations usually develop strategy on a 3-to-5 year horizon. There may be some longer-term objectives, but these are more likely to be aspirational, rather than definite in a rapidly changing environment.

The rest of this chapter describes the process and tools companies actually use, together with some specific examples.

5.5 The strategic planning process

There are as many strategic planning processes as there are strategy consultants, and there are a lot of these! Nevertheless, lying behind most processes there appear to be certain common steps. These are shown in Figure 5.1.

Figure 5.1

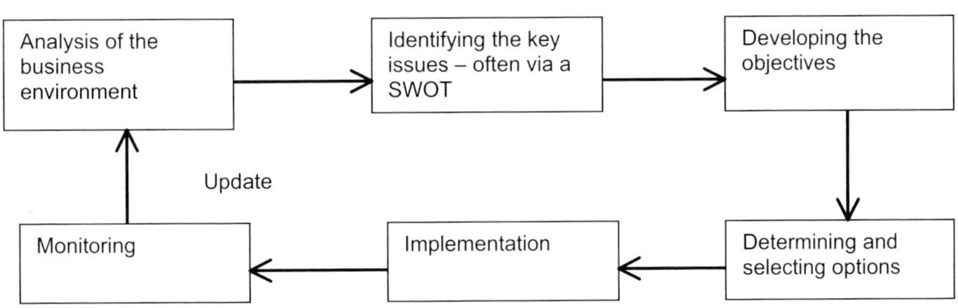

This is not surprising because, like any other management process, it follows the conventional cycle, ie evaluate the evidence, determine the actions, implement, and then monitor progress. In practice, strategic planning rarely happens in a tidy, logical order. It is usually spread out over many meetings and may go through several iterations before the strategy is finalized.

Operations usually update strategies annually, although they may revisit them more frequently in periods of exceptional change. Each step of the process is now considered in turn.

5.5.1. Analysis of the business environment

a) External analysis

Input is given on the key external factors that will impact the organization over the planning horizon. Typical headings will be:

- Political/legal/regulatory
- Economic
- Social
- Technological
- Environmental
- Insurance market/competitors

Some writers refer to this as a PEST analysis from the initial letters of the first four headings.

A thorough external analysis will require considerable research and may involve input from consultants who have knowledge of organizations responding to diverse challenges.

b) Internal analysis

A similar approach is taken for the internal analysis. To do this, the operation is broken down into manageable chunks, which may vary considerably, depending on the level of strategy, eg:

- Corporate strategy – portfolio of major activities such as regional operations, property and casualty, health, life, etc
- Regional strategy – individual businesses and functions in the region
- Business strategy – product lines and supporting services in a business.

5.5.2 Analytical tools

a) Boston Matrix

This well known tool, developed by The Boston Consulting Group (BCG), is typical of a number of matrices that can be used to describe a business (or product) in its market. It plots a business's relative market share against the 'attractiveness' of the market itself (usually measured by market growth). The business will fall into one of four quadrants labelled Seedcorn (traditionally shown as a question mark in the original BCG work), Star, Cash Cow or Dog (see Figure 5.2); which map the four market positions in which a business can find itself. The theory is based on the notion that fast-growing businesses are inherently more profitable in that there would be less pressure to compete on price. Hence, high market share in a high-growth market represents an attractive position. Seedcorn businesses need investment to become Stars for the future. When the market matures and growth (and the associated need for investment) slows, the Stars become Cash Cows. These Cash Cows can then be used to subsidize the Seedcorn businesses. The aim is to produce a balanced, substantially self-sufficient portfolio of businesses.

In an insurance example, a Seedcorn business might be a small insurance subsidiary in the growing Latin America market. The Cash Cow might be a larger business in the mature US market. Profits and expertise from the US should be used to support the development of a smaller subsidiary.

Businesses in the various quadrants need different types of management and targeting. For example, Seedcorn businesses will need managers with marketing skills and be given high growth targets, but Cash Cows will need to be run to maximize profit through efficiency and cost management.

Figure 5.2

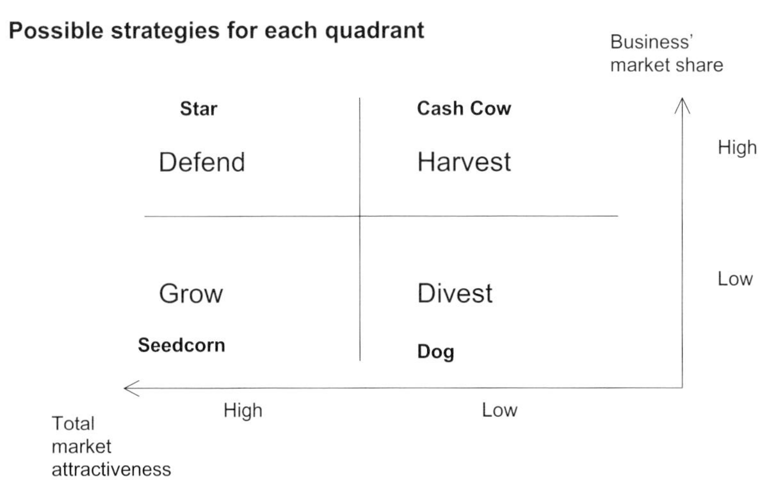

The Boston Matrix is highly graphic and easy to assemble, but relies on the assumption that growing market share makes a business more profitable. Because this is not always the case in insurance, some care is necessary when interpreting results.

Figure 5.3 shows a simplified version of a real matrix used by a P+C insurer to analyse its European portfolio.

Figure 5.3

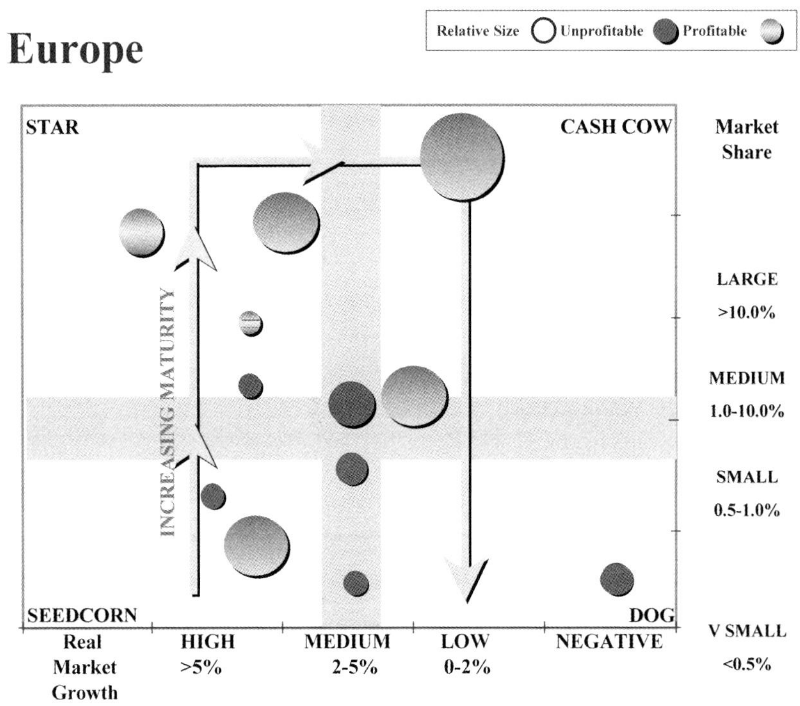

b) The 5 Forces Model

This is a popular tool designed by Michael Porter of Harvard Business School to cluster information from the business environment analysis under a set of dominant market forces. Considering each of these in turn gives an indication of the opportunities and threats impacting the operation and helps management to develop a response with an appropriate strategy.

The five forces are:

Force	Insurance example
1. Threat of new entrants	Supermarkets, aggregators
2. Bargaining power of suppliers	State of the reinsurance market
3. Threat of substitute products	Alternative risk transfer, captives
4. Bargaining power of customers	Purchasing leverage of large corporate customers, major brokers
5. Rivalry between existing players	State of the underwriting cycle

c) Benchmarking

Companies use published material from trade associations, regulators, research organizations, the trade press, management consultants and others to make a quantitative assessment of their activities against their peer group. Where possible, this benchmarking is extended to measurement against leading companies outside the insurance sector.

Of course, there is always a danger that one is not comparing like with like, but benchmarking has an important role in any strategic planning process.

NB – Benchmarking in insurance tends to be more difficult than in banking due to variations in the way costs are allocated or held centrally between companies.

> 'The company had been so successful, for so long, it stopped comparing itself with competitors and started gauging itself by internal measures. That's a recipe for trouble.'
>
> Lou Gerstner, IBM

d) Scenario planning

This technique was developed originally by the Shell Oil Company and has gained some acceptance in the insurance industry. It is not intended as a method of predicting the future, but rather as a way of analysing how a step change in the business environment would impact the operation and its market. This helps to identify the competences required and to devise appropriate defensive or aggressive strategies. For example, an insurance company might explore the proposition that the government will reduce its involvement in social welfare – How would the insurance company respond? What could the company do to benefit or limit the downside risk?

> 'Scenario planning avoids the dangers of simple point forecasts by allowing users to explore the implications of several alternative futures. By surfacing, challenging and altering beliefs, managers are able to test their assumptions in a non-threatening environment. Having examined the full range of possible futures, the company is well positioned to modify its strategic direction as events unfold.'
>
> Darrell Rigby
> *Management Tools and Techniques*, Bain & Co 1999

e) Value chain analysis

Value chain analysis was developed in the 1980s by the business schools, particularly Harvard and Cranfield. Basically, an industry can be regarded as a series of sequential steps, each adding value to the end customer proposition. In a simple manufacturing company the components might be as shown in Figure 5.4.

Figure 5.4

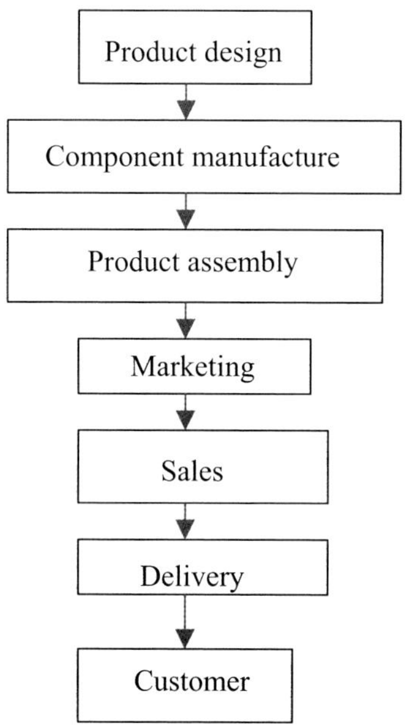

Each step potentially requires different competencies and has a different set of drivers for success. In the past, economic logic encouraged operations to vertically integrate much of the value chain within the company, or even within individual divisions. This gave rise to the so-called silo structure, which can result in the loss of potential scale benefits, and various internal conflicts of interest or uneasy compromises, because the range of different competences and drivers have to be balanced across the business.

Recently there has been a tendency for value chains in some industries to begin to disaggregate – a process facilitated by improvements in communication technology. This is causing companies to look at what they should be doing themselves (and what could be done better by others) and to outsource non-core activities.

Most insurance operations now tend to include some sort of value chain analysis in their planning to seek to ensure that every activity adds value in its own right, has the right competencies, and decide whether it would be better off outsourced. The insurance value chain in discussed in more detail in Chapter 7.

f) Stakeholder model

The theory behind this model is that the management of an insurance operation acts essentially as trustees of the company's resources. It is responsible for allocating them to satisfy the needs of the various stakeholders and managing a series of what should be mutually beneficial relationships (see Figure 5.5).

Figure 5.5

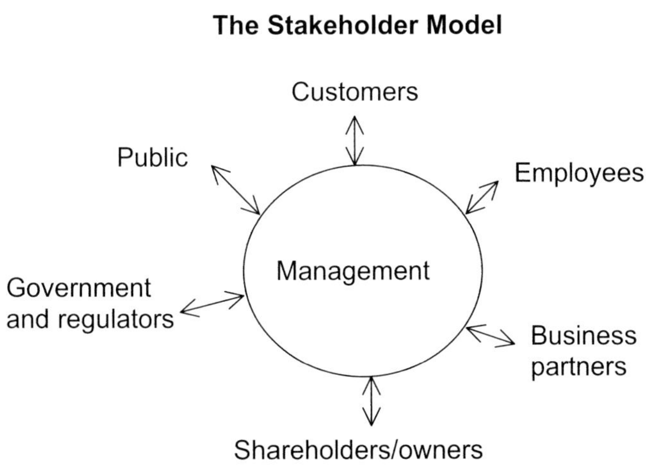

This model helps an operation to understand the various interests that need to be taken into account and allows decisions to be made on what the strategy will deliver for each stakeholder group. An operation could well place more emphasis on one set of the stakeholders at the expense of others. For example:

- An economic value added (EVA) strategy emphasizes the needs of the shareholders.
- A customer-focused strategy emphasizes the needs of the customer.

This situation is totally acceptable, but in the long run the interests of all the stakeholders will have to be addressed, at least to some extent, for an organization to be successful. This proposition is discussed later in the context of business ethics in Chapter 17.

Stakeholder relationships

'Management are the trustees of a company's resources. They are responsible for satisfying the needs of the various stakeholders and managing what should be six mutually beneficial relationships. It is a bit like the old circus act where you have to keep six plates spinning on the top of six different poles all at the same time.'

CEO, major UK P+C insurer

For a mutual company, its owners are some or all of its customers. Potentially, a customer who also owns part of the company may have somewhat different needs to someone who is just a customer, or just a shareholder. Where not all customers have ownership rights over the company, you then have to separately manage the stakeholder needs of the two separate sub-sets of customers.

5.5.3 Identifying the key issues

The next step in the strategic planning process is to take the large number of issues raised in the analysis of the business environment and prioritize them.

The best-known tool for helping with this exercise is the SWOT Analysis. The key internal Strengths and Weaknesses and the key external Opportunities and Threats are drawn up into a four-quadrant matrix. A typical SWOT for a health insurer might look like the one shown in Figure 5.6.

Figure 5.6: SWOT for a hypothetical UK Health Insurer

Internal

Strengths	Weaknesses
• Market share • Sales force • Strong brand • Provider relationships	• Rising expense ratio • Inadequate technology • Ageing product portfolio • Reserving

External

Opportunities	Threats
• Acquisition of competitor • Total health care packages • Rehabilitation • Outsourcing	• Government attitude to private sector • New entrants • Economic recession • Rising health costs

Note – This company may appear to have a reasonably strong current position but has to make choices about where to invest in an uncertain market of the future, eg acquisition, reserve strengthening, new propositions. Can it afford to do everything?

> 'Strategy is about making choices.'
>
> Professor Michael Porter, Harvard University

As with many of the techniques used in planning, the real benefit of a SWOT analysis is not so much the final list of issues, but the deeper understanding of the business that is provided as managers work through the exercise.

5.5.4 Developing the objectives

Having analysed the business environment and identified the key issues, the management of an insurance operation should be in position to begin to articulate a clear set of strategic objectives. If it is merely updating an existing strategy this step should be relatively straightforward. If there is to be a major change of strategic direction it could well be much harder.

In an insurance operation there will always need to be a hierarchy of objectives. They may be broad or narrow in scope; they may be long term or immediate. In strategic planning it is normal to start with the long-range, operation-wide objectives and these are subsequently translated into individual units' objectives and short-term targets.

Nomenclature may vary, but insurance operations often use some sort of Mission (or Vision) Statement. This can be quite short like 'To be the blue chip UK insurance company' or it may be something much longer and more complex.

Actual mission statements from the insurance industry

- 'We will remain a major and growing autonomous quoted company with its core activity in insurance, operating predominantly in the UK supported by selective representation in the major overseas insurance markets which, over time, will produce a better geographical spread. Through a commitment to management, financial strength, quality of products and service, we will ensure that the expectations of our shareholders, customers and staff are fully met.'
- 'To help individuals achieve financial comfort and security throughout life, for themselves and for their dependents; to create a business environment which gives effective service and good value to our customers; to offer satisfying jobs and careers to our staff and to meet the reasonable expectations of our shareholders.'
- 'To provide a superior return on shareholders' capital by offering risk protection, investment and financial services to corporate and individual clients on an international scale. We endeavour to satisfy clients' needs through efficient and cost-effective services and by being fair and considerate in all our dealings.'

One powerful technique, sometimes called 'the light on the hill', is to write an imaginary statement from the Chairman in five years time looking back over the recent past and outlining the operation's main achievements. This can be helpful in defining a framework of objectives, clarifying where it is you want to get to and the key steps to get you there from the current position, and can prove to be highly motivational when it comes to communicating the final strategy.

Extracts from an insurer's 'light on the hill'

Overall

- The leading and most influential commercial insurer in the broker market.
- One of the largest direct personal lines providers.
- ROC exceeds target X%
- Achieve underwriting profit
- World-class customer service benchmarking results
- Brand recognition Y%
- Broken down silo structures and become one company

Underwriting and risk selection

- Industry leading underwriting results throughout the cycle
- Superior technical pricing and risk selection techniques
- Retained the best technical experts
- Region-wide common processes

Claims service and claims management

- Single claims function
- Demanding targets for indemnity cost savings and service standards

Customer relationship management

- Adopted best practice approach and drove it through the operation
- Targeted specific customer segments and measured success

Our people

- Identified and empowered a new set of leaders
- Clear direction supported by good communications
- Culture that recognized and rewarded performance

Capital and risk management

- Took tough decisions to improve performance
- Applied streamlined business models
- Controlled costs
- Assessed price v risk, and investment v reward
- Reduced business services overhead

Technology and services

- Simplified technology
- Simplified processes
- Rationalized locations

5.5.5 Determining and selecting options

Gap analysis

To create strategic options an analysis is necessary. Essentially, management asks the questions for each objective:

- Where are we today?
- Where does the objective want us to be?
- What is the gap?
- How could it be filled?
- What are the options?
- What are the pros and cons of each?

Gap analysis is particularly associated with John Argenti in the pioneering days of modern corporate planning in the 1960s. However, the principle is still as valid today.

For example, if an insurance operation has a decided on a particular growth objective which is not achievable by organic growth of its existing book alone, it must look at how to bridge the gap from the current position. This could include steps such as geographical expansion, new related products, or even diversification (see Figure 5.7).

Figure 5.7

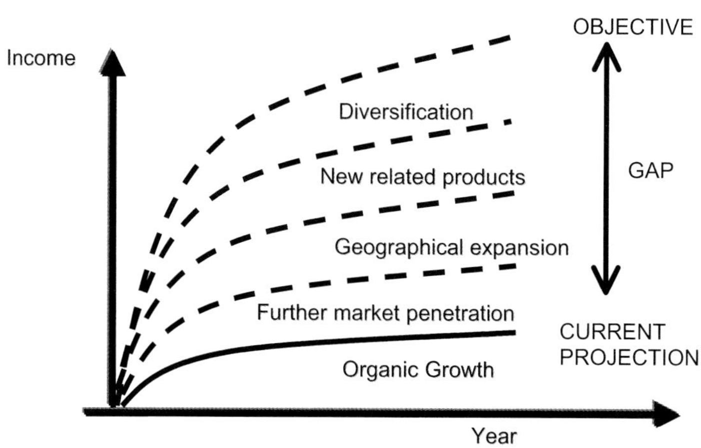

Option generation

The generation of strategic options is the most creative part of the strategic planning process. A common approach in insurance is to use one or more of the following:

a) Planning awaydays

The management team takes a few days away from the office to concentrate on brainstorming and evaluating options. Facilitators are often useful to ensure that all objectives are addressed – including the difficult ones!

b) Consultants

There are many strategic consultants operating in the insurance sector ranging from giants like the McKinsey & Co and the Boston Consultancy Group down to sole traders. They bring a range of skills and experience of dealing with similar problems in other companies and sectors.

c) Task forces

A team of people with the appropriate skills is charged with analysing the problem and reporting back with recommendations.

d) Hothouses

This is a variation on the task force when a team with fresh minds (eg new graduates) is asked to develop new and radical solutions. Hothouses became particularly popular with many companies during the Internet boom.

Option selection

The questions asked at this stage are:

- Does it meet the strategic objectives?
- Does it pass the financial appraisal and meet the required returns?
- Are the risks acceptable?
- How will the market react?

One method of testing how the market might react is to play war games. Managers are divided into teams, each team pretending to be a major competitor. After careful briefing, the teams are asked to respond to an imaginary press release announcing the option. This is a simple but surprisingly powerful and productive technique.

Modelling

As an aid to decision-making it has become common for insurance companies to simulate their performance using computer models. The effect of changing external and internal variables on possible outcomes can be studied. Similar models may also be used by regulators and major brokers to assess a company's strength and security.

Of course, the validity of the exercise will depend on the assumptions made, the quality of the data input and closeness to reality of the model itself.

At some point the options will probably need to be discussed with the board before final approval can be given. This is an important event and the senior management will normally take great care in making the presentation. By way of example, the outline of the plan presenting options to the main board of an international insurer is shown in the Appendix to this chapter.

5.5.6 Implementation

The basic steps of implementation are:

a) Allocate responsibility

Be clear who is responsible for delivery, who is accountable for success and ensure that they are empowered to make things happen.

b) Develop an action plan

Break down the activities necessary to achieve the objectives, understand their interrelationships, determine the sequencing of activities and allocate the resources.

c) Communicate

It is important to let all those who will be affected know what is happening as soon as is practically possible. Preferably, involve key staff in the planning phase to ensure buy in to the changes.

d) Build in a monitoring process

Establish clear and unambiguous measures of success and review progress towards achieving them frequently.

Reasons for failure

Unfortunately, many strategies fail or are only partly successful, particularly in large and complex organizations such as insurance operations. There may be a variety of reasons apart from the obvious one of poor planning, but two in particular seem to recur:

- Lack of a perceived reason for change

Unless there is a compelling reason for change, large organizations have a habit of quickly reverting to old behaviours. Really difficult change processes are almost impossible to implement without an acknowledgement 'from all key executives of the existence of a burning platform', ie recognition that the company risks total failure if it does not change in the way proposed.

- Lack of leadership

Major change needs committed, highly visible leadership who remain focused on the strategy and are prepared to drive it through the organization. Middle management often finds it very difficult to implement strategy without clear and active support from the top.

5.5.7 Monitoring and dealing with variances

Measuring the progress made in implementing a strategy is essential to ensure delivery, deal with problems at an early stage, and respond to changes in circumstances. This process is relatively straightforward for a small unit. but becomes increasingly difficult in larger, more complex organizations.

The traditional approach was for senior management to concentrate mainly on financial measures. However, in recent years more holistic monitoring methods have become accepted, usually based on a 'balanced scorecard'. This arose out of the work by Kaplan and Norton at Harvard Business School who proposed integrating conventional financial measures with appropriate customer, process and organizational capability measures.

In this method, key performance indicators (KPIs) and milestones showing a balance of predictive and actual outcome measures are built into a monthly report for the board. The report contains a mixture of tables and graphs, each supported by a brief commentary and possibly a traffic light status coding:

Green	=	On schedule
Amber	=	Attention required
Red	=	Behind schedule

Depending on the type of information involved, the individual items may be updated monthly, quarterly or annually. Normally a specific board member would be responsible for each item, and for carrying out any remedial action necessary to meet targets.

Example

Balanced scorecard used by a P+C insurer.

Financial

- Return on capital
- Operating ratios
- Growth
- Pricing movements
- Reserving movements
- Cash flow
- Cost savings
- Claims leakage
- Competitor performance
- Distribution mix

Processes

- Key project milestones
- Adverse internal audits
- E-business
  - Intermediary EDI %
  - Direct customer usage %
  - Suppliers EDI %
- Service Functions
  - Service Levels achieved

Customers

- Customer satisfaction
- Intermediary satisfaction
- Customer complaints
- Media profile

People

- Competency levels
- Training costs
- Culture change milestones
- Employee satisfaction survey
- Employee
  - Numbers
  - Turnover
  - Absences

Select bibliography

S Diacon (Ed), *A Guide to Insurance Management*, Macmillan 1990, Chapters 1, 2 and 4.

R Koch, *The Financial Times Guide to Strategy 2nd Ed*, F T Prentice Hall 2000.

Richard Lynch, *Corporate Strategy*, Pitman Publishing 1997.

M Goold, A Campbell, M Alexander, *Corporate Level Strategy: Creating Value in the Multibusiness Company*, John Wiley & Sons 1994.

Harvard Business Review on Measuring Corporate Performance, Harvard Business School Press 1998, cites R Kaplan, D Norton, *The Balanced Scorecard*, Harvard Business Review 1992, Vol 70 No. 1 pp71-79.

Appendix to Chapter 5

Strategic options presentation for an international insurance group.

GROUP STRATEGIC DIRECTION

Section 1:
Background

- Rationale for change
- Benefits for stakeholders

Section 2:
Market environment

- Political factors
- Socio-demographic factors
- Technological factors
- Industry factors
- Demand, market growth
- Underwriting cycles
- Major customer segments
- Competitors
- Investment markets

Section 3:
Current group position

- Capitalization
- Portfolio balance: product, geographic, etc (including Boston Matrices)
- General insurance
- Life assurance
- Re-insurance

Section 4:
Financial objectives

- ROC
- Solvency
- Embedded value
- Growth (including stochastic models for different scenarios)

Section 5:
Strategic marketing plans

- Value propositions
- Target segments

Section 6
Cross-regional views

- General business task force
- Life and investment business task force
- Fund management task force

Section 7
Summary and strategic options

- Summary and key issues
- Strategic options:
  a. building on the status quo
  b. global segmentation synergy
- Impact and risk analysis of options
- Conclusion and recommendations

These are the main headings from the 82-page document presented by the executive management to the main board. It was the result of six months' work led by the chief executive, supported by the strategic planning department and several task forces.

Figure 5.8

The generic strategic planning process

- There is no single, right way to plan
- The process should be iterative
- An annual, 3-year rolling strategy is most common
- In times of great change the review may need to be more frequent.

Steps	Tools (examples)
External analysis ↓	PEST Boston matrix Directional policy matrix Porters 5 forces Value chain analysis
Internal analysis ↓	
Key issues ↓	SWOT
Objectives ↓	Vision Mission Financial objectives
Strategic options ↓	Away days Consultants Working groups
Selection ↓	Financial appraisal Risk appraisal
Action plans ↓	→ Budget
Implementation ↓	
Monitoring	Balanced scorecard KPIs

Cycle (Monitoring → External analysis)

EnablEd Ltd

Six

Commonly applied insurance strategies

Objectives

On completion of this chapter, and wider personal research, the reader should be able to:

- understand a range of corporate and business strategies employed in P+C insurance
- explain the use of size, portfolio, bancassurance and geographical spread strategies
- discuss the use of commoditization, call centres and cross-selling in an insurance context
- compare organic growth, acquisition and strategic alliances as methods of changing a portfolio.

6.1 Introduction

Strategies may be classified broadly as:

- corporate strategies: which originate in the centre, eg the holding company, and operate across, and add value to, the whole organization.
- business strategies: which aim to give competitive advantage to each business in its individual market. They are usually developed by the businesses themselves.

Insurance is similar to most other industries in so far as its operations tend to position themselves either as:

(i) generalists: with a broad base of propositions and segments, or

(ii) niche players: focused on a narrow selection

They also seek to gain advantage over their competitors by some combination of:

(i) low cost, and

(ii) differentiation

These themes recur in the following examples, which have been chosen to give some idea of the current thinking in the industry.

Corporate strategies

The examples here are those relating to:

a) size

b) portfolio

c) geographical spread

d) organization

We shall look at each in turn.

6.2.1 Size strategies

An insurance operation should decide what size it needs to be to compete effectively.

Large insurance operations should be able to create advantage through scale economies, experience and market power (see Figure 6.1).

Scale economies

Costs can be spread over more policies and so reduce the expense ratio. Investment in IT systems can be more cost effective.

Experience

Larger organizations potentially benefit from greater experience. In insurance this means that the underwriting accounts should become more predictable. They can also afford to have more technical specialists in-house, who can add value.

Figure 6.1

The Virtuous Circle of Scale

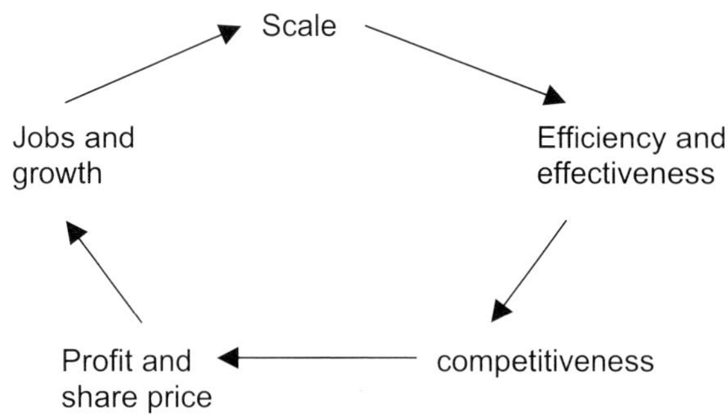

Creating advantage out of scale is never easy but the rewards can be compelling. It creates a virtuous circle. Success breeds success.

Proper use of scale can produce efficiency and effectiveness. The outcomes are:

- a better competitive position
- more profit
- higher share price
- more growth, and
- more jobs

This gives us more scale and the cycle continues.

'Great companies do not shrink their way to success.'

Dr. Jules Goddard, London Business School

Market power

This may manifest itself in the potential to:

- influence market **pricing.** As a dominant player it can hold prices at a lower level to put pressure on companies with higher expense ratios. Alternatively, it can use its reputation to charge premium prices or to lead prices upwards.
- exploit **buying power** over suppliers, for example in reinsurance and claims procurement.

A typical insurance market in equilibrium is likely to show the characteristics depicted in Figure 6.2.

Figure 6.2: Generic market profitability model

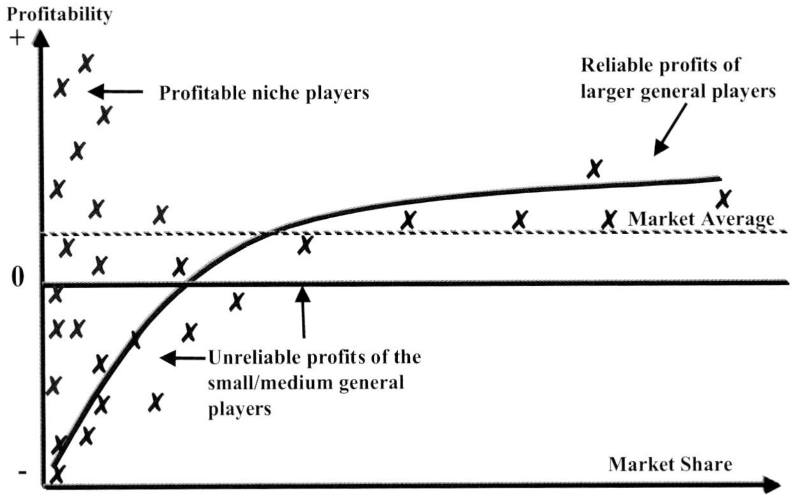

Source: - City University Business School

> 'Efficiency scores are strongly associated with insurer size, with clear evidence of a U-shaped relationship, ie both small and large insurers appear to have higher efficiency scores.'
>
> Professor Stephen Diacon, University of Nottingham 2002

Above-average profitability is achieved by very large generalists and by some niche players. Medium-sized generalists are unable to obtain the advantages of either the larger players or those of the successful niche players. Over time they become very vulnerable to acquisition by players wishing to grow.

On the other hand, **niche players** need to be able to defend their positions from the lower costs of their large competitors. The underlying dilemma of the niche is growth: the larger it becomes the farther it moves from its core specialism. There is more than an element of truth in the old saying 'a niche is a tomb'.

Case study – A niche is a tomb: collapses of Municipal Mutual (1993) and Iron Trades (1990)

Niche marketing can be a highly successful strategy, allowing a company to out-perform larger generalists. However, when the niche becomes unprofitable, the company may find itself trapped. This is exactly what happened to two famous UK companies.

Municipal Mutual

Specialized in local government risks, building a profitable business from its close relationships at Town Halls. It was the undisputed leader in its field for many years until the 1980s when the environment changed. Increased litigation against councils, school arson, latent defects in building design and finally terrorism claims turned what had been a profitable niche into a loss maker. Attempts were made to diversify into other classes of business, both in the UK and abroad, but to no avail and solvency collapsed. In 1993 existing business was transferred to the Zurich and the rump put into run off.

Iron Trades

Specialized in the heavy engineering and ship-building industries and was a pioneer of employers' liability insurance. The niche remained profitable for almost a century, but the decline of heavy industry in the UK, together with the increase in occupational disease litigation, especially deafness and asbestosis, took their toll. Diversification came too late and, as in the case of Municipal Mutual, the business was split into two companies. Existing clients were taken on by one company which was subsequently sold along with the Iron Trades name to the Australian insurer QBE. The rump company, formed to run off the pre-1990 liabilities, was named Chester Street. This unfortunately went into liquidation in 2001, causing hardship to many long-term claimants.

Disadvantages of size

Size of course has its own disadvantages. Problems of communication, coordination and motivation occur and large companies can become slow, inflexible and vulnerable to faster-moving niche players.

Problems of size

'You may think that you are a shark in your waters but the piranhas will get you.'

Anon

'It is a biological law that, the larger an organism, the greater is the ratio between its mass and its surface and the less exposure to the outside there is for the cells inside.'

Drucker

'The bad news is that huge companies like us can't compete against small, nimble companies. The good news is, at this rate we'll be the smallest company around!'

Dilbert, Scott Adams, 1997

In very large organizations, the management may become rather in-bred and divorced from the outside world and the organization's customers.The easiest way to overcome this is to recruit from outside.

6.2.2 Portfolio strategies

The exact balance of the portfolio dictates the whole nature of the operation. Examples might include:

Corporate portfolio balance

- Insurance v other financial services (bancassurance)
- Manufacture v distribution of insurance (value chain)
- Life v general insurance (composite)
- General insurance v risk-related services (diversification)

The balance within the general insurance account eg

Business portfolio balance

- Commercial v Personal
- Property v Casualty
- Home v Motor
- Long tail v Short tail

Is the subject of business strategy.

The factors that may dictate the design of a portfolio are:

Design factors

- Business opportunities in the different elements, and potential synergies between them
- The operation's core competencies
- The needs of the existing customer base
- The spreading of risk

The Boston Matrix, described in Chapter 5 is a useful tool to assist in portfolio design. It works on the premise that different products or businesses have different characteristics according to their position in the business cycle. A largely self-sustaining, balanced portfolio is possible by reallocating resources between them.

The main options for growing a portfolio are organic growth, acquisition or strategic alliance.

a) Growth by organic means

The organic approach is the most straightforward, especially if there is an existing business that can be developed. The main disadvantage is that it can be slow and the business or product might take an unacceptable time to attain critical mass. The steps taken (price reductions, increased advertising, etc) are likely to be expensive and may reduce profitability in the short run. If there is not an existing entity, a start up will be necessary. This may require competencies that are not readily available in the operation and so involve head-hunting specialists from outside.

b) Growth by acquisition or merger

> **M & A**
>
> 'The weight of research evidence indicates that the majority of corporately sponsored acquisitions, alliances, new ventures and business re-definitions fail to create value.'
>
> Michael Porter, Harvard Business School
>
> 'Merger (integration) costs are frequently higher than expected and firms may struggle to achieve the forecast cost-side synergies.'
>
> Managing Risks: Practical lessons from recent 'failures' of EU Insurers
> William McDonnell, FSA 2002

Purchase of, or merger with, a competitor's business is often the first choice of management. It provides a rapid answer to acquiring volume but, unfortunately, the majority of acquisitions and mergers in insurance fail to deliver fully the expected benefits. In the case of acquisitions, once an acquisition opportunity arises it may develop a momentum of its own, especially if there are several bidders. In these circumstances some of the basic rules may be overlooked.

Mergers and acquisitions: Basic rules

A merger as opposed to an acquisition implies

- parity of size
- consent of both parties

The attractions are a better understanding of the target and it may be cheaper because of less write-off of goodwill.

Golden rules

1. Know why you are doing the deal

- Understand how the transaction fits your strategic aims in terms of size, spread, products, distribution, expertise, expenses, etc.
- Can these be satisfied in another way?
- How much will it cost, how much will it save, and can it be justified to the shareholders, customers and staff?
- Articulate it all in a clear set of objectives.
- Everything that follows must contribute to the achievement of those objectives.

2. Know what you are merging with/buying

- Do your homework on the target.
- 'Skeletons' are inevitable, so face up to them from the start. Insurance, being a long-term business, is more susceptible than most to skeletons.
- Are the key employees included in the deal?
- Are the reserves adequate?
- 'Marry in haste, repent at leisure.' (proverb)

3. Plan the integration thoroughly

- Appoint a senior executive to lead the integration and have him or her establish control immediately.
- Appoint senior management early.
- Use dedicated task forces drawn from each business unit and function.
- Communicate frequently to the stakeholders.
- Understand and resolve differences in culture between the two companies.

A case of not knowing what you are buying

Some years ago, a major insurer bought a small company in another country, believing it to be a self-contained insurance company. Only after the deal was signed did the insurer learn that the acquisition was in fact only an underwriting agent, and therefore did not own its customer base.

M & A – What goes wrong?

In his studies of M&A over a cross-section of industries, Peter DiCiero of City University has suggested that the success rate has been disappointing:

- half of all acquisitions fail to achieve the promised benefits
- half result in the same or lower profits
- three-quarters take 10 years or more to recover the cost of the deal

The main reasons are probably:

- inadequate screening and due diligence
- insufficient attention being paid to post-acquisition integration

He also believes that the expectations from M&A are usually too high, ie:

- cost synergies are overestimated
- revenue enhancement is overestimated
- up-front costs are underestimated

Finally, not enough time is spent on planning the human aspects, as opposed to financial. factors.

M & A in insurance appears to be no different to that in other industries.

City University

Culture Differences

When a major, fairly old fashioned, insurer purchased a risk-related services business, it underestimated the difference between its own conservative culture and the more relaxed attitudes of the new subsidiary. The shock came in the first Christmas after the deal when the subsidiary sent greetings cards to all the parent company's most important clients. Inside each card was a contraceptive bearing the message 'For the best protection, come to us!'.

Some clients were not amused.

c) Growth by strategic alliance

A strategic alliance is an arrangement between two or more parties that meets their separate and mutual needs. The main types, in order of degree of commitment, are as follows:

Strategic alliance

1. Contractual alliance

The parties form a binding agreement for a specific project, but have a limited role in each other's strategy.

2. Minority investment

Stronger ties are cemented by equity transfer (cross shareholding).

3. Joint venture

A new, jointly-owned business is created, separate from the principal parties.

Strategic alliances have an advantage over acquisitions in that they:

- are cheaper
- reduce the risks of a difficult integration
- allow an easier exit, if needed.

They may be used as a trial stage in advance of an eventual merger. All types of alliance require:

- a strategy that clearly benefits both sides
- agreed rules for decision-making
- excellent communication.

Perhaps the most topical portfolio strategy is Bancassurance.

Bancassurance

The term *bancassurance* in its widest sense means the selling of banking and insurance products through the same channel. This has been possible for many decades as banks and building societies have been agents for both life and general insurance companies.

In the narrow sense, bancassurance means the joint ownership of banking and insurance operations so that the bank effectively becomes a manufacturer of insurance products. This definition is probably the more usually understood today.

In Germany, the word *allfinanz* is used in much the same way although it often relates to an insurance company owning a bank.

The attraction to a bank in **selling** insurance through its branch network is obvious. It can earn risk-free commission income and provide a wider proposition to its customer base. The question is why have bancassurers chosen the route of manufacturing insurance, not just selling it?

Although there had been a few examples of banks manufacturing insurance as early as the 1960s, the main interest started in the late 1980s. This was due to the coming together of several factors, namely:

a) Deregulation allowing companies in one area of financial services to become involved in others. (This process has been slower in some countries, eg the USA).

b) Improvements in information technology, which increased the effectiveness of cross-selling.

c) A growing appreciation of the value of strong brands and large customer bases.

At the time, there was a general feeling that a 'financial services revolution' was beginning and the traditional market structure was about to disintegrate. Financial institutions of all types took steps to secure their distribution and defend their customer bases.

Some banks took the view that controlling more of the insurance value chain could strengthen their hold over the customers as well as producing opportunities to make scale economies and insurance profits. The logic applied to general insurance, both personal and commercial, but the overwhelming initial interest was in life assurance.

Life assurance was perceived to have several advantages, ie it was:

- a growth area because of socio-demographic forces
- stable and profitable
- less complicated than general insurance
- complemented the savings and investment products of the bank

Banks soon began to develop their own life assurance operations by acquisition, joint venture or, in a few cases, from scratch.

In some countries this strategy has proved to be highly successful but in others, particularly the UK, the initial promise has failed to be fulfilled. An investigation into bancassurance by Ernst & Young in 1999 (Insurance Executive – Issue One 1999 – Ernst & Young) suggested that banks were seen as 'credible sellers of insurance' but had never really mastered manufacturing of insurance products.

They listed the following problems:

Problems experienced by UK bancassurers

- Too many product offerings causing confusion at branches and difficulties in prioritization, eg life, general insurance, unit trusts, deposits, loans, credit cards.
- Low closing ratios and transaction values compared with specialist life companies.
- Low productivity.
- Products not best of breed.
- Costly and complex IT systems.

About this time independent financial advisers began to regain the initiative in the UK market and the whole life industry experienced difficulties regarding mis-selling. As a result, some bancassurers withdrew from the market.

The manufacture of general insurance by banks is much less common, possibly due to an unwillingness to carry the underwriting risk on the balance sheet. At the time of writing the best known example in the UK is RBoS, which owns Direct Line, and HBoS, which now also writes its own motor business.

The long-term future of the bancassurance model is presently in the balance. E-based distribution models, whereby a range of complementary banking and insurance products are supplied by partners alongside the company's own products, may well prove to be more successful. A typical example in the UK is egg.com, which has been set up by Prudential Assurance.

6.2.3 Geographical spread strategy

The underlying attractiveness of a market for insurance depends on a combination of factors. One insurer uses a quantitative assessment process as follows:

Market attractiveness assessment

Countries can be compared quantitatively by applying weighted scores to each of these factors:

1. GDP size
2. GDP growth rate
3. Inflation rate
4. Political/social stability
5. Size of general insurance market
6. Catastrophe potential
7. Insurance penetration – premium as a percentage of GDP
8. Freedom of operation (regulation, tariffs, etc)

The choice of geographical spread will depend on the operation's aims, ie:

- to grow by replicating the home model in attractive foreign markets
- to follow multinational customers
- to spread risk

At the time of writing, a few companies have selected global strategies (eg AIG, AXA), others concentrate on a specific region such as Europe, Latin America or Australasia, and a majority restrict themselves to just one country, or a very small number of countries. Some of the long-established insurers have no obvious geographical focus, their current portfolios being the result of a number of mergers and acquisitions over the years.

It is worth remembering that, when trading conditions become difficult, it is usually the overseas subsidiaries that are the first to be sold off to support the home operation.

It will be interesting to see how developing maturity of the Internet will affect geographical spread strategies. It will undoubtedly become easier for countries to be serviced remotely. At present the limiting factors are regulation, market practice and language.

6.2.4 Organizational strategies

Most large insurance operations are multi-business organizations controlled by a holding company. Such operations are obviously much more complex than their smaller competitors and require carefully thought-through organizational strategies.

Holding companies often destroy value by creating bureaucracy, incurring costs and, sometimes, making poor decisions on behalf of the constituent businesses. If this value destruction outweighs the added value of the holding company the company should be broken up and the businesses sold to competitors who can make better use of them.

There is no absolute right or wrong way for an operation to organize itself to ensure success. However, there are some common factors that are often found in world-class companies of any industry, and it is becoming evident that some of the best insurance operations are taking a similar approach. The factors are as follows:

- Holding companies should have a clearly defined group strategy that is understood by all the stakeholders.
- The holding companies do not prescribe the business strategies of their businesses but instead provide a strong policy framework within which the businesses are empowered. This is described by Ashridge as **'strategic control'** and represents a mid course between centralization and decentralization, adopting the best of each. It helps the businesses to respond to the needs of the customer and allows the holding company to make pan-organizational changes rapidly and obtain scale advantage where possible.

Changes in organizational structure

'Vertical, integrated silos prevent economies of scale and distract businesses from concentrating on core competencies.

New organizational structures are being based on a number of business units focused on customer segments.

These are supported by shared infrastructure and outsourced services.

There is a framework of policy, not subsidiary independence, and no central dictat.'

Ashridge Management School

- Acceptance that it is not possible to be world class in everything, everywhere. Therefore, even the largest of generalists are **selecting where they wish to play** and then taking a leading position in these areas.
- The front end of world-class companies is **customer oriented** because the requirements of geographical markets differ and holding companies are remote from customer needs. However, businesses are not allowed to reinvent the wheel in every location. **Common business models** are used and, wherever possible, local customization of standard solutions.
- Realization that the **core intellectual capital** is the lifeblood that needs to be developed, protected and shared. Such knowledge is a source of innovation and a protection against making the mistakes of the past. Nevertheless, in the spate of mergers and acquisitions that has occurred over recent years, many companies have shed intellectual capital in an effort to reduce processing costs. The better companies try to maintain strong intellectual capital which they leverage and share.

Intellectual capital

'Over my career, I have learnt that it is knowledge and experience of insurance that determine long-term success. Quality here is our rarest commodity and I think it was something that was eroded in the consolidation of the market in the mid 1990s as companies focused on attacking expense ratios. As we all know, the loss ratio is the biggest single component of the operating ratio. Weakness in underwriting, risk management or claims management eventually comes back to haunt insurers. On the other hand, application of deep expertise in these areas has a greater leverage on the bottom line than anything else.'

UK P+C CEO

Actual knowledge sharing requires a process of identifying key knowledge, identifying the key audiences, and then bringing the two together effectively, via technology such as e-mail and intranet sites.

> ### Knowledge sharing pitfalls
>
> One of the leading knowledge-sharing consultants has said that companies commonly make the following mistakes:
>
> - They pay more attention to managing the medium (intranet, etc) than the message (the content).
> - They believe that knowledge sharing can be used to reduce the number of managers and experts in an organization.
> - They believe that merely putting an intranet site in front of a person is all that is necessary to create knowledge sharing.
>
>   The sad fact is that:
>   - people frequently don't have the time or understanding to use them.
>   - inexperienced staff 'do not know what they don't know' and so need constant supervision and guidance.

- Successful companies tend to positively select, develop and rotate what they believe to be their greatest asset – their **people**. They develop a culture that is appropriate to the organization as a whole and the chosen brand strategy. This usually includes shared values and a common approach among all decision makers.
- Achieving **scale advantage** is relatively straightforward within a single business, but it is much more difficult in a large, complex operation. Nevertheless, some large insurance companies are generating real efficiency and effectiveness. They do it by leveraging their purchasing power, simplifying the spaghetti of systems, sharing processes and outsourcing where others can do things more effectively. Such companies concentrate on core similarities, rather than local differences. The watchword for back-end processing is simplicity. Any business not using a company standard process must prove that the benefits outweigh the loss in scale advantage, ie a reverse onus of proof. The best companies understand the trade-off between scale advantage and local empowerment.
- The area that really seems to make the most difference between the 'world class' and the 'rest' is in **driving** to success. The winners tend to be those who have clear metrics for those few selected things that really matter, impose stretching targets on the businesses, and actively monitor progress.
  - They take rapid and decisive action when performance differs from plan.
  - They do not waste effort and resources on measuring and managing the irrelevant.
  - Above all, they understand the value of clear business goals.

6.3 Business strategies

The examples of business strategies chosen here are:

a) commoditization
b) securing distribution
c) call centres
d) cross-selling

a) Commoditization

Commoditization of insurance is particularly suitable for large operations with a strong brand, and is mainly targeted at personal and SME business. Banks and other corporate intermediaries are attracted to it because they can partner with low-cost insurance 'manufacturers' and they also do not need to build up much internal insurance expertise to develop products.

The aim is to produce high-volume, simple products and compete on price and brand. This involves taking steps to:

- achieve a low cost position
- strengthen sales capability
- differentiate on brand image

If there are product variations these should, as far as possible, be restricted to basic, augmented and superior.

b) Securing distribution

There have been many instances in recent years of insurers attempting to secure distribution by taking an equity interest in, or even purchasing outright, a distributor such as a broker or real estate agent. The practice began in the UK in the 1980s, with a number of insurers buying chains of estate agents in the hope of taking advantage of the so-called 'golden moment' when a customer buys a house. At that moment there is a unique opportunity to sell life assurance, home insurance and other financial products. Having an interest in an estate agent theoretically provided:

- a new profit stream,
- influence over distribution,
- raised barriers for competitors,
- a wider proposition to the customer.

The main attraction to the estate agent firms (which were mostly partnerships) was that many partners saw this as an opportunity to liberate their capital and it also provided financial backing at a time when significant investment was needed in technology.

Insurers also began to buy brokers in the hope of securing personal lines distribution, eg Sun Alliance purchased the high street broker Swinton, and Norwich Union acquired Hill House Hammond.

In practice, most of these ventures were less than successful due to:

- conflicts of interest and culture,
- loss of entrepreneurial management in the distributor
- the distributors experienced profit downturns in phase with those of the insurers.

At the time of writing, a variation on the strategy has recently been resurrected by a number of insurers, who have been taking equity interests in commercial brokers.

c) Call centres

Call centres are used in many industries, and have been found to be a highly effective way of servicing personal and, increasingly, SME business. Essentially, smart systems deliver easy-to-understand propositions to front line telephone advisers who match the needs of the customer to the relevant product. The telephone advisers are supported by managers who are responsible for performance and consistency of service. This requires expertise in:

- call forecasting and matching resources
- call management
- call recording and monitoring
- customer relationship management
- sale completion techniques.

The big challenge is to keep the customer-facing staff motivated and focused, and to ensure that the turnover of staff is low.

d) Cross-selling

The compelling logic of cross-selling is that it should be both easier and cheaper to sell an additional product to an existing customer than to secure an entirely new customer. In order to do this an insurer usually takes the following steps:

- build a **brand**
- surround each chosen customer segment with appropriate **products**
- create a customer **database** whereby an individual's product holdings and potential needs can be determined
- develop **tactics** for exploiting cross-selling opportunities, eg a mail shot at renewal
- provide an **incentive** for the customer to switch from their existing insurer, eg a discount for holding multiple products.

Most personal lines insurers are actively engaged in cross-selling. A few are remarkably successful but most struggle to achieve much more than an average of 1.5 policies per customer. The reasons appear to be as follows:

- There are few really strong brands in insurance. It is interesting to note that, after some TV advertising campaigns, recognition of the insurer's name may rise by a few percentage points, but very often its competitors' sales also increase in the same proportion. In other words, brands are so weak that advertising sells insurance in general, rather than for the company specifically.
- Some products are much easier to cross-sell than others. For example, it is relatively easy to sell roadside assistance services or legal expenses as add-on products to a motor customer. On the other hand, the gap between general insurance and life, savings or loans business may be much harder to bridge.
- Creating a useable customer database, which includes all the relevant information in an easily accessible form, is a problem for many long-established insurers. New entrants can design their systems from scratch, but existing insurers are having to reorganize their databases and use sophisticated software than can provide a 'single view' of the customer across various existing systems.
- Most customers have yet to be fully convinced of the benefits of one-stop shopping for insurance. Many, especially motor customers, like to shop around for the best deal.

Cross-selling

'One of the disadvantages insurers have relative to other financial services sectors is the relative infrequency of contact. This contrasts with, for example, the high level of contact that policyholders have with their banks.

Andersen Consulting

Insurance diversification 1985–1995

In this decade insurers experienced a wave of diversification. The aims were to create synergy, control distribution and develop new profitable income streams – especially counter cyclical businesses. The target businesses included the following (see Figure 6.3):

Figure 6.3

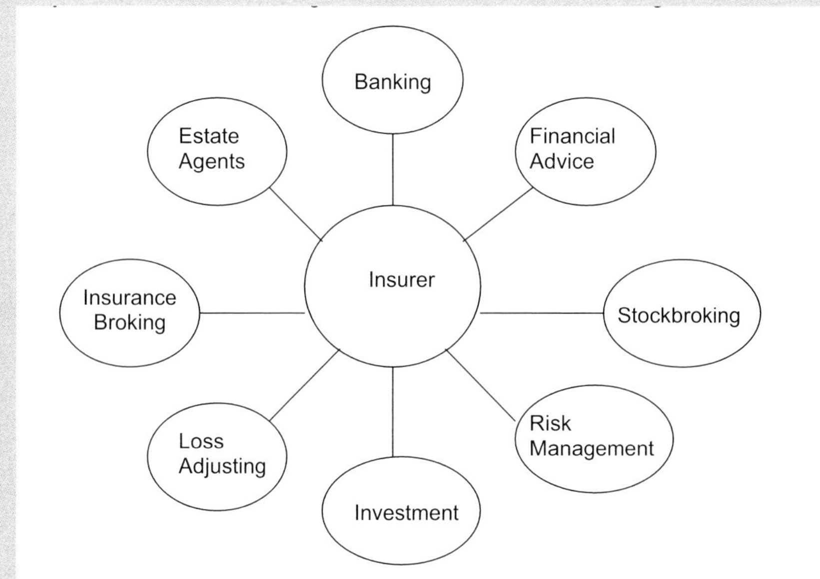

Much of this diversification was unsuccessful. The reasons included:

- Inability to control a diversified group
- Not understanding the acquired business
- Culture clashes
- Conflicts of interest
- The acquisition was reactive and not thought-through
- It was not counter-cyclical
- Synergy was illusive.

Select bibliography

N Genetay, P Molyneaux, *Bancassurance*, Macmillan 1998.

G Benoist, *Bancassurance: The New Challenges, Geneva Papers on Risk and Insurance Vol 2*, No 3, July 2002.

S Diacon, K Starkey, C O'Brian, *Size and Efficiency in European Long-Term Insurance Companies, Geneva Papers on Risk and Insurance Vol 27*, No 3, July 2002.

Mergers and Acquisitions, *Insurance Trends,* ABI October 1998.

R Cadugan, B Keiser, *A review of the Insurance Industry Market Attractiveness of Eastern Europe, Journal of International Insurance Vol 1,* No 2, 1999.

J Gora, *Planning and Managing Insurance Merger Integration,* LOMA 1999.

A Newman, *Call Centres: Where Training is Paramount,* CII Journal, May 2001.

Seven

Introduction to the value chain

Objectives

On completion of this chapter, and wider personal research, the reader should be able to:

- understand the insurance value chain;
- appreciate the dynamics associated with each position in the chain;
- explain the forces that might give rise to disaggregation;
- speculate on some of the new models that might appear in the future.

7.1 Introduction

As previously noted, the value chain is a conceptual way of breaking a business down into components and then looking at each element separately in terms of the value added, its core drivers and its relevance to the organization's key objectives.

Historically, many companies, including most insurers, have created vertical organizational structures that, in the simplest terms, design and develop products, manufacture those products and distribute them to customers. These are supported by business services functions (finance, IS, etc) that provide services to the whole organization, but are not directly part of the design/manufacture/

distribute structure. The key challenge presented by value chain analysis is that each component is essentially driven by different success drivers as can be seen in the simplified value chain in Figure 7.1.

Manufacture: the drivers for manufacturing (**processing**) are: economies of scale, volume and cost effectiveness of processes.

Design and development: is about using **core intellectual capital** to create new and better products that can be sold at a profit. Its core drivers are know-how and speed of innovation.

Distribution: is driven by meeting the needs of the customers, the scope (appropriateness, attractiveness) of the offering, and effective customer relationship management (**CRM**).

Each has fundamentally different drivers and therefore, potentially, should be managed in a different way with different incentives to the other parts.

Figure 7.1

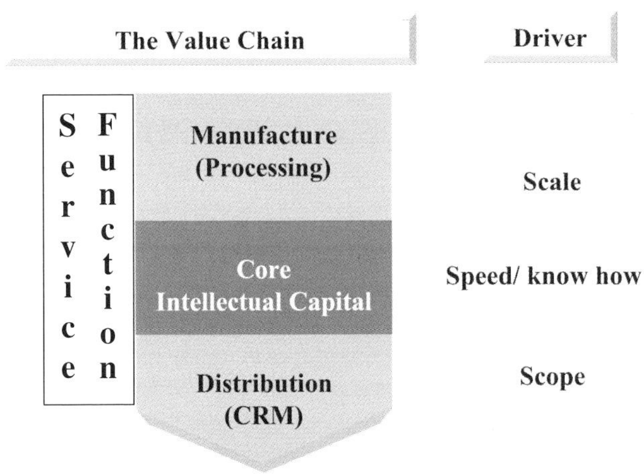

Translating this concept into the key elements of an insurance operation:

Manufacture: Policy and claims processing/administration (including front-line underwriting and claims notification, routine handling and payment processes), procurement (supplier management).

Design/product development: This is the core insurance intellectual capital – technical underwriting and claims management skills, risk management, product design and pricing, etc.

Distribution: Intermediary management, call centre and Internet 'shop window' presentation and design, marketing, customer relationship management, sales management.

Having identified each component of the value chain, each needs to be separately evaluated/benchmarked to assess:

- how much value do they add to the business?
- are they currently world class at what they do?
- can they be managed/performed more effectively by others without compromising the objectives of the entire operation?

This creates challenges to the old, vertically integrated model:

'The key issue is future disintegration of the traditional insurance value chain; the specialist will always beat the generalist on skill and efficiency levels; you have to decide where to compete.'

Prudential

'Each stage of the value chain will have to be ruthlessly scrutinised to assess whether the insurer has got sustainable competitive advantage; if not, find who can do that part of the business better, and sell it to them; otherwise you will eventually lose out.'

AXA

'The market environment is undergoing significant change as the evolution of the internet removes barriers of time, space and distance.'

IBM

'Companies should seek to identify and commercialise the intangible capital latent in their organizations, and in this way also develop new business for the marketplace. To do this insurers need to re-think their value chains. The conventional view is to regard each business line – commercial property and casualty, personal property and casualty and so on – as a large, integrated value chain, complete with all the necessary functions: product development, distribution, etc. But such a perspective disguises the wealth of opportunities that can reside within the functions of a high-performing business.'

McKinsey

> 'To survive, companies need to breakdown their value chain into processes and decide:
>
> - In which parts of the value chain are they world class?
> - In which parts do they wish to become world class?
> - Which parts are going to need external help (partners) to become world class?
> - Which parts are they going to 'buy in' from world-class suppliers?
>
> Mike Christophers, Strategy Consultant

As a result, the logic of maintaining the whole value chain is weakening. Companies in recent years have expended lots of energy and resources re-engineering and re-designing core processes, but there are limits to such gains. As noted above, the drivers for the three core elements conflict and bundling them into a single organization forces management compromise.

Scope, speed/know-how and scale cannot be optimized continuously between and across all functions and thus trade-offs are required. By definition, trade-offs are likely to lead to sub-optimal behaviour or performance.

7.2 Challenges for management

Using the term 'silo' to denote a business structure comprising processing, intellectual capital and distribution, we shall now examine some different options available to organizations. (The challenges for business service functions are dealt with separately in Chapter 16.)

7.2.1 Starting from multiple silos

Most large insurance organizations are not a single business, comprising just one vertical silo, but are made up of multiple silos, each facing a different segment of the market, eg:

- Personal: intermediated/direct
- Personal: motor/household/other
- Commercial: London market/large corporates/medium size/SME
- Commercial: property/motor/liability/marine

Each silo is largely self sufficient, and full profit responsibility is vested in the manager of each silo.

Management is therefore additionally challenged (ie in addition to the value chain challenges noted above) to look at how the value chain drivers can be managed more effectively horizontally across the organization (see Figure 7.2).

Figure 7.2

Managing across silos

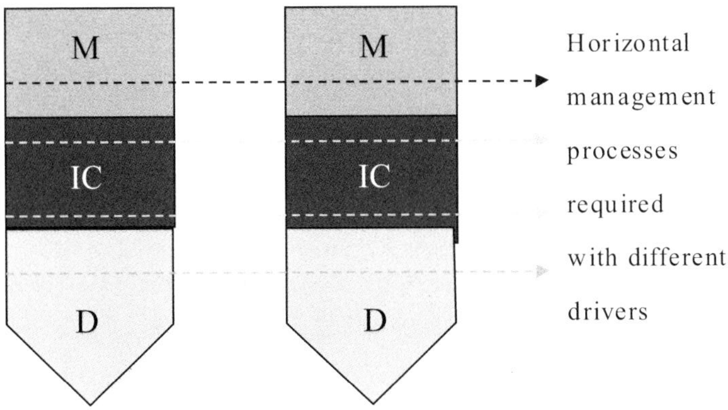

This could mean:

- combining processing activity across silos to generate scale economies.
- looking at how core intellectual capital can be grown/shared/managed across silos.
- creating shared distribution or CRM processes for shared customer segments.

Where any such change occurs, to maximize the overall value created to the organization, there will be some reduction in the clarity of the existing roles. The managers who previously had full profit responsibility for their vertical silo will now find that other managers are managing activities horizontally across the business, and potentially impacting their ability to deliver.

Additionally, those managers managing horizontally will not have clear profit responsibility for a 'vertical' market segment, but will need to be measured and incentivized on deliverables/criteria relevant to their value chain component.

This then becomes matrix management, rather than the more conventional hierarchical management, and requires management to work together in a different, more team-oriented way.

7.2.2 Challenging the need to do it all

Historically, most insurers conduct all parts of the three core elements of the value chain themselves, within one basic insurance operation. However, if you truly want to maximize the value of the business overall, it may not make business sense to do so.

If you are not 'world class' (and are not capable of achieving world class) in any area of the business, management should challenge itself to justify why it should continue to perform that particular function within the business operation, and therefore consider outsourcing the function to another company.

Reasons to retain non-world class functions:

- The function is a key differentiator for the business and employs core intellectual capital that should be retained within the business.
- There are no organizations available to outsource the function to on a cost-effective basis and in a way that does not damage the interests of the insurer.
- Even though not world class, the function is better than that available to competitors, can retain that advantage over time, and the synergies of running the function internally balance any cost advantages of outsourcing.

Reasons to consider outsourcing non-world class functions:

- The function is not a key differentiator for the business and does not utilize core intellectual capital that should be retained within the business.
- There are reliable external suppliers who can perform the function more efficiently and cost effectively.

As discussed in Chapter 16, the concept of control will play a key part in any decision making regarding outsourcing of activities to third parties. To operate an effective insurance business, management must establish and maintain control over all key elements of the business. Where activities are outsourced, control of those activities becomes more complex and needs to be managed differently from similar functions retained within the business (ie through contractual service level agreements/standards, regular monitoring/checking of the performance of the third party, etc). Supplier management then, potentially, becomes an additional requirement of core intellectual capital.

7.2.3 Maximizing the leverage of world-class activities

If an organization is world-class (or can be brought up to world-class) in a specific functional area of the value chain, and that function contributes significant value to the organization, management should look at ways of leveraging/maximizing the value generated from that function, potentially at the expense of putting less focus on other, less valuable business functions (ie focus on what you are good at/creates the greatest value).

Examples of ways to maximize world-class capabilities:

- Ensure that the expertise is shared across the organization to bring all similar functions up to world-class.
- Look to increase throughput through this function (even if this additional throughput does not flow through the rest of the business), eg insource/perform the function for other companies for a fee.

- Look for new areas of business (markets, customer segments, products, etc) where the capabilities can be applied for profit and move into these areas (eg via acquisition of existing market operators who do not have equivalent world-class capabilities).
- Look at ways of developing/growing and maintaining these world-class capabilities into the future (what it takes to be world-class does not remain fixed, but will move forward over time).

7.2.4 The challenge of different drivers

As noted previously, each element of the value chain has different drivers and thus, theoretically, should be managed/incentivized using a different set of criteria/measures to other elements. This challenges senior management (those with responsibility for delivering the overall objectives of the business (profit, return on capital, etc)) to create a more complex incentivization structure for management, rather than the more normal approach where all managers are measured in terms of contribution to the current year's profit.

The way that the insurance price is created in the first place is described in Chapter 11. If we assume that for each premium and every insurance product sold, the price could then theoretically be broken down into the following components linked to different elements of an insurer's value chain:

Core, risk-based, insurance premium:	anticipated long-term cost of claims and claims management and handling costs + expense allowance for technical underwriting/pricing + targeted underwriting profit (based on the required rate of return for the product)
+	
Distribution allowance:	commission paid to intermediaries + expense allowance for marketing and branding, CRM, distribution management, proposition assembly, etc
+	
Processing allowance:	expense allowance to cover front-line underwriting, general policy administration, premium collection, claims notification
=	**the recommended street price for the risk.**

Conceptually, therefore, the key drivers for success (and therefore the incentivization bases) for each core element of the insurance operation should be based round the following:

	Drivers
Technical Underwriting/Pricing:	To create a range of marketable products at a price the market will bear that will generate the required, long-term level of underwriting profit/return.
Claims management:	To **manage** claims effectively to minimize the total cost necessary to comply with the terms of the policy and satisfy the customer.
	To **handle** claims efficiently and effectively and live within the expense allowance built into the core risk premium.
Distribution:	To deliver the company's products to the marketplace in the most appropriate manner that maximizes both the volume and price achieved in the target market segments.
	To operate within the distribution allowances generated from the products sold.
Processing (including front-line underwriting):	To ensure that only acceptable risks at acceptable prices are written.
	To operate within the processing allowances generated by the business written and deliver the required level of customer service.

(NB Breaking down the insurance premium in this way can facilitate management's thinking on whether to retain in-house or outsource components, because each component can now be separately measured for effectiveness, which may not be the case in most insurers.)

Issues that arise from this theoretical construct:

- A process needs to exist to separate out the elements of each premium and allocate them to each functional area, so that the relevant costs can be allocated against them for performance measurement. **This is a fundamentally different and more complex way of accounting than is usual in an insurance operation**.
- Should either the distribution or processing functions vary the recommended street price, this variation should be borne by their own revenue/cost base, and not impact other areas of the business, ie if they sell at a greater price they retain the increased proceeds, if they sell at a lower price they must find the shortfall from their expense allowances. (Each area should be measured only on what it directly influences.)

- There will need to be a constant dialogue between all areas:
  - to ensure that the core, risk-based premium required by the technical underwriters allows an acceptable street price to be achieved to generate the appropriate/targeted volume of attractive risks.
  - to understand the development/movement of pure claims costs and the expense cost for each area, and to update the pure risk premium and street price accordingly.
- The overall underwriting driver is the long-term underwriting return, not that of any one year. Over what period you measure long-term return and how you utilize such a measure to motivate new starters/people planning to leave within a short time, creates a range of challenges. But, as noted elsewhere in this book, short-term/single-period results may not reflect the true profitability (and therefore adequacy of pricing) of an account.

7.3 The value chain concept is a tool to stimulate thinking, not a strategy in itself

The value chain concept is an intellectual tool to challenge management to think about each core element of the business, the value each creates and their core drivers and, potentially, to look at how to change the way functions operate to increase the overall value created. Like all other theoretical tools, its application to each business will be unique and how individual management teams utilize it and develop action plans from it will also be unique.

7.4 The impact of technology

The true ability to deconstruct the value chain in a highly-complex, high-volume, data-processing environment such as insurance has only really become feasible in the last decade or so with the significant developments in communications technology.

It is not just the Internet that has been key, but developments in satellite communications (both voice and data), fibre optics, etc mean that it is now relatively easy and cheap to transmit substantial volumes of voice and data traffic over considerable distances. It is now feasible to have call centres servicing the UK market based on other continents, such as the USA or India, and for volume processing to be conducted thousands of miles away from front-line staff, and for it all to be 'joined up' to provide effective customer service.

The changing face of insurance

'In classic marketing terms we are experiencing both horizontal and vertical integration, as well as the deconstruction of value chains. Insurers, banks and intermediaries are all having to give careful thought to their positioning. No less heart searching is going on in the boardrooms of loss adjusters, claims administrators, specialist software houses and other service providers. Business strategy is all about making choices so I do not think there ever will be one simple, right answer. What may work for one company may well not work for another. Perhaps the common denominator for all the winners is that, whatever they do in the value chain, they will have to do it excellently, at the lowest possible cost. And, of course, waiting in the wings will be a new breed of insurance providers – the so called virtual companies, where everything is outsourced.'

Paul Spencer, UK CEO, RSA

Claims handling

'Claims handling in property and casualty could emerge as a separate business, for example, opening up new profit opportunities for top practitioners in the field. Companies that handle claims poorly could then improve their performance by outsourcing to a best practice claims operation.'

McKinsey

Select bibliography

A van Rossum, *The Debate on the Insurance Value Chain, Geneva Papers on Risk and Insurance Vol 27,* No 1, Jan 2002.

Richard Lynch, *Corporate Strategy,* Pitman 1997, Chapter 18.

M Porter, *Competitive Advantage,* Free Press 1985.

R Normann, R Ramirez, *From Value Chain to Value Constellation,* Harvard Business Review, July/ August 1993.

J Rayport, J Sviokla, *Exploiting the Virtual Value Chain,* Harvard Business Review, Nov/ Dec 1995.

P Evans, T Wustner, *Strategy and the New Economics of Information,* Harvard Business Review, Sept/ Oct 1997.

Eight

Insurance products

Objectives

On completion of this chapter, and wider personal research, the reader should be able to:

- outline the main types of insurance products, both property and casualty;
- appreciate how they have developed over time in response to market forces;
- speculate on how they might develop in the future.

8.1 Introduction

The main categories of insurance products are:

- *Life Insurance* Alternatively known as long-term insurance due to the extended period of most of the contracts. It includes life, pensions and permanent health insurance.
- *General Insurance* Alternatively known as non-life insurance or property and casualty (P+C) insurance. This covers all other types of product, most of which are written as annual contracts.

General insurance itself may be sub-divided in a number of ways depending on the context.

a) Statutory classes

Regulators will usually define statutory classes for reporting purposes, and industry statistics tend to be based on these. Unfortunately, these classes rarely correspond exactly with the way products are structured. As a result, company accountants compiling their annual statistical reports have to break down the figures for each of their products and reassemble them to fit the statutory requirements.

UK statutory classes

- Accident and Health
- Motor
- Marine
- Aviation
- Transport
- Property
- Third Party Liability
- Miscellaneous and Pecuniary Loss
- Non Proportional Treaty
- Proportional Treaty

b) Internal company organization

Companies may organize themselves in different ways and the sub-division of classes may well reflect this, eg:

(i) Primary insurance, reinsurance

(ii) Commercial, personal (customers)

(iii) Property, casualty, marine and aviation.

8.2 Key elements of an insurance product

Insurance products have developed over three centuries in response to the perceived changing needs of customers. Consequently there is little standardization and even policies with similar names may vary between insurer and from country to country. As a result, managers should take considerable care when attempting to benchmark underwriting accounts.

Some products are built around specific perils, some around the subject matter affected by the peril, and others around the type of customer.

Key elements of insurance products

Element	*Examples*
Peril	Fire, earthquake, theft, liability, sickness, accidental damage
Subject matter	Premises, person, inventory, ship, motor vehicle, business, jewellery
Customer type	Commercial, personal
Customer segment	Home owner, tenant, shopkeeper, building contractor

Products may be written for a single peril or a narrow group of perils. The UK Standard Fire Policy and the Motor Third Party policy are typical of these so-called monoline policies. However, the majority of products sold are packages, or comprehensive policies, providing cover for a wide range of perils appropriate for particular customer types or segments. Often these packages include non-insurance products and services such as legal advice, breakdown assistance or loss control inspections.

This packaging, for example in a Home Insurance policy or a Commercial Combined policy, is a more customer-driven approach than a simple monoline policy but it does pose particular challenges to management.

a) there may be pressure to give package discounts

b) there may be cross-subsidization, intentionally or otherwise

c) management information may be inadequate to identify how the individual parts affect the overall result.

In the brief outline that follows some of the more common products are described under the split: Property, Casualty and Marine and Aviation.

(NB Students should have some degree of familiarity with these products but a detailed knowledge is not necessary.)

8.3 Property insurances

Standard Fire Policy and Additional Perils

Property insurance in the UK developed from the original **Standard Fire Policy** which was designed to cover a building, plant, machinery and stock against fire, lightning and certain types of explosion. At a later date **Additional** or **Special Perils** covers became available in response to the growing awareness among customers of the limitations of the original policy. In their eventual form, additional perils include the following:

Additional Perils

Chemical perils	Explosion, spontaneous combustion, heating or fermentation
Social perils	Riot, civil commotion, strikers, locked-out workers, persons taking part in a labour dispute
Natural perils	Storm, tempest, flood, hail and thunderbolt, earthquake, subterranean fire, subsidence, landslip
Miscellaneous perils	Bursting or overflowing of water tanks, apparatus or pipes, aircraft and other aerial devices or articles dropped therefrom (excluding sonic booms), impact by vehicles, horses or cattle.

Commercial All Risks insurance

A widely used approach, especially for larger risks, is commercial **all risks insurance**. Wordings may differ, but the general principle is to provide cover for all risks of physical loss or damage to the property with certain exceptions, eg:

- Wear and tear
- Inventory shortages
- Machinery breakdown
- Dishonesty
- Money shortage

All risks policies usually carry large deductibles.

Theft insurance

Specific theft policies are still issued, especially for high-risk businesses such as jewellers. However, as is the case with fire cover, theft is more usually included as part of a wider package. Commercial policies generally restrict cover to theft involving forcible entry to the premises. The intention is to exclude pilferage by staff or customers, which is very difficult to control. Personal policies tend to cover theft of property irrespective of the thief's method of entry.

Business Interruption insurance

This is technically a pecuniary insurance but is almost always written in the property department. **Business Interruption** is otherwise known as **Loss of Profits** or **Consequential Loss** insurance. The purpose is to indemnify a business for those costs that cannot be stopped or reduced in proportion to the reduction of sales caused by a fire, machinery breakdown or other insured peril. Cover may include:

- loss of gross profit
- wages
- additional costs of working.

Commercial Combined

This is a the common package for small businesses. In addition to the conventional property covers, the following may be included:

- Book debts
- Business interruption
- Employers' liability
- Public liability
- Money
- Motor
- Transit

Contractors All Risks insurance (CAR)

CAR has been developed in response to the demand for compulsory insurance for large- scale building and civil engineering works. Standard contract conditions have been published by the Institute of Civil Engineers and the Royal Institute of British Architects and these have been given widespread use. The policy indemnifies the insured for loss or damage to property as a result of any cause, with the following exceptions:

- war, civil commotion
- consequential loss
- cessation of work
- defective design
- defective material or workmanship
- breakdown of plant
- lack of maintenance

Engineering insurance

This deals with the insurance of plant and machinery and is focused mainly on loss or damage within the plant itself. Insurers offer an inspection service with or without insurance cover and a greater proportion of premium is spent on this than on the payment of claims. In some countries the regular inspection of plant (eg cranes, boilers, lifts) is a statutory duty and the insurer may be authorized to carry this out. The main covers are as follows:

- ♦ Explosion: for boilers and pressure vessels
- ♦ Breakdown: for mechanical, electrical and electronic plant and machinery
- ♦ Accidental damage: for specific machinery, caused by storm, flood, impact, collision
- ♦ Consequential loss
- ♦ Machinery in transit.

Home insurance

Home insurance, otherwise known as Household or Homeowners insurance is a package based originally on property insurance. Policies for buildings and contents may be given separately, because buildings insurance may be a condition of a mortgage. In recent years the extent of the package has expanded considerably and includes related services as well as property and liability covers. The following is an example of what is available under a modern Home insurance policy.

Homeowners policy

1. Standard perils – fire, storm, water damage, malicious damage, theft, subsidence, falling trees and branches and flying objects hitting the home
2. Contents in the garden
3. Contents temporarily away from the home
4. Students contents away from home
5. Contents when you move
6. Short-term accommodation costs
7. Locks and keys
8. Metered water and oil
9. Freezer contents
10. Accidental damage to satellite dishes, TVs, videos, etc, and mirrors
11. Accidental damage to drains, pipes, cables, glass and sanitary ware
12. Tenant's legal responsibilities and improvements
13. Occupier's personal legal responsibilities
14. Employer's legal responsibilities
15. Owner's legal responsibilities

16. Legal fees for removal of squatters
17. Money in the home
18. Misuse of credit cards following theft from the home
19. Theft from outbuildings
20. Business equipment
21. Wedding and Christmas gifts
22. Visitors' personal belongings
23. Reinstatement of title deeds
24. Full accidental damage cover
25. Valuables
26. Emergency assistance
    - emergency repairs
    - overnight accommodation

Optional extensions
- Trees, shrubs, plants, lawns
- Pedal cycles
- Legal expenses

8.4 Casualty

8.4.1 Accident insurance

This includes a range of covers including personal accident, credit, fidelity and contingency insurance.

Personal Accident (PA)

PA provides compensation for accidental injury or sickness. It may pay a capital sum in the event of death or specific injuries (eg loss of limb) or a benefit for up to 104 weeks if the insured is prevented from undertaking his or her normal occupation (NB sickness cover beyond 104 weeks is known as permanent health insurance and is written by life companies).

PA may be restricted to accidents only and is often included as part of a travel policy.

Credit insurance

This is cover for businesses against the non-payment for goods and services supplied on credit terms, ie bad debts.

Fidelity insurance

Cover for businesses against losses caused by the dishonesty of employees is known as fidelity insurance. It includes loss of both money and stock.

Contingency insurance

Contingency insurances include a wide range of miscellaneous covers that do not fit into the main classes, for example, missing beneficiary indemnity, abandonment of events, golf hole-in-one, and also includes film stars insuring parts of their anatomy, etc.

8.4.2 Liability

Companies, organizations or individuals may become legally liable for bodily injury or damage to property caused by their acts or omissions. The liability may arise out of negligence, statute or contract. The potential for third parties to make a liability claim varies depending on local culture, custom and the pre-disposition of the legal system to support such actions. In some countries, particularly the USA, the opportunity to initiate a successful action by a plaintiff, and the size of the award, are much higher than in other countries. Some of the specific insurances in this class are as follows:

Public Liability (PL)

Public or general insurance covers liability of a business to the public as a result of its operation, for example, pollution, injury to a visitor, or damage to a third party's goods in its custody.

The equivalent insurance for an individual is known as personal liability and this is usually included as part of a Home insurance policy.

Product Liability (PL)

This covers liability arising out of goods sold, supplied, repaired or serviced by the insured. It needs to be underwritten with great care, particularly for pharmaceuticals, vehicle components and goods exported to the USA.

Professional Indemnity (PI)

Cover for negligent acts and advice as part of a professional service is known as professional indemnity. It is taken out by lawyers, accountants, surveyors, brokers, etc. PI for doctors is particularly expensive.

Employers' Liability (EL)

This covers an employer's liability to employees for injury or sickness. It is a compulsory class in many countries. In some parts of the world (eg Australia, New Zealand and certain US states) the cover provided is well beyond that of negligence and is called Workman's Compensation.

Directors and Officers (D&O)

D&O covers the personal liability of directors for the way in which they run their companies. This is a growing area of insurance that has been given fresh impetus by the corporate scandals of the early 2000s.

8.4.3 Motor

Motor insurance arose from the need to cover liability in respect of road accidents involving steam traction engines and the basic principles were adapted for motor vehicles. Since then, damage to the vehicle itself has been included and more recently a range of additional covers have been made available.

Private car insurance

The minimum statutory insurance in the UK is for third party liability but this is usually combined with cover against loss by fire or theft. The more common comprehensive policy includes accidental damage and broken windscreens and may be extended for personal accident, medical expenses, personal possessions, legal expenses and roadside assistance.

Motorcycle insurance

This is essentially similar to private car insurance.

Commercial vehicle insurance

Businesses take out cover for their trucks, vans, buses, salesman's cars and vehicles of special type under commercial vehicle policies. Where ten or more vehicles are insured a **fleet policy** may be used whereby the rating is based on the claims experience of the fleet itself rather than on standard premiums.

8.4.4 Marine and Aviation

These are highly specialized classes of insurance operating under their own legislation in their own markets. Marine is the oldest type of insurance and uses terminology that often differs from property and casualty insurance. Aviation is obviously much newer, but because it developed out of the marine market it has much in common with that class.

Marine insurance

Marine insurance basically provides cover against the perils of the sea, eg sinking, stranding, heavy weather damage, fire, collision, thieves and piracy. The subject of the insurance may be the **hull**, the **cargo** or the **freight** (the payment for carriage of the cargo). Cover may be given during construction of a vessel or for subsequent voyages or periods of time. Marine policies may also be written for oil rigs and pleasure craft.

Ship-owner's liability for collisions are also covered by marine policies, but only to the extent of three-quarters of the loss. The remaining quarter must be carried by the ship-owner who usually places this risk in a mutual association known as a protection and indemnity (P&I) club.

Goods in Transit insurance

This provides cover for the owner or the carrier of goods for damage or loss incurred during inland transit. It is an area where insurers are very vulnerable to acts of dishonesty and much attention is paid to the quality of the carrier.

Aviation insurance

This covers hull, passenger liability and third-party liability, usually on an all risks basis. The insured may be airlines, companies, private owners and flying clubs.

8.5 Operational management issues

a) Property

Property insurances are among the more stable classes in terms of underwriting result, although they can be subject to accumulations of risk and natural catastrophes. It is often difficult to persuade the market to carry premiums with sufficient margin to accommodate potential catastrophe losses. This is becoming more critical as the weather changes associated with global warming become more evident.

b) Casualty

Personal Accident has been a profitable class, but the ease by which it can be added to other purchases (eg credit cards) has led to it becoming commoditized and margins squeezed.

Fidelity and Contingency insurances are niche areas requiring specialist expertise.

Liability insurance is by far the most difficult class to underwrite on a consistently profitable basis. With constantly emerging risks, a changing legal framework and a long-tail contract, underwriters need to be able to assess and price the risk and persuade the insured to pay premiums that will provide for an uncertain future pattern of claims.

Employers' Liability has been particularly unprofitable for some years. More recently, PI has been hit by very large losses for accountants, lawyers and management consultants resulting in withdrawals from the market. D&O has become a potentially high-risk class, especially for large businesses, since the Enron case.

c) Motor

Motor is perhaps the most commoditized of all classes. Underwriting profits are rare and barriers to entry are low. The emergence of direct writing has forced premiums down for **private motor**. **Commercial vehicle** has always been highly competitive and motor fleets are frequently 'churned' by brokers, to obtain the lowest quotation.

Broking and the power of the photocopier

Some years ago a broker confided in the authors his method of marketing a motor fleet risk at renewal. He indicated that he would photocopy the details of the risk and send a copy to his mailing list of 40 companies and 30 Lloyd's syndicates. 'Amongst that lot,' he said, 'someone is certain to make a mistake!'

d) Marine and aviation

The Marine market is very cyclical, periodically producing very large losses, particularly for hull insurance. It is sobering to realize that one in five ships eventually sinks. Cargo is more profitable but, like goods in transit, requires a thorough knowledge of the carriers. Aviation insurance has been subject to considerable loss over the last decade and most risks are now insured by pools.

Select bibliography

A Couchman, R Litton (Ed), *Kluwer's Handbook of Insurance*, Kluwer 2003, Chapter 2.

M Dans, J Hood, B Stein, *Insurance non-Marine*, Witherby & Co 1997, Appendices.

A Fitner, J Trupin, *Commercial Insurance*, Insurance Institute of America 2002.

Appendix to Chapter 8

Figure 8.1

Product development opportunity: Computer risks

As the role of technology in business continues to increase so will the perceived risks. Examples are shown below.

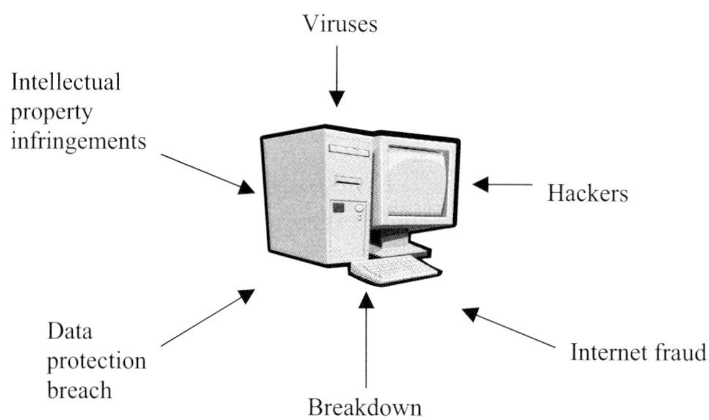

These obviously create opportunities for insurers but, as in all new areas, they are faced with problems regarding how to assess the risks and set premiums commensurate with the ultimate exposure.

Note: Multiple perils imply a package solution rather than a series of mono-line products.

Nine

The management of the front end I. Market analysis and segmentation

Objectives

On completion of this chapter, and wider personal research, the reader should be able to:

- understand how the principles of marketing are applied in an insurance operation;
- explain the importance of branding and segmentation in insurance;
- describe the marketing mix in an insurance context.

The 'front end' of an insurance operation is the part that markets the products and services to the customer. In this chapter the reader is reminded of the theory of marketing and segmentation and shown how it applies to insurance.

9.1 Introduction

> 'Business without marketing is called adventure.'
>
> Ray Wiltshire

Marketing involves the identification and anticipation of, and the putting forward of, value propositions that satisfy customer needs in a profitable manner. It should be the shared purpose of the whole operation from top management down to the most junior employee. It is not the sole responsibility of the specialist marketing teams.

The concept of marketing is not new. More than two centuries ago Adam Smith wrote:

> *'Consumption is the sole end purpose of all production, and the interest of the producer ought to be attended to only in so far as it may be necessary for promoting that of the consumer.'* The Wealth of Nations (1776)

What he was describing was customer focus – something still regarded as a novel concept in some insurance operations.

Compared with some industries, insurance has been slow to adopt marketing techniques. Too often some parts of the sector have failed to:

- React to the business environment
- Provide propositions relevant to the customer
- Manage its distribution
- Employ people who know what the company wants to achieve, what customers want and the values the company stands for.

Even now some insurance operations are still structured to 'push' products with attention focused on 'selling', an activity which relates more to the interests of the company than to those of the customer (although it has to be recognized that many insurance products are 'forced purchases' in the eyes of the consumer, in other words, consumers would rather not have to buy them at all).

Nevertheless, under the twin pressures of stronger regulation (focused around the concept that the products sold must meet the consumers needs) and competition from new entrants with stronger customer relationships, most companies are taking marketing more seriously.

9.2 The marketing process

The starting point for marketing is the company strategy. This should specify the financial objectives and make the high level decisions about the positioning of the company, ie:

- What are the markets where the company could deploy its resources more effectively than its competitors?
- The brand – what the company stands for, including its corporate ethics.

In some strategic planning exercises the top management will go down to a much lower level and determine main markets, customer segments, products and distribution. What happens after this will depend to a great extent on the company structure.

Usually, each major business will need to develop its own marketing strategy, which is likely to include the following elements (see Figure 9.1).

Figure 9.1

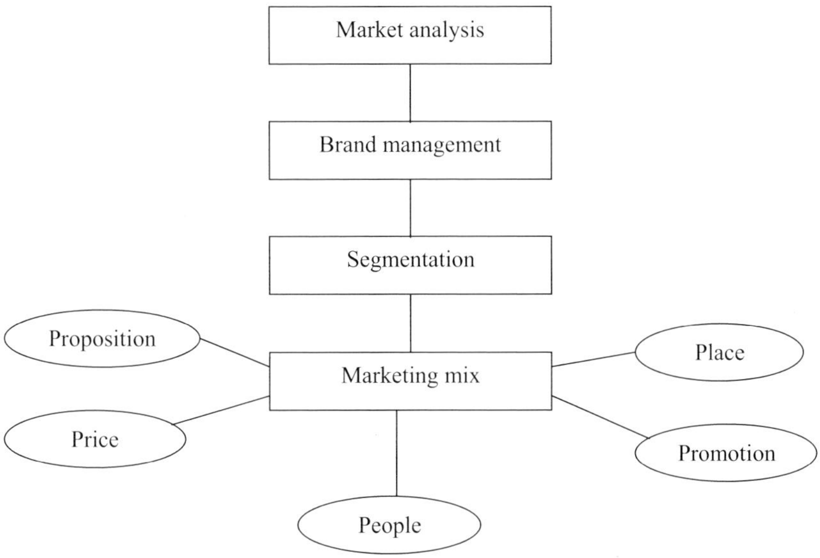

The specialist marketing function may have an input into all of the marketing strategy and usually has direct responsibility for some parts, eg marketing analysis, brand management and promotion.

Let us consider each element in turn.

9.2.1 Market analysis

The purpose of market analysis is to identify opportunities where the company would have competitive advantage. The approach is quite similar to that used in developing the corporate strategy only more detailed, and should go right down to customer level.

External and internal analysis of the business environment is undertaken to determine the following:

- Potential customers: type, volume, current spend
- Their needs
- What the competition is doing (ie how well existing suppliers satisfy these needs)
- Gaps: for both current and potential future needs

- Where the company could have competitive advantage
- How the company could make a sustainable profit
- How customers might respond to propositions.

There are two types of information source used in the analysis:

- Primary sources
  The company's bespoke data compiled for specific needs (eg customer surveys), often undertaken by specialist market research agencies.
- Secondary sources
  These include the large amount of internal data kept by the company as well as off-the-shelf information such as market statistics, demographic studies and analysts' reports on competitors.

9.2.2 Brand management

It is now taken for granted that a company must build a strong brand to be successful, particularly in retail markets.

> 'If I lost all of my factories and trucks, but kept the name Coca-Cola, I could rebuild my business. If I lost my name, the business would collapse.'
>
> CEO, Coca Cola

The issue in insurance, and also to some extent in banking, is that some companies equate brand with name recognition, and therefore assume that they already have a strong brand. As a result, their brand management is often limited to communication to increase name awareness and policing the appearance of printed material.

Conversely, other companies have been taking an approach similar to that used by successful retailers. This means attempting to create a distinctive, consistent experience of what the organization stands for and which is manifest in all it does for the customer in terms of products, service and behaviours. The aim is to deepen their relationship with the customer. Boston Consulting Group aptly described the situation as follows:

> *'Banks and insurers need to develop brand strategies that focus on what matters to the customer: the set of experiences around buying and using products and services in addition to the products and services themselves'.*
>
> *When the Experience is the Brand,* Boston Consulting Group

Of course, distinctive brand building is particularly challenging in insurance because the opportunity for continued customer contact tends to be limited to annual renewals and claims handing. However, this has not held back the most successful insurance brand builders such as Direct Line in the UK. The latter was able to build an image of convenience and low prices based on a powerful advertising campaign.

Insurance branding

Branding is seen by insurance operations as a powerful tool in building and protecting the business. It is a major support to sales, especially where buyers are not clear about all the features and benefits of competing products.

Brand strategies range from those promoting a single brand for the company to those that maintain local and product brands. The multi-brand approach is undoubtedly more expensive but it may be useful in overcoming channel conflicts between intermediaries. In addition, there is some evidence that the big global brands can have a negative impact in some markets where customers prefer to remain with the traditional, trusted names.

Andersen Consulting

9.2.3 Segmentation

Segmentation involves the identification of groups of potential customers with broadly homogeneous needs and attitudes, then selecting which groups and needs can be served profitably given current and expected market conditions.

The crucial questions are (now and in the future):

- What business are we in?
- What are we good at?
- Where can we offer more than, or something different to, our competitors?
- Who are our current, or potential, target customers and how many are there of them?
- What do they value?
- What are their current and future needs?
- What segment could they form?
- What are their current and (potentially different in the future) habits and expectations?
- What is their potential value to us?
- How could we communicate with them most effectively?

How can customers be segmented? Some of the main methods are described below.

1. Personal customers

Customer segmentation is generally more advanced in personal lines, probably due to the activities of the direct writers. Motor has led the way with home, travel and PA following on. Typical approaches used are as follows:

a) Perception of value

In a mature market, research is likely to reveal that a segment of customers, perhaps as many as 35%, are seeking the **lowest price** almost irrespective of other features. This segment can be served by simple, accessible commodity products and the insurer should aim to be a low-cost producer, ie maintain a low expense ratio and resist the temptation to spend money on product variations.

Most of the remaining customers are looking for **added value**. Price is of course very important but this segment seeks more from the relationship than merely obtaining a product at the lowest premium. This added value may be manifest in a variety of forms, eg:

- financial security
- additional services
- excellent customer service
- fit with their personal needs
- convenient touch points

There is also a very small segment – possibly 1 or 2% of customers – who appear to prefer **premium products** beyond the added-value proposition.

Case study – Exploitation of a premium segment

Chubb in the USA has for many years successfully targeted customers requiring premium products. The company specializes in insuring the homes of the wealthy and fully appreciates the associated issues of security, cover for works of art and high sums insured for valuables. At one time Chubb advertisements stated 'Congratulations! You are now wealthy enough to consider our insurances'.

b) Socio-economic groups

The socio-economic groupings used in the UK are:

A Upper class

B Professional

C_1 Junior managers/non-manual workers

C_2 Skilled manual workers

D Unskilled manual workers

And their many variations are often used in insurance, but mainly as an overlay to other segmentation systems. The absence of a large, affluent middle class which is, by volume, the main purchaser of insurance, has been a contributory factor to the slower take-off of some insurance markets, eg some parts of Latin America and Africa.

Personal customer Life Stage product opportunities

Product / Age	18 - 25	25 – 35	35 – 45	45 – 55	55 – 60	60 – 65	65+
General insurance	• Motor • Travel	• Motor • Travel • Home • PMI • Creditor • PA	• Motor • Travel • Home • PMI • Creditor • PA	• Motor • Travel • Home • PMI • Creditor • PA	• Motor • Travel • Home • PMI • Creditor • PA	• Motor • Travel • Home • PMI	• Motor • Travel • Home • PMI
Life assurance	• Personal pension	• Personal pension • Term assurance • 25-year endowment	• Personal pension • Whole-life assurance • Term assurance • 25-year endowment • PHI	• AVCs • Whole-life assurance • Term assurance • 10-year endowment • PHI	• AVCs • Whole-life assurance • Term assurance • 10-year endowment • PHI • Annuities	• AVCs • Annuities	• Annuities
Banking	• Current account • Instant access savings	• Current account • Instant access savings	• Current account • Instant access savings	• Current account • Instant access savings • Term access savings	• Current account • Instant access savings • Term access savings	• Current account • Instant access savings • Term access savings	• Current account • Instant access savings • Term access savings
Savings and investment		• Unit trusts • ISAs	• Unit trusts • ISAs	• Unit trusts • ISAs • Savings and investment bonds	• Unit trusts • ISAs • Savings and investment bonds	• Unit trusts • ISAs • Savings and investment bonds • Income bonds	• Unit trusts • ISAs • Savings and investment bonds • Income bonds
Loans	• Unsecured	• Unsecured • Mortgage • Secured • Home improvement	• Unsecured • Mortgage • Secured • Home improvement	• Unsecured • Mortgage • Secured • Home improvement	• Mortgage • Secured	• Equity release	• Equity release
Misc services	• Roadside assistance	• Roadside assistance • Financial planning	• Roadside assistance • Financial planning • School fees planning	• Roadside assistance • Financial planning • Wills • School fees planning	• Roadside assistance • Financial planning • Wills • Retirement planning	• Roadside assistance • Financial planning • Wills • Retirement planning • Long-term care advice	• Roadside assistance • Financial planning • Wills • Long-term care advice

Life Stage

← Young independents →
← Pre-family couples →
← Parents →
← Empty nesters →
← Retirement →
← Elderly →

c) Life Stage

An increasingly popular method of segmentation for personal customers is Life Stage. The population is broken down into a number of stages of a customer's life, each of which will have its special needs and purchasing triggers. The table on the previous page is fairly typical.

d) Attitudinal

People can be segmented on their attitudes towards savings, debt, credit, life and general insurance. Such systems are designed by market researchers who ask a large sample of potential customers to respond to statements such as:

> 'With insurance you always get what you pay for'
>
> 'You should claim what you can get away with'

A typical segmentation system, created by the Henley Centre, is shown in Figure 9.2.

Figure 9.2

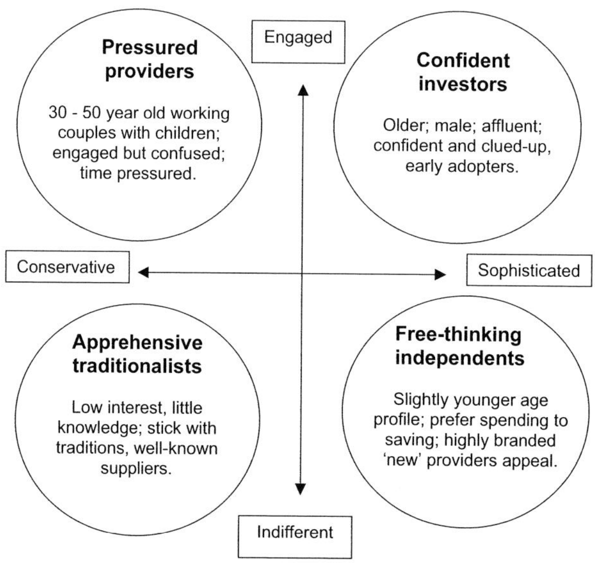

The real world

Personal customer segmentation systems such as those described above, combined with the many non-customer based systems (channel, postal address, etc), gives rise to the hundreds of different segments in use today.

Customer segmentation is undoubtedly of great value to an insurer because it can allow increased focus in terms of products, systems, etc with associated increased efficiency of operations. However, considerable care needs to be taken in its use because it is a blunt instrument. It should always be remembered that customers consider themselves to be individuals: they do not live up to their stereotypes; they do not act their age; and, they want to be different things at different times. There is no such thing as Mr or Mrs Average.

2. Commercial customers

Commercial customers are usually segmented using two factors: size and occupation.

a) Size

Small, medium and large businesses have their own distinctive needs. The small/medium-sized company (SME) has considerable growth potential and is targeted by many insurers. Such companies do not have much time and expertise available to deal with insurance matters so they are responsive to specially packaged products suitable for their common needs. At the other end of the scale, the large and multinational companies have very specialized needs and are usually highly informed buyers.

b) Occupation

This segmentation may be based on industry sector, or specific trades within a sector. Government statistics are a good starting point. These will provide a classification of industries, their turnover, growth, etc. The UK list, for example, is as follows:

Agriculture	Transport, storage, communications
Fishing	Finance
Mining	Public administration
Manufacturing	Education
Electricity	Health
Construction	Other
Retail	
Hotels and catering	

An insurer might prefer to target specific industries or trades, and design products accordingly.

9.2.4 Marketing mix

The marketing mix is the way the various elements and techniques of marketing are combined. There are lots of ways to describe this but a simple one involves the easily remembered five 'P's – Proposition, Place, Price, People and Promotion.

a) Proposition

In insurance, the proposition is a combination of both product and service. Regarding the **product** element, unless operating in a specific niche market, it is essential that an operation builds up a balanced portfolio of products to meet the multiple needs of customers, taking into consideration product life cycles so that new products become available to replace the old. These new products may be developed as a result of a range of drivers, eg:

- Customer feedback
- Competitor activity
- The company's own R&D
- Overseas subsidiaries' ideas.

Recently, there has been an attempt to widen the propositions being offered by bundling together existing products from the insurer and products offered by other suppliers (eg banks, car leasing companies, etc) to create much wider, single solutions to a broad set of customer needs. There are also early signs of new, genuinely hybrid products being introduced. For example some of the alternative risk financing propositions in commercial lines are hybrids between banking and insurance.

Proposition bundling

A carefree driving solution

One insurer is offering a simple way to find and run a car. By linking with a leasing company and using its own motor trade connections the insurer is able to provide a bundled proposition which includes:

- Selection/acquisition/provision of the car of choice
- Servicing and maintenance
- Insurance
- Breakdown cover

All delivered for a fixed monthly payment.

Because insurance products can be fairly easily copied by competitors, the main focus of differentiation in personal lines, other than price, has tended to be around service. This can be divided as shown in Figure 9.3.

Figure 9.3

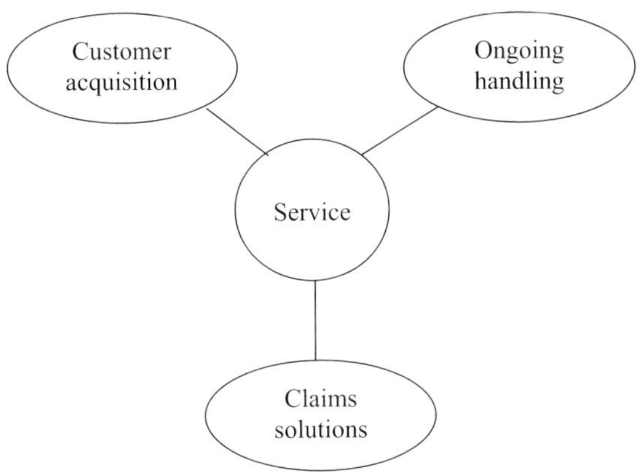

- Customer acquisition: providing information to and collecting information from the customer in support of the sales process, including quotations, policy documentation and payment collection set up.
- Ongoing handling: premium collection; ad hoc problem solving; mid-term changes to policy or policyholder information; renewal solicitation; win back; etc.
- Claims solutions: claims notification handling and immediate policyholder support; advice and support to manage and deliver the optimal claims solution; payment of suppliers, third parties, the policyholder; recovery of monies due from third parties; etc.

Each area provides an opportunity for the insurer to impress the customer with the quality of the service offering, but equally it also provides an opportunity to disappoint or annoy the customer with poor or inappropriate service.

Demand for better service and better value for money

'Consumers expect claims to be paid promptly and generously and they are demanding higher standards of service generally than they have been given in the past. The media have played their part by raising expectations and even teaching people how to complain. Above all, the consumer is increasingly expecting that more of his premium money will be returned as claim payments and less used to pay for the administration of the business.'

Professor Ralph Petty, University of Nottingham

b) Place

'Place' in the product mix relates to how the propositions are presented to the customer. In insurance this involves selecting the channels of distribution. There are basically only two categories: intermediated and direct.

From the insurer's perspective the choice will revolve around effectiveness (gaining access to the target customers) and efficiency. From the customer's point of view, the choice may depend on the perceived added value of the channel. Distribution is discussed in more detail in the next chapter.

c) Price

As previously noted, unlike most industries, the actual cost of an individual insurance sale is not known at the point of sale of the contract, and may be thousands of times larger than the premium. For example, a $1,000 public liability policy taken out in 1975 could result in claims totalling $10m for asbestos-related diseases in 2005. For this reason pricing in insurance is an extremely complex area. The technical aspects are very much the province of the underwriter, supported by the actuary. There is then the requirement for marketing specialists to become involved, particularly in fine tuning the technical pricing, to ensure that it reflects the target population and is a price the market is willing to pay. It is important to assess which markets you can successfully compete in – you cannot sell a product at a price customers are unwilling to pay.

You then need to determine whether you can still make an acceptable profit at the price the market will bear, or to exit that market segment. There are many examples of where marketeers have cut the prices calculated as being required on a technical basis by the underwriters, only for the company then to make substantial losses on the business obtained.

Pricing is dealt with in more detail in Chapter 11.

d) People

It is a sad fact that many of the marketing models taught in insurance have ignored the people element. This is unfortunate, because it is the company's staff and their skills that deploy the rest of the marketing mix.

The company needs to ensure that all staff:

- have the appropriate skills to deliver the marketing strategy
- fully understand what the proposition is in terms of the technical product, the level of service and the company's values
- fully understand who the target customers are.

If the business is sold via intermediaries, these will require to be similarly skilled in order to market 'on behalf of the insurer'.

e) Promotion

The final part of the marketing mix is promotion. This is the method by which the company, its brand and propositions are communicated to the stakeholders. It may conveniently be divided between Marketing Communications and Corporate Affairs, although there may be substantial overlap in some companies. The Corporate Affairs function is described in Chapter 16.

Marketing communications

These relate to the various ways in which the brand, brand values and propositions are communicated to potential customers. They include press, TV, radio, direct mail, Internet, SMS and digital TV, e-mail, sponsorship, sales support and community investment programmes. Advertising itself is a very high-profile activity, not only because of the large amount of money involved, but because it attracts considerable attention both outside and inside the company.

The key points in managing advertising are:

- There must be measurable objectives, eg increase sales to targeted segments by x% , increase brand name awareness by y%, cost per sale under £z, conversion of enquiries to sales at better than a%;
- There must be a clear message and the effectiveness of getting this message across to the targeted audience should be monitored;
- Media, timing and frequency are critical;
- Budgets should be carefully controlled.

Front-line staff (call centre operatives, etc) need to be fully coordinated with any advertising initiatives so that full advantage can be taken of the opportunities created and the customers will not be disappointed by the response they receive from the insurer. There have been recent examples where direct-marketing television campaigns have been so successful that call/contact centres have been overloaded, service levels have fallen as a result, and both potential business and customer goodwill have been lost.

9.2.5 Customer Relationship Management

The marketing mix is a robust management model, but there are some marketeers who feel that it is too inward-looking. They have put forward a more customer-centric model known as Customer Relationship Management (CRM).

There is a wealth of literature on the subject, but little consistency in definition. One might be tempted to assume that it relates almost entirely to technology, given the volume of articles published on CRM from technology solutions providers. In reality, however, it is very much more a management discipline, which technology solutions can then be applied to, to support key elements. But, as noted elsewhere in this book, technology is only a tool to deliver broader business objectives, not an objective in itself.

A useful description of CRM has been produced by the consultants Valoris, Abram, Hawkes.

CRM

- An organization-wide set of activities that focuses on how to deliver value to customers **and** the business.
- The allocation of resources, both human and financial, to customers in relation to the value the customer delivers (or might deliver) to the business.
- Organization-wide knowledge of each customer, their current and past holdings, their needs and preferences, and their value to the business.
- The promotion of alternative products and services to customers in the way they prefer, at the time they need them.

Valoris, Abram, Hawkes *Business Report,* Issue 34

This has been expressed diagrammatically as shown in Figure 9.4.

Figure 9.4

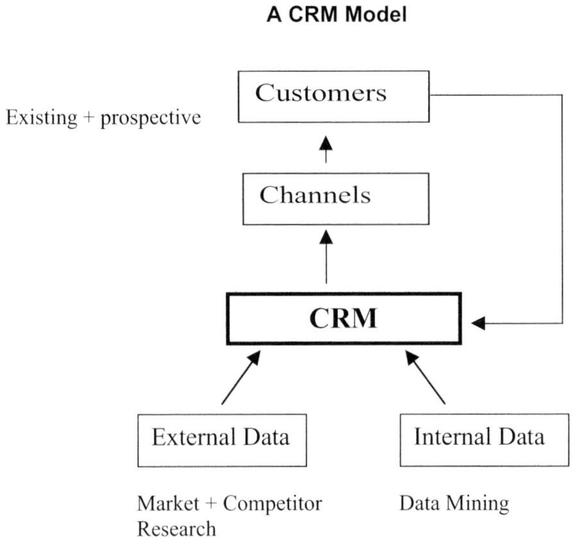

After N Russell-Jones,
Customer Relationship Management,
Institute of Financial Services (*ifs*)

As Neil Russell-Jones explained, CRM involves the coordination of a combination of the following key components:

- customer focus
- single (organization-wide) view of the customer and appearance to the customer/seamless service
- proactive rather than reactive offerings
- segmentation by profitability
- 'solutions' not 'products'
- retention of the 'best' (most profitable) customers
- performance-related staff remuneration
- excellent processes supporting the services offered
- having the right people with the right skills in the right place
- continuous learning and feedback.

These are all highly appropriate to the marketing of insurance, but it can prove to be rather more complicated than it initially appears to implement effectively. Two examples are:

- With insurance sales, there may be a long time lag between the sale and any subsequent claim(s). As a result, it is not easy to estimate the lifetime value of a customer, and there is a risk that short-term decisions might be made that are not optimal in the longer term. Staff may receive short-term performance-related rewards for putting, what turns out in the longer term to be, unprofitable business onto the books.
- Strong proponents of 'customer focus' can tend to lose sight of the need to provide customer service only so far as it is logical and cost effective for the business to do so. There can be a tendency for seeking to meet the customers' needs even where it is not in the organization's best interests to do so.
- The role of the intermediary within a CRM framework needs to be clearly understood and developed. At times, the intermediary is akin to a customer of the insurer in the way that the insurer will seek to manage and maximize the value of its intermediary connections. At other times, the role of the intermediary in delivering the insurer's CRM approach to the end customer will take precedence and will potentially need to be managed in a different way.

Select bibliography

I Youngman, *Competitor Analysis in Financial Services,* Woodhead 1998.

A Meidan, *Marketing in Financial Services,* Macmillan 1996.

(Marketing)

P Kotlar, G Armstrong, J Saunders, V Wong, *Principles of Marketing 3rd European Ed,* F T Prentice Hall 2001.

P Robertson, *Brands and the Insurance Industry, Insurance Trends,* ABI April 1999.

T Proctor, *Essentials of Marketing Research,* Prentice Hall 2000.

Neil Russell-Jones, *Customer Relationship Management,* Institute of Financial Services (***ifs***) 2002.

S Diacon (Ed), *A Guide to Insurance Management,* Macmillan 1990, Chapter 13.

Ten

The management of the front end 2. Practice

Objectives

On completion of this chapter, and wider personal research, the reader should be able to:

- understand how insurance products and services are delivered to the customer;
- describe the characteristics of the various channels;
- explain the duties of an agent in an insurance context;
- appreciate the management issues facing brokers.

In this chapter some of the practical aspects of managing the front end, and in particular the distribution of insurance products, are examined in more detail.

10.1 The distribution of insurance

General insurance is distributed either directly to the customer by the insurer or indirectly via intermediaries. There are also many examples of insurance being integrated into other sales processes, as with travel insurance bought alongside a holiday. The distribution mix of a modern insurance company can appear quite complex (see Figure 10.1). However, it becomes much clearer when one understands how it has evolved.

Figure 10.1

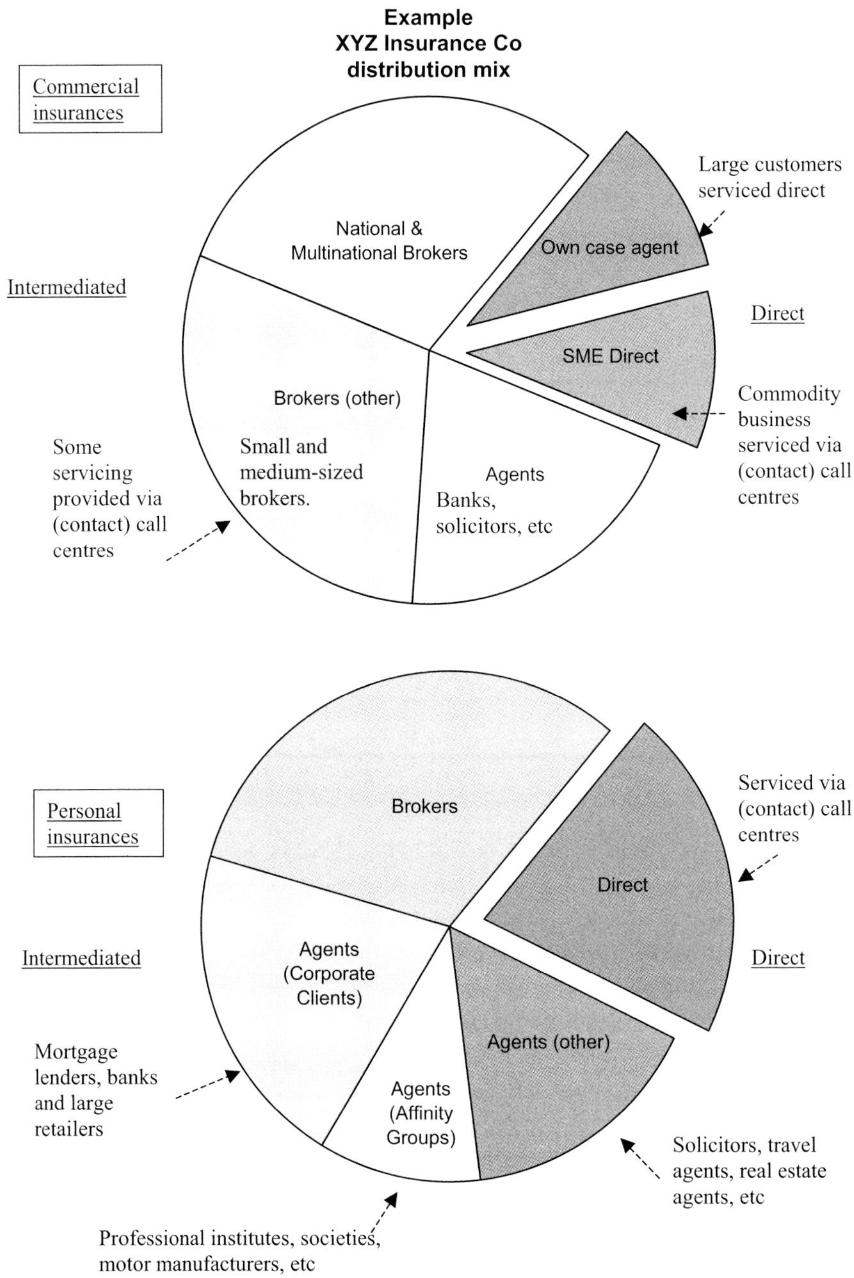
Example
XYZ Insurance Co
distribution mix
Commercial insurances
National & Multinational Brokers
Own case agent
Large customers serviced direct
Intermediated
Direct
SME Direct
Brokers (other)
Small and medium-sized brokers.
Commodity business serviced via (contact) call centres
Some servicing provided via (contact) call centres
Agents
Banks, solicitors, etc
Personal insurances
Brokers
Serviced via (contact) call centres
Direct
Intermediated
Direct
Agents (Corporate Clients)
Agents (other)
Mortgage lenders, banks and large retailers
Agents (Affinity Groups)
Solicitors, travel agents, real estate agents, etc
Professional institutes, societies, motor manufacturers, etc

10.1.1 The development of insurance distribution

A pioneering insurance company would have originally established an office in a major trading centre, a large city or port such as London. Here it would have dealt directly with commercial and personal customers, either face-to-face or by written correspondence. As the company succeeded and began to grow it would need to reach out to more customers in its home country and possibly abroad. It could do this by establishing a chain of branch offices and so duplicate the direct model already operated in its original base. This they did, but certain disadvantages became apparent that are still valid today.

Direct distribution:

- does not guarantee access to target customers
- requires substantial expenditure in establishing and maintaining a trusted brand
- can be expensive because it requires common infrastructure and expertise to be spread across locations
- requires customers, wherever located, to be able to access the insurer in a simple and convenient way.

(Even today in the UK, where Internet and telephone technology allow easy access to insurers and the current direct model has been around for 15-20 years, the majority (> 60%) of consumers still prefer the choice offered by intermediaries, or the simplicity of buying from a trusted source, eg their mortgage provider.)

The solution to these problems was to use intermediaries to bring potential customers and their business to the insurer.

10.2 Intermediated distribution

10.2.1 Agents

Insurers began to use agents to carry out defined tasks such as acquire customers, issue temporary insurance cover, undertake some of the administration and assist with handling claims. Agents were chosen for their trustworthiness and access to potential clients where their core business activities had linked insurance needs. This started with merchants, shopkeepers, lawyers and bankers and in due course spread wider to include real estate agents, mortgage lenders, travel agents, motor manufacturers and garages, etc.

The motivation for the agent was commission income and, in modern parlance, 'broadening their proposition' to existing clients. For example, a lawyer arranging a property purchase would be able to offer fire insurance cover at the same time.

Originally, agents would have represented a single insurer but, over time, some elected to take out agencies with several companies, to provide a greater choice for their clients. This led to the logical development of agency, the **broker**.

10.2.2 Brokers

Agents who work full time in insurance, have access to a range of insurers and have built up specialist expertise in some or many classes of business are known as brokers.

Today these range from large multinational brokers like Aon or Marsh McLennan employing thousands of staff, down to small local operations with one or two people. Many banks have established insurance broking subsidiaries in order to service commercial clients.

10.2.3 What does an agent do?

> **Legal duties of an agent to the insurer**
>
> The agent must carry out the conditions of the contract (which is usually in writing), act in good faith and account for monies. A higher duty of care is expected from a broker because the latter is deemed to have greater expertise than a part-time agent. An agent cannot normally delegate duties.

The amount of work carried out by an agent varies with the terms of the agency agreement. It could be little more than introducing business. At the other extreme, a bank or mortgage lender may have a large household insurance account for which it undertakes almost all administrative activities, which are integrated into its own processes. The insurer, or occasionally panel of insurers, specifies the underwriting criteria, agrees the net prices, carries the risk and is notified of the total income and claims on a periodic basis. The bank would regard the clients as its own and use its own branded products. As likely as not, the insurer would not know the identity of the individual policyholder unless he makes a claim, and the policyholder feels that he is dealing with the bank and would generally be unaware of a separate insurance company behind the product.

Since the deregulation of financial markets in the UK it has become relatively easy for a bank or mortgage lender to decide to carry the risk itself and drop the panel of insurers. This has already happened in a few cases, eg Halifax Bank of Scotland now carries its own risk for motor business and has set up as an insurance company in its own right for certain classes of business. (See also Bancassurance – Chapter 6.) Others have their own captive insurers to share part or all of the financial risks for insurance products, such as creditor and mortgage indemnity.

Whose agent?

Insurance is unusual in so far as agents may act for both parties, the customer and the insurer. For example, the agent or broker is the agent of the **customer** when:

- advising the customer on policy cover required
- advising the customer how to make a claim
- filling in the proposal form on behalf of the customer.

However, the agent acts for the **insurer** when:

- explaining the conditions and exclusions of the policy being offered to the customer
- collecting premiums
- undertaking a survey
- passing on claim payments
- issuing a cover note
- acting under a delegated authority arrangement.

Special types of agent

i) Affinity groups

Many affinity groups are exploiting the value represented by the membership of the group to obtain a good insurance deal for their members. An affinity group can be any collection of people with a common interest, having a regular means of communication. Examples include the professional institutions, motoring associations, societies, owners of a particular type of car. The organizers can become agents in their own right and produce a branded policy for their members, or arrange a discount for their members with the insurer on proof of membership.

The affinity group can earn introduction fees/commission on policies sold to members as an additional income stream.

ii) Brandassurers

Brandassurer is a name given to a number of new entrants to insurance distribution. They are companies with strong retail brands and large customer bases. They are selling simple commodity personal lines products under their own brands but manufactured by existing insurers. The benefits to the brandassurer are:

- commission income
- deepening their customer relationships
- enhancing their brands.

The insurer supplying the products sees this as an opportunity to access large volumes of business via brands that are stronger than their own. Typical examples of UK brandassurers are Tesco, Sainsbury, Virgin, Marks & Spencer, Kwik Fit.

10.3 Direct distribution

Intermediated distribution has been the successful model for general insurance in most parts of the world for most of the last 200 years. It therefore initially came as quite a surprise to the established players that the pendulum has recently swung back towards direct distribution, especially in personal lines. Though perhaps the real surprise for the industry commentators of the 1990s was the survival of the brokers, albeit that the major chains/brands were capturing an increasing share of the intermediated cake.

There has always been a proportion of business handled directly by the insurer. Large commercial property owners, for example, have preferred to be 'own case' agents with their own insurance experts and so make commission savings. In addition, most branches of insurers will have had a number of personal customers not attached to any agent who bought their insurance over the counter at the branch.

Direct customers could, if necessary, be attended to by the field force of 'inspectors' who were employed primarily to develop/support the intermediaries. In some countries, notably Sweden, the role of this 'inspector' sales force in handling direct business is still very strong. And 'telephone direct' has made little progress in France and Germany because of continued support for local agents by customers.

The resurgence of direct business began in the 1980s and has continued to gain momentum. There were two key factors.

i) Direct marketing

Following its success in other industries, insurers used newspaper and TV advertising, and used unsolicited, bulk mailings to stimulate a direct response to the insurer. Increasing selectivity based on the use of post coding and improved technology enabled insurers to achieve a high success rate. Although expenses are high as the portfolio is being built, the insurer does not have to pay commission. Retention levels also tend to be much better than intermediated business. However during periods of substantial price increases more customers naturally seek alternatives and move to new insurers in much larger numbers to take advantage of timing differences between companies' price increases. However, such market arbitrage is not limited to direct and is in fact easier via a broker who can access comparative quotes from a range of companies very quickly via their access to market-wide electronic comparative quotes systems for retail insurance products.

ii) Strong branding and offering 'something different'

Direct Line was the UK market innovator in direct personal lines general insurance in the 1980s and 1990s.

Direct Line built on the success of the direct marketers and exploited a general disenchantment in the public regarding the way that insurance was run. Its entry into the motor insurance market using the slogan 'Cut out the middleman' was regarded as a revolution – although the incumbent insurers pushing through very large price increases at that time had a major part to do with it. Even so Direct Line made little progress for its first five years before acceptance of its model became commonplace.

The basic model was that the insurer concentrates on highly-segmented and targeted customers, using strong advertising and branding to attract direct customers who were serviced through dedicated telephone call centres. Opportunities were then taken to cross-sell and up-sell products although, to date, most direct insurers have achieved relatively little success in such activity. Pricing was dynamic, ie rate changes could be made in hours rather than the traditional players' weeks, allowing an immediate response to changes in demand, potential aggregations and other factors.

This model, based around the telephone call centre, has proved to be extremely successful and has been copied by other insurers and applied to other financial services, eg direct banking.

Direct Line demonstrated first-mover advantage and within ten years of starting up had taken more than 10% of the UK motor market as well as a significant share of household insurance business. But in recent years retail growth has slowed significantly and it now relies on corporate partnerships and affinities for growth, but with significantly lower profit per unit. Other large UK direct insurers such as Churchill have also had to diversify into intermediated business to maintain growth. (Note: Churchill was acquired by RBoS, Direct Line's parent, in 2003.)

10.4 The impact of technology

Computer technology has had a major influence on the distribution of insurance. Not only does it offer the potential for reduced transaction costs, but it also enables an insurer or intermediary to target customers more precisely and broaden the proposition offered. Specific factors are:

a) EDI

Electronic Data Interchange is the name given to a number of ways by which a broker's computer network may be linked to that of an insurer to exchange information cheaply and rapidly. The stimulus to its widespread adoption was responding to the expense reduction challenge posed by the direct insurer.

Many brokers now have EDI arrangements with insurers for both personal and commercial business. In addition, there are several commercial networks whereby groups of brokers and insurers come together to form an electronic marketplace to share data, provide comparative quotations from a range of insurers for the same risk, and allow other elements for on-line data exchange.

EDI

'The advent of full cycle EDI accelerated both policy and claims processing and enabled brokers to achieve the levels of speed and efficiency of service that had previously been the exclusive territory of direct writers'

Front Runners in Internet Insurance 2000 – Datamonitor

b) Internet

The arrival of Internet technology in the mid 1990s attracted many new entrants to the insurance market and forced existing players to reconsider the way they do business. However, it should be emphasized that the 'e-channel' models are all basically agency/broking or direct distribution models. At the present date, for many customers, the web remains an information source but not necessarily somewhere to transact business. Predicting how this will change over time is one of the big questions facing insurers.

c) Further developments in digital communications

With the continuing development of mobile telephony (SMS messaging, third generation technology) and digital interactivity, eg digital TV, the ability to communicate with potential customers and for them to buy insurance and related products has increased and will continue to change as customers' lifestyles and habits change. Insurers will need to keep fully abreast of all relevant technological developments to ensure that their target potential customers have the ability to do business with them how and when they choose.

Technology is a threat as well as an opportunity

'On the technology side, such innovations as call-centre technology and the Internet are challenging the traditional distribution strongholds of multi-line insurers. They are also increasing customers' price sensitivity and lowering the barriers to switching insurance vendors.'

McKinsey Quarterly 1998 No. 3

Technology is a tool, not a channel in itself, but it is vital in supporting the distribution channels that are deemed appropriate to the business.

The impact of e-business on insurance is discussed in more detail in Chapter17.

10.5 Choosing a channel

Like much else in management, the choice of distribution channel to use will ultimately depend on effectiveness (reaching the target customers with the right product, correctly presented) and efficiency (cost of distribution).

- Some channels are much more effective in reaching certain segments, eg brokers for large commercial customers, and banks/mortgage lenders for home buyers.
- Some channels are particularly suited for selling certain types of product, eg direct marketing for simple, low-cost products like Hospital Cash, and direct call centres (contact centres) for commodity products like private motor or SME commercial packages.
- Direct distribution has an inbuilt cost advantage over intermediated distribution because it avoids commission; on the other hand central costs, particularly advertising/promotion/branding costs may be high. At the present date in the UK there are no major insurers who are solely direct distributors.

Other factors to consider when choosing a channel are potential conflicts. For example, an insurer relying heavily on broker business might experience adverse reaction if it sets up a direct operation that the brokers perceive as competition, hence the use of different brands, contact centres, processes – although this can preclude taking advantage of scale.

The overall advantages and disadvantages to an insurer of intermediated and direct distribution are outlined in the following tables.

Pro	Con
Intermediated distribution	
♦ Broadening existing 'network' to attract potential customers	♦ Commission cost (typically 10-20% of premium, but could be a lot more)
♦ Trusted expertise to help • customer select cover • risk improvement	♦ Some duplication of administration ♦ Holding premiums affects the insurer's cash flow and represents a credit risk
♦ Undertakes some administration	
♦ Suitable for most types of product and customer, particularly linked sales of insurance	♦ Broker tendency to re-market cases at renewal (churn), low loyalty to insurer
♦ Selling costs are totally variable	♦ Customer access only via the intermediary
	♦ Limited control over claims process/costs
Direct distribution	
♦ No commission	♦ Limited to customers who buy direct
♦ Access to customer allows • direct communication • cross-selling/up-selling opportunities	♦ Requires strong retail brand/franchise ♦ High up-front costs of marketing/ selling/brand building requires volume book of business for cost effectiveness
♦ Opportunity to manage claims process/costs	♦ Only suitable for simple/commodity products or bespoke business for very large customers
♦ Cash flow – premiums collected early	
♦ Potentially, higher renewal rate/ customer loyalty	
♦ Increased flexibility in terms of segmentation and pricing	
♦ No opportunity to share admin costs	

10.6 Key issues regarding distribution

- It is desirable to control access to customers; this allows you to directly influence their behaviour, cross-sell, etc. In most intermediary arrangements, access to the customer is controlled by the intermediary, reducing the control exercisable by the insurer.
- It is deemed vital to an insurer to control both front-line underwriting and claims handling. Any delegation of front-line underwriting or claims handling to an intermediary reduces the insurer's control and requires additional controls (audits, etc) to be put in place to establish adequate control.
- It is important to understand the drivers and economics of the intermediaries dealt with:
  - brokers will tend to re-broke their clients on a regular basis to demonstrate the value they add, damaging retention.
  - where broker panels are set up, the brokers may select against the insurers on the panel when placing business, or put another way, they interpret lowest price as the insurer saying they are most keen on writing those risks.
  - empirically, broker business tends to have 7-8% worse claims ratio in personal lines than direct business.
- Brand building and direct marketing spend (eg TV advertising) is very expensive and is incurred in advance of any new business it generates. A direct book needs a large volume of business to spread marketing costs to be viable. In the UK this figure is thought to be > 1 million policies.
- It is vital to manage the marketing spend, particularly for direct business, to understand the importance and impact of brand, and to ensure the customer proposition is clearly differentiated from the competition. Measurement of the effectiveness of marketing spend is crucial, yet very difficult to deliver.

10.7 Management issues for the broker

The challenge facing brokers

'Brokers have to position themselves in the eyes of the customer as the professional adviser. They must differentiate themselves from intermediaries who do not add value. This will mean having a better understanding of what the customer needs and satisfy it.'

Peter Taylor, Speech to BIIBA 1996

10.7.1 Introduction

Broking is a resilient sector that has survived for two centuries by adapting to the changing needs of the customer. It was originally focused on the Marine market but eventually spread to all classes of insurance. The large international and national brokers began to appear immediately before World War II and the present market gradually emerged over the succeeding decades, viz:

Types of broker

- International brokers
- National brokers
- Regional and High Street brokers
- Chains of High Street brokers
- Specialist brokers
- Banks, building societies, motor organizations acting as brokers.

Lloyd's brokers are brokers who are authorized to place business in the Lloyd's market.

The basic value proposition of a broker is to advise the client and place the business with the most appropriate insurer. This will always be a subjective judgment but factors include:

- Financial security and reputation of insurer
- Cover available
- Premiums
- Capacity
- Flexibility
- Service
- Claims handling
- Geographical spread.

10.7.2 The threat from direct

The success of direct business led to much speculation about the demise of broking. In practice this has not occurred on the scale suggested by the pessimists.

Commercial business remains overwhelmingly broked. There is a small amount of SME business handled by direct writers and a number of large companies place their insurances direct with insurers, although most of these retain brokers for advice.

Direct writers have made considerable inroads into personal lines business, but this has flattened out in recent years as brokers have lowered their own costs through EDI.

10.7.3 Commission v consultancy fees

A by-product of direct writing has been an increased public awareness of commission levels. A response to this has been a trend for larger brokers to charge consultancy fees in cases where they might once have charged commission. This approach is more transparent and enables clients to understand what they are getting for the money they pay.

10.7.4 Added value services

Commercial brokers have been extending their propositions beyond that of advising the client on cover and then placing the business with an insurer; in particular, they have led the industry into the field of risk management with activities such as:

- loss control advice
- surveys
- captive insurance company management
- risk financing and other non-insurance solutions.

Such added value services deepen the relationship with the client and create new sources of revenue.

10.7.5 Globalization

This has given the opportunity for the international brokers to provide global insurance programmes for their multinational clients. There are two types of policy involved:

- **admitted policies:** where policies are written in each country where the client operates. (These may be backed up by a Difference in Conditions Policy (DIC) designed to fill any gaps left by the variations in local cover.)
- **non-admitted policies:** where there is a single master policy providing cover for all the countries required.

Non-admitted policies are obviously more convenient for the client, but they often upset local market relationships for the brokers and in some countries they are illegal.

In order to take advantage of globalization, international brokers need to be large, have a broad geographical spread and have considerable expertise. This demand for these competencies has been a major contributory factor in the consolidation of the sector.

UK Intermediaries: trends

Commercial lines

- Brokers still dominate
- Large are growing at the expense of medium-sized
- Large are tending towards advice and fees for service
- Small are tending towards personal service
- Total number is reducing

Personal lines

- Direct continues to grow but has slowed
- Banks and building societies are providing commodity distribution
- Large motor specialists have emerged, eg AA, Swinton
- Traditional intermediaries are finding personal lines expensive to handle
- The e models have yet to make a real impact

Implications

There is over-capacity of intermediaries: rationalization and fragmentation continues.

10.7.6 Technology

The need to keep pace with new technology such as EDI, point of sale, administration and customer management systems has placed a large burden on brokers, particularly the smaller ones. This has led to many mergers and withdrawals from the market by those brokers unable to make the necessary investment to remain competitive.

At the other end of the broking spectrum, technology has created a number of electronic marketplaces whereby brokers offer risks and insurers accept them.

10.7.7 Regulation

Like insurance companies, the intermediary sector is increasingly subject to more rigorous regulation with the associated compliance obligations and costs. In the UK, for instance, the FSA is introducing stricter solvency and conduct of business rules for brokers from 2004, and under the EU Mediation Directive intermediaries will need to demonstrate specified levels of competence.This may lead to a further shake out of intermediaries, and a fall in the number of intermediary businesses, particularly the smaller operators, who may find that the cost of implementing/complying with the new regulations make their businesses no longer viable.

Select bibliography

B Webb, C Harrison, J Markam, *Insurance Operations and Regulation,* Insurance Institute of America 2002, Chapter 3.

G Dionne, *Handbook of Insurance,* Kluwer 2000, Chapter 22.

P Wright, R Oak, *Insurance Brokers An Industry Accounting and Auditing Guide 3rd Ed,* Institute of Chartered Accountants 2002.

S Diacon (Ed), *A Guide to Insurance Management,* Macmillan 1990, Chapter 10.

Eleven

The management of underwriting – 1. Key concepts

Objectives

On completion of this chapter, and wider personal research, the reader should be able to:

- understand the underwriting process;
- outline the basics of assessment and acceptance of risks, policy terms and condition;
- understand the fundamentals of pricing in P+C insurance;
- explain how premium rates are built up.

11.1 Introduction

Underwriting, along with investment, is the main source of income and profit to an insurer and the main exposure of potential loss to its balance sheet. As such it should be regarded as a critical activity and be subject to careful management.

Underwriting is the process of assessing, accepting and pricing risks, applying policy conditions and managing exposures. Although the actual practice and terminology may vary between the different classes, the underlying principles are much the same.

The title 'underwriter' is commonly applied to a wide range of people from a specialist carrying out bespoke liability underwriting for large multinational clients to a junior operative inputting data into a call centre computer program for motor insurance. For commodity classes like the latter, however, the real underwriting will have to be done at the account level by a professional who sets the rules and designed the program.

Most underwriting is performed in-house by an insurer, to maintain control, but there are two notable exceptions:

a) Some insurers will give a level of **underwriting authority**, within strictly defined limits, to specific intermediaries, eg banks. Where this is the case, commission is higher to reflect the increased work involved from the intermediary, and there may also be an element of profit sharing between the insurer and intermediary, to provide an incentive to maintain the quality (profitability) of the book of business written in this way.

b) The provision of **binding authority** to selected brokers is more common. This gives the broker authority to accept risks on behalf of the insurer and hold cover. However, the insurer will generally issue the policy and retain control over final pricing.

Prior to discussing the practicalities of underwriting management it is necessary to gain a little more insight into the underwriting process itself.

11.2 Proposal

Risks may be presented to an underwriter in a variety of ways, eg:

- a telephone call to a personal lines call centre
- a written proposal form through the post from an agent/broker
- an online proposal through an e-channel
- a broker slip in the Lloyd's market
- a formal presentation of a large commercial risk by a broker.

Choice of cover

Responsibility for ensuring the most appropriate cover lies with the insured or with the intermediary if the latter is providing advice. Nevertheless, the underwriter can provide addtional guidance and must never, knowingly, mis-sell products.

11.3 Assessment

Whatever way a risk is presented, it is the job of the underwriter to assess it. This means understanding the risk, determining whether or not it should be accepted and under what conditions.

In practice, the underwriter will be relying to a great extent on an underwriting manual which will provide advice/best practice on how to deal with most of the risks that are likely to be offered to the insurer. This will normally include: pricing guidelines, alternative terms and conditions, target segments, risks to avoid, etc. The manual (paper or electronic) reflects the insurer's underwriting policy and is designed to influence the individual and aggregate decisions of the front-line underwriters and, ultimately, determine the composition of the portfolio of risks written.

In assessing the risk, the underwriter will obviously need to know the identity of the proposer, the insured activity, the extent of cover required, the location of the risk and the previous claims experience. Beyond this there will be a considerable amount of information needed that is specific to each class of business and particular risks. Broadly, this falls into two categories relating to **physical hazards** and **moral hazards** that can influence the probability and severity of loss.

a) Physical hazards are the tangible factors that arise out of the nature of the risk itself. For example, in motor insurance these might include the model of the car, annual mileage, type of use, etc. In employer's liability, the insured trade, manufacturing processes, materials handled and condition of premises are highly relevant. In product liability, information will be needed on the type of products, customers, markets and quality control procedures.

Physical hazards

1 A proposal for property insurance for a new furniture warehouse may reveal that it is located on a riverside industrial estate prone to flooding. The underwriter will need to decide whether the risk is acceptable, whether flood cover should be excluded, or whether a higher premium should be charged.

2. An engineering components manufacturer reveals that some of its components may be used in aircraft engines. The catastrophe potential of the failure of these items would merit extremely high premiums.

b) Moral hazards are the intangible human aspects of a risk that are much more difficult to ascertain. They include the potential for fraudulent claims, carelessness and, in the case of commercial insurance, poor management. There is still an element of truth in the old saying that 'you insure people rather than things'.

Moral hazards

1 A city-centre tobacconist asks for theft cover for his shop but is unwilling to install an alarm on the grounds of cost. (For some reason such proposals often appear to be made late in the afternoon before the current policy is due to expire.) The underwriter would do well to decline this risk because the proposer does not give sufficient priority to the protection of his property.

2. An existing motor policy holder asks for cover for an additional vehicle, a sports car, and names his 19-year-old son as the additional driver. The underwriter will have to make a judgment as to whether the son is really the main driver but is using the father's policy to avoid a high premium or possible declinature.

Experience shows:

Fraudulent or seriously inflated claims are far more common than is generally believed, even by experienced insurers. A few years ago, the police asked a major UK motor insurer if it would assist them in some research on the causes of car theft. It was agreed that, for a period of one week, all policyholders making claims for stolen cars would be asked to come to the office to attend a short interview with a policeman to record the circumstances of the loss. Much to the insurer's surprise, one in seven of the claimants immediately withdrew the claim because they had 'found the car'!

11.3.1 Risk control surveys

The initial presentation of the risk may not provide enough information for the underwriter to make an assessment. In a significant proportion of commercial cases and in some of the higher-risk personal cases the underwriter will ask for a risk control survey. This could be carried out by one of the insurer's own surveyors, a broker's surveyor or possibly by an independent specialist.

The surveyor will visit the proposer, discuss the risk in some detail and write a report with recommendations on how the risk could be improved. In some ways the surveyor can be described as 'the eyes and ears of the underwriter'. Survey reports play a major part in the larger and more complex cases in property, business interruption, liability and motor fleet insurance. Depending on the instructions from the underwriter and the customer service proposition of the insurer, the surveyor can be involved in anything from a simple inspection of the premises to working closely with the insured to develop a full risk-management programme. Some of this work could be subject to a separate fee.

A typical fire insurance risk control survey might include the following information.

Risk control survey (Fire)

a) **Description**

- Premises and activities
- Construction and condition
- Stock
- Hazardous goods
- Fire-protection system

b) **Assessment**

- Estimated maximum loss (EML)
- Reinstatement cost
- Quality of management
- Security
- Adequacy of sum insured

c) **Risk improvement**

- Recommendations and requirements

Surveys as marketing opportunities

When visiting the insured, it is not at all unusual for the surveyor to be able to give advice on the extent of cover, the probability of underinsurance, etc, as well as risk improvement actions.

In some cases an even stronger relationship can develop between the insured and the surveyor. The authors know of one example where, when a surveyor, a professional engineer in his own right, visited a complex bio-engineering plant to assess a public liability risk, the insured was so relieved to find an insurer who understood the risk that he transferred his employer's liability and property policies to the insurer, even though this meant a substantial increase in premiums.

11.4 Acceptance

Having assessed the risk, the underwriter will make a decision. This is essentially that shown in Figure 11.1.

Figure 11.1

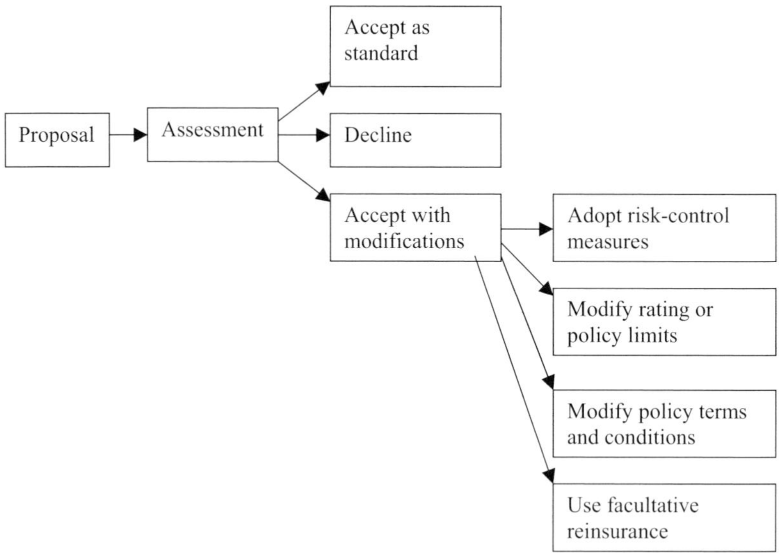

- If the risk is **accepted as standard** a quotation will be given to the insured/intermediary and, if accepted, the case proceeds to policy issue.
- If the risk is **declined**, the insured/intermediary will need to be informed without delay. (NB Any such declinature must be disclosed by the insured when they apply to another insurer because it is considered to be a **material fact**.)
- If the risk is **accepted with modifications** the following options are possible:
  - **Adopt risk-control procedures**, eg install burglar alarms, fit sprinklers, fit guards to dangerous machinery – depending on the type of insurance and as identified by the risk control survey.
  - **Modify rating or policy limits.** The rate might be increased to reflect higher risk, or lowered to attract especially good business. The sum insured or limit of indemnity could also be changed to reflect specific issues relating to the risk, eg to avoid under- or overinsurance.
  - **Modify terms and conditions.** This might include increasing the deductible, or excluding certain types of loss. These options are discussed in more detail later in this chapter.
  - **Use facultative reinsurance.** Where the risk falls outside the existing treaty arrangements, facultative reinsurance might be used to enable the risk to be written by the insurer. The whole subject of how reinsurance is used is dealt with in the next chapter.

The underwriter's decision to accept or decline risks, either at proposal, or renewal is critical to the future profitability of the insurer. Unless active selection of risks takes place, rejecting poor risks and ensuring that every risk is properly priced, the quality of the book will rapidly deteriorate.

> 'If the insurance company does not select those applicants that it desires to insure, it will have to depend on prospective insureds to select it. This will quickly lead to adverse selection, with loss-prone applicants most likely to be among those seeking coverage. The selection process enables the insurer to ration its capital to obtain optimum spread of loss exposures by geographic distribution, class and line of business.'
>
> The Insurance Institute of America

The phenomenon known as **adverse selection** occurs when an insurer receives more business from those with a higher risk of loss than would be expected from a random sample. It may occur in the normal course of competition – if the insurer's competitors are actively 'cherry picking' the better risks the insurer will suffer unless it takes defensive action. (A similar situation may arise in banking when a bank will find that its lending book will deteriorate if it is not as selective as its competitors.)

Adverse selection may also occur when potential customers with a higher risk of loss recognize a greater need for cover, and so a higher proportion than the population in general seeks insurance. For example, it is highly likely that the availability of genetic testing will stimulate more demand for life, sickness and medical insurances from those identified as being prone to life-threatening diseases.

The underwriter's main method of defence against adverse selection is active and prudent underwriting, involving adequate pricing and an element of screening of risks. However, great sensitivity is required if whole segments of potential customers are to be declined, and people are denied cover by the market in general. This can easily lead to criticism of insurers for unethical or antisocial behaviour, eg 'red-lining' of flood plains or high-crime areas.

11.5 Assessment at renewal

Renewal of a policy also provides an underwriter with the opportunity to reassess a risk. Particular attention is paid to any changes that might have occurred during the year and the insured's loss experience.

Reassessment of an employers liability risk at renewal

Claims paid plus reserves (£)

	Year notified				
	1998	1999	2000	2001	2002
1998	5,000 est	–	–	–	–
1999	10,000 est	2,000 est	–	–	–
2000	10,000 est	2,000 est	1,000 est		–
2001	14,000 (paid)	2,000 est	5,000 est	30,000 est	–
2002	–	2,000 (paid)	5,000 est	50,000 est	1,000 est

This method of displaying claims experience is known as triangulation from the shape of the table. For simplicity, it is assumed in this example that there has been one claim a year for the last 5 years. A claim was notified in 1998 and a reserve estimate of £5,000 placed on it. This was increased to £10,000 in 1999 but the claim was finally settled in 2001 for £14,000. A claim notified in 2001 and reserved at £30,000 has had the reserve increased to £50,000 in 2002.

The table provides the underwriter with a view of how claims have moved (or 'developed') over the period and will help in the assessment of whether the policy should be renewed and at what premium. In practice, an insured may have a large number of claims at various stages of development. The table would then be more complicated, but the principles would be the same.

11.6 Policy terms and conditions

The wording of a policy defines the scope of cover and hence the future claims. The underwriter must exercise considerable care, using clauses that have been tested in the courts. Any insurance contract also has **implied conditions**, eg insurable interest, utmost good faith, contribution. These do not have to be written into the policy document but often are there for absolute clarity.

However, there are a number of **express conditions** that an underwriter might apply to make a risk more manageable, including the following:

Deductible

This is also known as an excess. The insured must pay the first part of any claim. The purpose is twofold:

- to discourage small claims and so keep costs down by reducing 'money swapping';
- to give the insured a financial interest in the management of the risk.

> **Deductible**
>
> 1. The use of a deductible (eg £1,000) in subsidence claims in home insurance policies has proved to be a very successful solution to what was becoming a serious issue in a period of climate change. It enables the insurer to pay out on major structural faults (for which the cover was originally designed). However, minor cosmetic problems caused by the natural settlement of buildings are absorbed by the policyholder as a routine maintenance cost.
> 2. Large deductibles are common in professional indemnity insurance to ensure that the policyholders have a major interest in taking care that the advice/service given to a client does not expose the firm to undue risk.
> 3. Large commercial insureds may elect to take substantial deductibles by way of self-insurance in order to reduce the premium. A motor manufacturer, for example, may well carry a property damage deductible of £100,000 on each of its plants.

Warranty

A warranty requires an insured to do, or not do, certain things and is often linked to a specific trade. A breach would make the policy voidable. Warranties may arise out of the survey report and are intended to deal with a particular hazard, eg daily removal of waste products from a factory. Others may be classified as common sense, eg sprinklers to be regularly tested.

Exclusion

Most policies carry standard exclusions, eg war risks, nuclear risks. Some like the standard fire policy also carry automatic exclusions (earthquakes, riot, civil commotion, etc) which can, if necessary, be insured for an additional premium. In addition, the underwriter may wish to apply specific exclusions, eg the policy will not cover certain buildings owned by the insured.

War risks

Cover for war risks is available in the Marine and Aviation markets because ships and aircraft may move in and out of the war zone and losses are likely to be isolated. War risks on land are generally not covered because many properties and businesses may be affected and insurers could be subjected to enormous aggregations of risk. Such risks tend to be dealt with by government compensation schemes.

Note on alternative wordings

The underwriter may have a choice of policy wordings to use in any particular set of circumstances. These have been developed out of experience and market practice. Brokers may well ask for specific wordings for their clients.

Claims incurred v claims made

One such example of alternate wording is in liability insurance. Most policies in the past have been written to cover claims incurred (or caused) in the policy year. This has meant that someone exposed to the cause of an industrial disease, say asbestosis, in the policy year may make a claim against the insurer years or even decades later. The use of a wording specifying claims made means that the current insurer will pay for any claims that are made (ie notified) in the current year, irrespective of when the cause of loss occurred. The impact on an insurer's ongoing liabilities will be very different for these two wordings.

11.7 Pricing

The principle of insurance pricing is to determine a price for each risk that reflects the perceived exposure in terms of impact and frequency, and makes an appropriate contribution to expenses and profit. As in some other aspects of insurance, the terminology used in pricing varies considerably between markets and even between companies in the same market. In the following section we have used expressions that would be recognized by most underwriters wherever they operate.

Insurers have been in business for many years and have built up a wealth of experience. In the majority of cases they will therefore have a good idea of the level of premium required. This information is put into an underwriting manual (or computer program) for the guidance of the front-line underwriters. This will include instructions on how to build up a premium and the terms and conditions to be applied for the various types of risk that are commonly presented to the company.

Pricing in different countries

'In most countries insurers can make their own pricing decisions. Only in highly regulated markets is the price derived from a predetermined formula. However, in some markets insurers fix their prices in consultation or cooperation with each other (for example, by forming rating bureaux or tariffs); in other countries this collusive behaviour is limited, or even prohibited by anti-monopolistic legislation.'

Walter Karten, University of Hamburg

In a few simple classes of insurance, with relatively homogeneous risks, a **flat rate** is used. For example, in motor a flat rate is set down for a certain model of car and this is adjusted by the underwriter in response to a limited number of risk factors, eg claims experience, driver's age, annual mileage, business use, etc.

In more heterogeneous classes, including most commercial insurances, a more flexible method is used that is responsive to differences in the size and complexity of risks. The principle is:

Book rate = premium base x premium rate

The **premium base** is some convenient base on which to measure the size of the risk. Depending on the type of insurance, it could be the sum insured, the annual turnover or wages roll.

The **premium rate** is a multiplier to reflect the hazard associated with the risk. It is usually expressed as a rate per cent or per mille of the premium base.

If the risk is made up of a number of different activities separate calculations may be done for each and a cumulative book rate built up.

A **book rate** is designed to deal with the average risk of its kind. The pricing can be further refined to suit the individual circumstances of the risk by applying loadings for adverse features and discounts for good features, such as good quality management. All this results in the figure widely referred to as the **technical premium**. This is the point from which an underwriter will negotiate/decide on a final quoted premium, taking into consideration the prevailing market conditions.

This may sound complicated and it may be better explained using an example. This is an EL quotation for a medium-sized builder that undertakes construction, alteration and repair work and uses sub-contractors. The quality of management and claims experience in this case is excellent.

Employer's Liability Quotation: for a builder

	(Premium base)	(Premium rate)	(Book rate)
Turnover			
– New construction	£2,000,000 @	0.25% =	£5,000
– Alteration & repair	£3,500,000 @	0.37% =	£12,950
– Payments to sub-contractors	£1,000,000 @	0.09% =	£ 900
			£18,850
		Less discount for quality	
		25% =	(4,712)
		Technical premium	£14,138

The technical premium built up in this case is £14,138. The underwriter might be able to negotiate a premium of say £13,500 in a soft market and £14,500 in a harder market.

In theoretical terms, in a stable market, the pricing of insurance will move towards the intersection of the supply and demand curves. In practice however, an insurance market is seldom, if ever, in equilibrium, and few insurers can be really confident about the minimum price they should charge for a risk.

11.7.1 Producing the book rate

So far this section has dealt with the mechanics of pricing a risk when someone else has already provided a book rate. How was that rate produced in the first place?

In theory, a book rate is built up as shown in Figure 11.2.

Figure 11.2

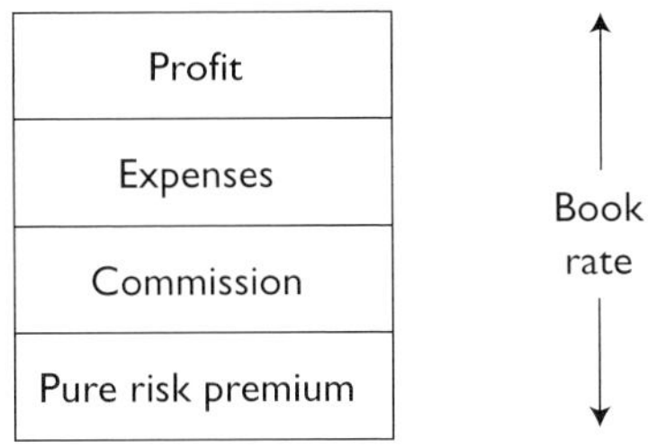

The **pure risk premium** is a quantitative assessment of the liability of the risk to the common pool, ie a measure of the probability, severity and timing of the loss potential (including the insurer's expenses to handle the claims). To this is added loadings for commission, the other expenses of the insurer (in acquiring, servicing and processing the insurance business and a share of 'corporate' expenses) and desired profit.

Calculating a pure risk premium goes to the very heart of underwriting. There are two approaches underwriters may take.

a) First principles

Developing rates from first principles involves creating and combining models of the probabilities of loss frequency and loss severity and converting this into a pure risk premium. (This means effectively multiplying the predicted number of claims per policy by the average size of claim.) This is a quite difficult mathematical exercise, because loss frequencies tend to follow an approximately Normal distribution, whereas loss severity is more likely to approximate to a skewed, Poisson type, pattern – small losses are much more common than large.

It should be noted that very similar models are used by the actuaries when they are calculating and setting loss reserves – see Chapter15.

In P+C insurance, as compared to Life, where rate-makers can use well-established mortality tables, the underwriters are often using partial or totally fragmentary information. They will therefore have to make the best of what is available and must use their skill and knowledge to make up for inadequacies in the data.

This means that an underwriter will have to gather incident statistics from relevant sources (national fire statistics, weather records, crime statistics, etc), make comparisons with their experience of similar risks, and attempt to model the pattern of potential claims. Any catastrophe potential will also need to be built in. If there is likely to be a delay in recording or settling of claims, as there is in subsidence and the liability classes, this needs to be considered along with the investment income that will accrue in the reserves.

Perhaps the most difficult challenge is modelling future claims patterns when the business environment is changing. For example, what assumptions in calculating the pure risk premium should an underwriter make about the effect of global warming on flood risk, or future legislation changes on a liability risk?

There is no single right way or wrong way to produce a rate from first principles. However, over the long-term, the most successful underwriters have managed consistently to combine good statistical modelling with a flair for anticipating changes in the environment.

b) Burning cost

Burning cost is intended to link the premium for a particular policyholder closely to his particular claims experience. In its most simple form, the underwriter looks at the risk's last 5 year's claims, takes an average, and expresses this as a percentage of the premium. The risk is said to be 'burning' at this loss ratio. (This is in all likelihood an echo of the method's origins in fire insurance.) After adding an allowance for claims inflation and any other known changes to the claims environment, the underwriter will translate burning cost into the pure risk premium.

This is essentially retrospective rating and considerable care is needed if it is to be used as a guide for future performance. (It has been compared to steering a ship by looking at the wake.) It is however an acceptable pricing mechanism for some types of reinsurance where the previous year is being priced in arrears. This approach clearly works against the law of large numbers, so any results need to be checked against other methods.

> 'Historical data generally is unreliable for estimating probabilities of rare, usually catastrophic, future events.'
>
> JF Outreville
> *The Theory and Practice of Insurance*

> **Pricing**
>
> 'It is obvious that a rating scheme (*a set of price calculation formulae for specific risks*) cannot produce certainty in result. Experience, judgment, highly refined schedules and careful scrutiny of hazards can all lead to tentative conclusions, but none can be predictive with precise accuracy. This is the dilemma. An insurance policy for a known cost today must insure against tomorrow's uncertainties with unknown costs.'
>
> American Institute of Property and Liability Underwriters

The effect of pricing

There are always opportunities to tempt the short-termist into making quick killings in what is in practice a long-term market. However, claims will catch up, necessitating strengthening of reserves.

As the market is so cyclical, particularly for commercial risks, holding or changing rates can have a disproportionately large effect. Similarly, in commodity classes such as motor, the timing of a rate increase can result in a large movement of premium in or out of the business.

Derek Archer, Sun Alliance

'Rates based on past experience are valid only if the conditions that pervaded in the past remain unchanged during the period of the contract.'

JF Outreville
The Theory and Practice of Insurance

11.7.2 Investment income

At one time, investment income was not taken into consideration in the rating process. Any investment gains were considered to be in addition to, and distinct from, the underwriting profit. In recent decades competitive pressures combined with strong stock market returns have tempted some insurers to build projected investment income into the book-rate calculation.

In its extreme form this is known as cash-flow underwriting, where insurers may actually price for an underwriting loss, hoping to make an overall profit once investment income and gains are taken into account. Investment income obviously has more impact in the long-tail classes, when reserves are held for extended periods and higher risk (and potential return) investments may be selected.

This is increasingly a high-risk approach given recent stock market performance and the expectation of low levels of interest rates and investment returns in the future.

11.8 Exposure management

The final part of the underwriting process is to manage the exposure from an individual risk or from the aggregation of exposures that build up in an account. The first line of defence against overexposure is at the selection stage. For example, the underwriter should avoid taking on too many risks in, say, the same flood area (property) or the same trade that could be subject to the same industrial disease (EL).

The second line of defence is reinsurance. This is dealt with in the next chapter.

Select bibliography

S Diacon (Ed), *A Guide to Insurance Management*, Macmillan 1990, Chapters 8, 11 and 12.

B Webb, C Harrison, J Markam, *Insurance Operations and Regulation,* Insurance Institute of America 2002, Chapter 4.

G Dionne, *Handbook of Insurance,* Kluwer 2000, Chapter 19.

S D'Arcy, N Doherty, *The Financial Theory of Pricing Property – Liability, Insurance Contracts,* Huebrier Foundation 1988.

D Weeks, *Insurance Fraud: A New Collective Approach to Tackling the Problem,* Insurance Trends, ABI Jan 2002.

Arson Attacks on Homes, Insurance Trends, ABI July 1999.

Arson in Schools, Insurance Trends, ABI October 1998.

N Dodd, *Applying Psychology in the Reduction of Insurance Fraud,* Insurance Trends, ABI July 1997.

R Derrig, *Insurance Fraud, Journal of Risk and Insurance* Vol 69, No 3, Sept 2002.

Twelve

The management of underwriting – 2. Reinsurance and ART

Objectives

On completion of this chapter, and wider personal research, the reader should be able to:

- explain how and why reinsurance is used;
- describe the basic types of reinsurance;
- outline the use of alternative risk transfer techniques.

12.1 Introduction

> 'The reinsurance mechanism is not a bottomless well into which the insurer tosses undesirable business. A valued axiom is that, an insurer, over time, eventually pays in premiums all that it ever recovers from its reinsurer.'
>
> American Institute of Property and Liability Underwriters

Reinsurers insure insurers, much in the same way as bookmakers are able to lay off their large exposures and/or accumulations of bets with other bookmakers.

The main reasons a primary insurer might purchase reinsurance are:

- To lower its exposure to either a single large risk or an accumulation of similar risks in the event of a catastrophe event occurring.

- To allow it to write a volume of business greater than that possible with its existing capital (increasing capacity).
- To provide an alternative source of capital (financing).
- To attempt to smooth the peaks and troughs of the underwriting cycle.
- To gain access to underwriting intellectual capital possessed by the reinsurer.
- To facilitate entry to or exit from a particular market or class of business.

A company buying reinsurance from another company is said to be conducting **outwards reinsurance** or 'ceding' a risk. The company providing the cover, the reinsurer, is said to be conducting **inwards reinsurance**. The vast majority of inwards reinsurance is undertaken by specialist reinsurance companies such as Munich Re, American Re, General Re and Swiss Re. Primary insurers may also be involved, running it as a separate profit centre or to comply with market practice, eg in the London Marine Market.

Alternative risk transfer (ART) is the name given to a broad range of non-conventional risk transfer techniques that mostly originated in the reinsurance market, but have been extensively developed by the large brokers. Some, such as captive insurance companies, have been in use for many years, but others, like those involving capital market products are relatively new.

There are two main types of reinsurance: **traditional** and **non-traditional**.

12.2 Traditional reinsurance

12.2.1 Facultative

At one time all reinsurance was facultative, that is negotiated on a case-by-case basis. These days its use tends to be restricted to cover a specific risk (eg a large chemical works) that falls outside the normal acceptance limits of the primary insurer. This may be due to its catastrophe potential, or because it is specifically excluded from an existing treaty. The risk is individually underwritten, and the retention and pricing agreed between the parties.

12.2.2 Treaty

The high administrative cost of facultative reinsurance has led to it being largely replaced by automatic arrangements known as treaties. In treaty reinsurance the primary insurer purchases cover for a class of insurance, eg property, public liability, motor. Pricing and conditions are agreed before hand. The primary insurer does not have the right to select what is ceded and the reinsurer cannot refuse cover. The main sorts of treaty are:

Figure 12.1

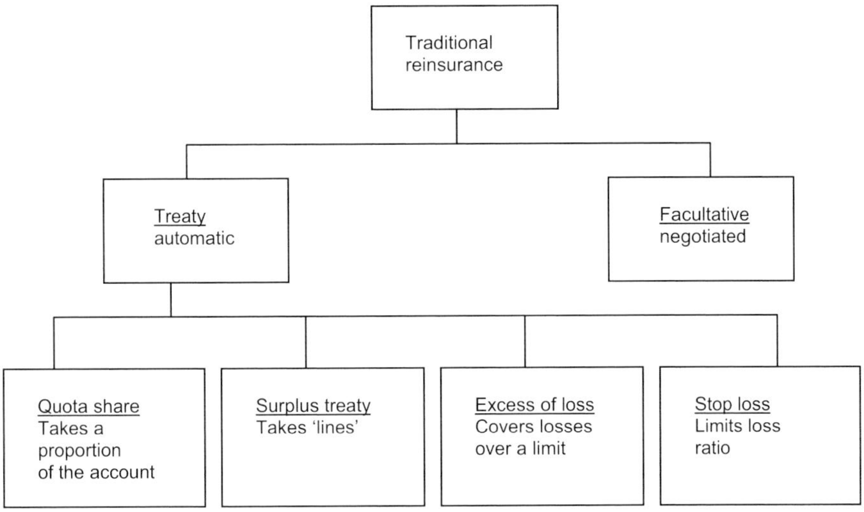

Quota share

This is particularly suitable to protect new entrants or companies with restricted capital. The primary insurer agrees to share a proportion of the whole account (eg 10%) with the reinsurer. This means that the reinsurer accepts a proportion of the premium and pays an equivalent proportion of the losses. An advantage to the primary insurer is that it is able to write more business without increasing its capital or reducing its solvency. Reinsurance is therefore being used as surrogate capital for the primary insurer.

Surplus

After assessing the potential exposure, the primary insurer decides the proportion of the risk it is prepared to retain, eg £100,000. This is called a line. The remainder of the risk is divided into lines of equal size and are ceded to the reinsurer(s) for automatic acceptance. In the case of a very large risk there may be several layers of treaties to accommodate all the lines.

Excess of loss (XL)

This provides protection from the impact of a very large loss or a catastrophe. The reinsurer agrees to pay any loss in excess of an agreed retention. As in the case of surplus, XL may build into multiple layers.

Stop loss

The reinsurer agrees to pay all losses once the primary insurer's loss ratio exceeds a certain value.

Quota share and surplus treaty are sometimes described as proportional reinsurance because the primary insurer and the reinsurer are sharing risks in an agreed proportion. Pricing is also in proportion, but the insurer will often compensate the primary insurer for the original acquisition expenses through an **overriding commission**.

Non-proportional treaties, ie excess of loss and stop loss, are normally priced retrospectively using burning cost methods.

LMX spirals (London Market Excess of Loss)

A dangerous practice arose among the London Market excess of loss retrocession underwriters in the early 1990s. They would participate at multiple layers on excess of loss contracts for the same risk. This involved taking a relatively small amount of the risk, passing the remainder on to the next underwriter, and taking more at later stages as the reinsurance programme was built up. The aim was to maximize commission for both the brokers and the underwriters, with apparently low exposure.

The problems were, firstly, that the customer's original premium soon got whittled away by the process, as more and more retrocession commissions were paid, leaving less and less risk premium for the subsequent layers; and, secondly, if a catastrophe did occur, the impact on the network of reinsurers was totally unpredictable. A large claim would slowly spiral up through the market, each underwriter paying its share then waiting for the claim to break through to the subsequent layers and the underwriter then having to pay again. If, as often happened, the higher layers ran out of reinsurance cover, or some underwriters became insolvent, the underwriters at the primary layers found themselves responsible for the residual loss. A number of underwriters, most notably the Lloyd's syndicate Gooda Walker, lost huge sums in this way.

In the litigation that followed the debacle, the courts made it clear that such spirals ran counter to a basic principle of reinsurance, which is the spreading of risk. Instead, they funnelled the risk onto the unlucky underwriters that were left stranded when cover failed. In an attempt to prevent such things happening in the future it was ruled that an underwriter owes a duty of care to the owners of his business. The extent of this duty will vary according to the circumstances, but at least in the case of LMX the underwriter must ensure:

1. potential aggregation of risk is carefully monitored
2. premiums must comprise:
   - a basic risk premium
   - appropriate loadings for administration expenses, brokerage and profit
   - a loading for random fluctuations

Failure to do this could lead to a finding of negligence against the underwriter.

12.3 Non-traditional reinsurance

This may also be known as financial or finite reinsurance. It tends to be cheaper than traditional reinsurance with reduced risk transfer and often involves access to other capital markets. Contracts may run for several years to smooth losses and may additionally involve arrangements for sharing profits and investment income. In some countries, the generally accepted accounting principles may cancel out the financial benefits of this type of cover.

12.4 Alternative risk transfer (ART)

Non-traditional reinsurance is just one of a range of non-conventional risk tranfer/financing techniques that are included in the rather imprecise term ART. The products can be used to protect insurers or, often, large customers, who are bypassing the insurance market. ART became a major talking point in the 1990s, with some commentators predicting the demise of the insurance market for larger commercial risks. However, many of the products have since fallen out of favour because of unease about their reliability.

A good example of an ART product is a catastrophe bond. The principle underlying the product is that finance should be both more available and cheaper in the capital markets than in the reinsurance market. The reinsurer or bank therefore issues a security to the customer that is dependent on a catastrophe event. If the catastrophe event occurs the bond is 'forgiven' – effectively contributing to the cost of claims.

12.4.1 Captive insurers

Captive insurance is another technique that falls under the heading of ART.

A captive is a wholly-owned insurance company set up to write part or all of its parent's insurance business. Some of the larger captives may also write business for other companies. Captives are subject to the same regulation as conventional primary insurers. For a very large commercial organization wishing to retain many of its own risks a captive can prove to be an effective funding mechanism.

The concept of a captive is not new and probably dates from the early 20th century. The main drivers in their development have been:

- non-availability of adequate cover at an acceptable price in the primary market;
- desire to retain premiums within the organization;
- avoidance of the costs incurred by an external insurer, eg acquisition/commission, infrastructure, profit;
- direct access to the reinsurance market for part of the risk;
- taxation benefits.

A key factor is that reserves put aside by a commercial company to pay for potential losses are not tax-allowable expenses, whereas insurance premiums paid to an insurer (including a captive) are allowable.

Popular locations for captives are off-shore tax havens such as the Bahamas and Bermuda, whereas reserves can be established on a tax-free basis.

The main risks to the parent company setting up a captive are inadequate funding of the captive itself, investment risks, foreign exchange risks and changes in local legislation.

The size of the captive sector varies with the underwriting cycle. A period of low market rates encourages a shrinkage in the volume of retained risks. However, an underlying, steady growth has occurred, particularly in the USA where captives now represent a significant proportion of the total commercial market.

Select bibliography

R Carter, *Reinsurance 4th Ed*, 2000.

R and S Kiln, *Reinsurance in Practice 4th Ed*, Witherby 2001.

H Geman (Ed), *Insurance and Weather Derivatives*, Risk Books 1999.

R Bellerose, *Reinsurance for the beginner 4th Ed*, Witherby & Co 1998.

A Punter, *New Solutions for the Financing of Corporate Non-Life Risks,* Insurance Trends, ABI October 2002

Sigma 2001 No 3, *Capital Market Innovation in the Insurance Industry.*

Sigma 2003 No 1, *The Picture of ART.*

R Derrig, *Insurance fraud, Journal of Risk and Insurance,* Vol 69, No 3, Sept 2002.

P Bawcutt, *Captive insurance Companies 4th Ed*, Witherby & Co 1997.

B Poutney (Ed), *Handbook of Risk Management,* Kluwer 1999, Chapter 8.

Developments in Excess of Loss Reinsurance, Advanced Study Group Report 244, CII 2000.

N Golden (Ed), *Rational Reinsurance Buying,* Risk Waters Group 2000.

Thirteen

The management of underwriting – 3. Practice

Objectives

On completion of this chapter, and wider personal research, the reader should be able to:

- explain the reasons for the instability of P+C insurance results;
- explain how an underwriting function and its portfolio are managed;
- describe how reinsurance is managed;
- describe how underwriting activities can be controlled and monitored.

13.1 Introduction

The approach to the management of underwriting will depend to a great extent on the structure of the operation and how it fits into the insurance value chain. For example, if underwriting is run as a stand-alone business, the underwriting strategy is effectively the business strategy and will tend to drive the marketing, distribution, IS and other business activities. In larger, more complex organizations, made up of a number of customer-focused businesses, underwriting is more likely to be treated as a technical function managing across the organization through a framework of policies. Underwriting management in this situation must liase closely with colleagues in the businesses to ensure that there is an integrated strategy.

In the interests of simplicity it will be assumed in this chapter that underwriting is a technical function creating policy for the businesses. This means that key assumptions about required ROC, growth, degree of risk aversion, target customer segments, distribution mix and the broad shape of the portfolio would have been decided in conjunction with the other parts of the business management team through the strategy development process described in Chapter 5.

13.2 Prerequisites of underwriting management

To manage underwriting effectively it is important to understand, among other things, the impact and drivers behind the underwriting cycle, the impact of changes to liability in recent years and the potential impact of 'catastrophes' (very large claims events usually impacting many insureds at the same time).

13.2.1 Underwriting cycle

As previously noted in Chapter 3, insurance is often cited as being the most cyclical of all industries. It has been this way for at least 50 years and most national markets demonstrate the phenomenon. At one time there were distinct differences in phases where the USA was usually ahead of the UK, which in turn might be a year ahead of some of the other European markets. However, with the globalization of capital these differences are gradually disappearing.

Underwriting cycles

'Underwriting results follow a cyclical pattern caused by external factors affecting capacity – such as catastrophic events and investment performance. In addition internal factors – such as insurers striving for market share during times of robust investment results – contribute to the cycle. The cycles average about six years in length and are synchronized across countries and to some extent across lines of business.'

Swiss Re, Sigma No 5, 2001

Figure 13.1

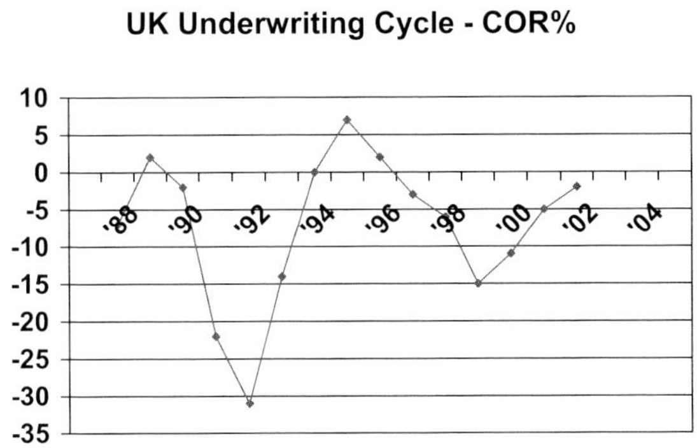

The UK cycle, shown above, is a useful example to study. Over the period shown, UK insurers made an average underwriting loss of around 7% p.a., relying on significant investment returns to provide an acceptable return on capital.

> 'Because there is no real product competition, companies periodically engage in price competition.'
>
> JF Outreville
> *Theory and Practice of Insurance*

It is easy to take the view that insurance is just like some other financial markets, driven by fear and greed with periods of overshoot. Although there is undoubtedly an element of truth in this, the cycle is influenced by a number of drivers that can affect the amplitude or wavelength.

a) Investment income

As previously stated, an insurer has two sources of income: underwriting and investment. Consequently, periods of good investment returns tend to encourage what is known as cash-flow underwriting and depress the underwriting result. On the other hand, poor investment returns mean that underwriting needs to earn more in its own right, so premiums are driven upwards. (The recent prolonged period of low interest rates and stock market falls has therefore emphasized the need for good-quality underwriting.)

b) State of the economy

A buoyant economy will mean that there is more money available to pay premiums. This will tend to reinforce an upswing, whereas a recession has the opposite effect. Also, in a recession, the number of fraudulent and arson claims tends to increase, so further reducing profitability.

c) Reaction to major claims

After a period of major claims (eg the World Trade Center disaster) there may be a concentrated effort in the market to push premiums up to a more economic level.

d) Capital

Insurers tend to exhaust their capital at the bottom of the cycle – a factor that has frequently led to companies leaving the market at that stage. The need to take advantage of the upswing and restore solvency has resulted in three distinct periods in recent history when companies have raised capital: 1986-87, 1992-93 and 2002-3.

The sum total of all these factors is a UK market whose profitability seems to follow a cycle with an average wavelength of about 6-7 years. Such cyclical behaviour is not in the interest of customers, who require greater stability of pricing, and it is certainly not in the interest of insurers, who carry a high level of fixed costs and have shareholders expecting real returns every year.

13.2.2 Liability and emerging risks

As noted in Chapter 1 the whole area of liability is a major challenge, both to society as a whole and the insurance industry in particular, as supplier of liability covers. We have:

- an increasingly litigious society;
- the feeling by both consumers and governments that there is always someone to blame;
- the belief that consumers must be protected at all costs (even from their own greed, stupidity or naivety);
- increasing value of awards for all types of injury alongside a broadening of the definition of the term 'injury', allowing new types of claim;
- 20:20 hindsight being applied to actions of perhaps decades earlier;
- new types of risk emerging, with no certainty as to their impact or prevalence;
- aggressive marketing by lawyers to encourage people to make claims, including 'no win – no fee' deals; and
- increasing extension of the scope and value of liability covers, both covers written perhaps many years ago, which may be re-interpreted by the courts, and ones being written today.

The increased uncertainties and costs of this type of cover are leading the industry to impose substantial premium increases, which has given rise to criticism and bad publicity as the cost of liability cover threatens the viability/profitability of many insured businesses. As noted previously, this is a problem that society as a whole needs to address or accept, not one for the insurance industry on its own to solve. But, unless the current environment changes, there is likely to be limited appetite or capital to write a significant number of liability risks and those that are written will be at a high price.

Emerging risks

Risks are emerging in society that need to be closely monitored by insurers. They may give rise to substantial claims in the future and so require consideration now in terms of pricing and underwriting practice. The following are examples of some of those with a high profile.

Stress

Stress is the body's response to pressure. A person may be able to cope with pressure until some critical point is reached when exhaustion and illness results. Stress at work is a common occurrence and has begun to give rise to employers' liability claims.

Toxic mould

This is a group of naturally occurring fungi that can grow within buildings and emit chemicals that can cause illness in susceptible people. Changes in building practice have given rise to an increase in toxic mould, particularly in the humid southern states of the USA. To date, there have been 9,000 claims, including one settled for $4m which involved the demolition and rebuilding of a house. Such incidents have led some US insurers to withdraw from home insurance.

Electromagnetic radiation

The link between cancer and exposure to electromagnetic radiation emitted from power lines and cellular phones is presently under investigation. Results are inconclusive but there is much media speculation and public concern which could eventually lead to a flood of claims against electricity suppliers and telephone companies.

Environmental pollution

Pollution is normally covered in a public liability policy on the basis of negligence by the factory owner. However, the EU is planning to introduce strict liability for putting right environmental damage (including loss of biodiversity) caused by pollution. This will lead to more frequent and much larger claims.

Genetically modified organisms

Genetic engineering is in its infancy and no one yet knows what risks are involved. If problems do occur, either to human health or to the environment, these are likely to be of the long-tail type, similar to asbestos.

Phil Bell, Chairman, Liability Committee, ABI

13.2.3 Catastrophes

It is widely accepted that both the frequency and severity of man-made and natural catastrophes are increasing and that this represents a serious threat to the viability of the insurance industry and the society it serves. This increased volatility is illustrated below (see Figure 13.2) in the global data for catastrophes compiled by Swiss Re.

Figure 13.2

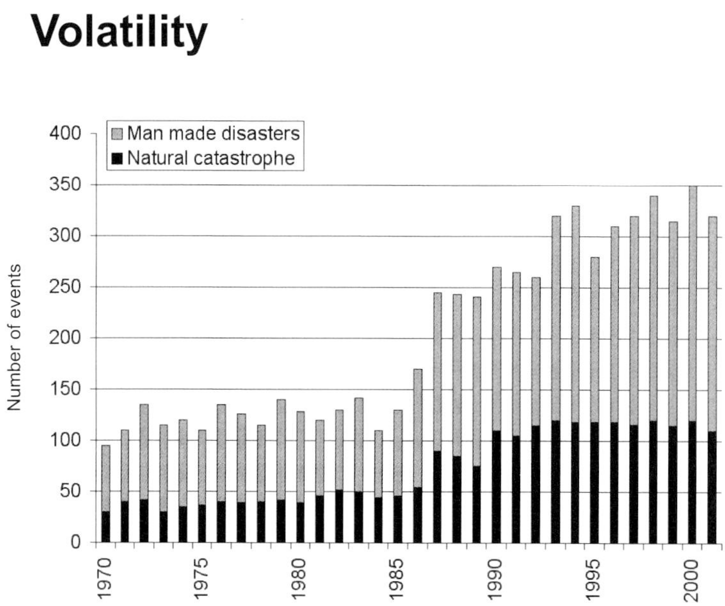

Source: SwissR

Two key causes of major catastrophes in recent years have been international terrorism and climate change. It is sobering to realize that, although the potential of both were widely predicted, in neither case was the impact fully built into the industry's property insurance rating. This is at least partly because the public is unprepared to fund new exposures until after the event has occurred.

Volatility

Methods available to reduce the volatility of the result of a P+C insurance operation include:

Portfolio management

- change the mix of products, customers, businesses, territories
- use another insurer to provide parts of the total proposition and so earn commission income rather than carry the underwriting risk for those parts

Reinsurance

- to smooth extreme results

Catastrophe/equalization reserves

- support the poor years with reserves set aside in good years

Variable expense base

- outsource a substantial part of the operation so that business volumes can be reduced at the bottom of the underwriting cycle without the handicap of having high fixed costs

It should be noted that while reinsurance can, to some extent, reduce the effects of volatility on a primary insurer's result, it does not remove the absolute necessity to have prudent risk selection, rating, and exposure limitation procedures.

13.3 Managing underwriting – overview

The aim of underwriting management is to ensure that underwriting achieves its financial targets and the desired portfolio is created and maintained. To do this it must create an organization with a deep understanding of risk, able to predict the severity, frequency and time pattern of claims in a business environment that is constantly changing. The history of insurance is littered with examples of insurers who have got this badly wrong, damaged their capital position and have either been taken over or gone into liquidation. For this reason the underwriting organization must have the following intellectual capital.

- An effective **Research and Development** capability to monitor the business environment and anticipate how risks will change and what new risks will emerge. There is a wealth of historic data available from a range of sources. Information on new or currently unknown risks is obviously much harder to obtain.

- Excellent **Management Information** so that trends in claims can be identified, analysed and effective remedial action taken.
- **Actuarial Support** to undertake statistical analysis and model the potential outcomes.
- A core of **Experienced Underwriters.** Underwriting is in many ways similar to lending in the banking sector. Although sophisticated mathematical techniques are frequently used, many of the most difficult decisions may be subjective. For this reason insurers need a core of people who have the perspective that comes from working through several underwriting cycles and have learnt the lessons of making short-term decisions in a long-term business.

The way this intellectual capital is applied in the organization is via a set of policies. These may be implied or explicitly written into various manuals. The appropriate parts also need to be communicated to the intermediaries so they clearly understand the requirements of the insurer.

13.4 Policy framework

The elements of underwriting that might be included in the framework of policies are shown in Figure 13.3.

Figure 13.3

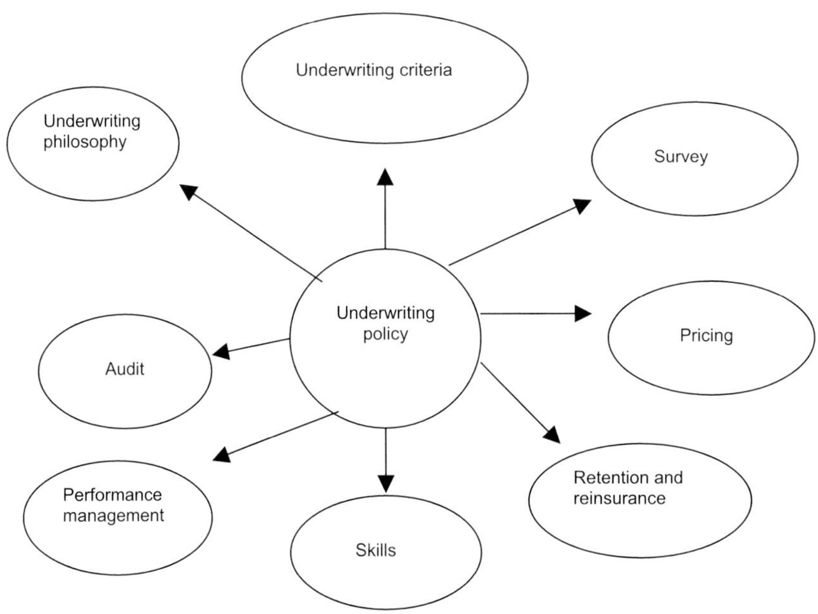

13.4.1 Underwriting philosophy

This should cover the aims for each account, what position is sought in the market, product mix, levels of authority and, in general terms, what sort of risks the insurer in trying to attract. It sets the tone of the entire underwriting organization.

13.4.2 Underwriting criteria

Underwriters need detailed instructions and criteria such as:

- Standards to apply to new, renewal and interim underwriting
- Classification of risks
- Unacceptable risks
- Wordings and other conditions
- Maximum limits of indemnity/sums insured/Estimated Maximum Loss (EML)
- Exposure measurement and recording
- Pricing procedures
- Standard deductibles
- Procedures and controls if underwriting authority is to be delegated to a third party.

It should be remembered that, in underwriting, refusing risks is just as important as acceptance. In this respect it is unfortunate that many inexperienced underwriters confuse 'customer focus' with always saying 'yes'.

13.4.3 Survey

The survey policy needs to specify where risk control surveys are needed and the specific features that should be reported on. The value of a risk control survey is two fold. Not only does it provide valuable underwriting information but, in many cases, it also improves the risk, so benefiting both the customer and the insurer.

Note. Risk control surveys may also be useful as marketing tools and may be provided as an additional, fee-based service, separate from the insurance business. The policy needs to clearly establish the operation's objectives in these areas if they are to be pursued.

13.4.4 Pricing

The methods of pricing and how these are expressed in the underwriting manual were discussed earlier. Beyond this, however, underwriting management must determine its overall pricing policy. For example:

- Does it want to be a lead or follow office? Does it set the rates in the market, or follow those of others?

- How should it behave, in pricing terms, at the various stages of the underwriting cycle?
- What flexibility is it prepared to give to the front-line underwriters to deviate from the technical rate?

Pricing is critically important. Its impact on the end result is far more than cost cutting or increasing volume which are the other favoured drivers used by account managers in financial services. This is clearly demonstrated in the following research findings by Boston Consulting Group.

Pricing is a bigger profit driver than volume or cost

Impact on return on equity of a 1% improvement in profit driver

Profit	Banking	Fund management	Insurance (non-life)	Insurance (life)
Price	6.8%	3.5%	12.0%	15.0%
Volume	1.8%	1.7%	5.2%	7.7%
Cost	2.3%	1.8%	2.6%	1.3%

Source – Boston Consulting Group 2002

This suggests that, for non-life (ie P+C) insurance, a 1% improvement in overall pricing produces a 12.0% improvement in the bottom line, more than double the benefit of a 1% increase in volume (5.2% improvement) and more than four times the benefit of a 1% reduction in the cost base (2.6% improvement).

13.4.5 Retention and reinsurance

Underwriting management needs to decide how much it is prepared to accept on a net basis per loss, how circumstances might arise to create unacceptable aggregations of exposure, and what is the maximum probable loss for the account. Working on these criteria, it should develop a policy for outwards reinsurance. It should be able to answer questions such as:

- Why does the company need reinsurance?

- Where will it prove cost effective?
- From whom should it be bought?

The first question is not as straightforward as it might appear. Although reinsurance is primarily designed to limit an insurer's underwriting exposure, ie protect its balance sheet from unbudgeted loss, it can also be put to other specific uses: eg as a capital substitute, to facilitate market entry or exit, and to access reinsurer's expertise. It can also be used for 'fronting' – to enable a company to benefit from another's licence for the class of business or territory concerned. This is particularly common in the case of insurers helping captives who may not have the appropriate authorization.

Note on the management of reinsurance

Reinsurance, both outwards and inwards, requires exceptionally careful management because of the large sums involved. In outwards reinsurance it must always be remembered that the existence of a contract does not absolve the primary insurer from its original policy obligations. If there is non-recovery from the reinsurer, through contract failure or bad debt, the primary insurer must pay the loss in full. To avoid this, best practice would suggest:

- The maintenance of a list of approved reinsurers which takes into consideration their solvency and credit rating. (Weaker reinsurers may not fulfil their obligations after a major market catastrophe.)
- The building of long-term relationships with reinsurers to ensure mutual trust.
- The use of staff with in-depth knowledge to negotiate with the reinsurers to minimize the risk of contract failure through non-disclosure or misrepresentation.
- Continuous dialogue with the reinsurers regarding any material changes, eg reserving, including movements in IBNR.

The management of inwards facultative reinsurance is similar to that of primary underwriting, ie acceptance, pricing and aggregation and exposure. Acceptance is particularly difficult, because the reinsurer must rely to a great extent on the quality of the primary insurer's underwriting, hence the importance to both sides of building long-term relationships. The management of treaty reinsurance is different in so far as the reinsurer has no control once the treaty is signed. Here mutual trust is even more important.

13.4.6 Skills

Insurers should have a policy to ensure that their underwriters have the appropriate skills to perform their specific role effectively and limits set on their authority. In the UK, for example, the regulator has specified that there must be an approved person in charge of underwriting and he or she has a formal duty to ensure the competence of all underwriters. This has led to companies designing competency frameworks whereby each job has minimum skill criteria that have to be demonstrated before a person is permitted to operate in that role. In some operations the senior underwriter may establish a process of issuing formal licences defining the authority and limits of each person.

All this has given a fresh impetus to technical training and knowledge sharing.

Re-establishing underwriting as a career

A number of major insurers have decided that reducing loss ratios is more important than expense ratios and are investing in reversing the neglect of underwriting. Key actions have included:

- defining competencies for the underwriting job family
- better employment packages for underwriters
- support for professional qualifications
- assessment for every underwriter
- licensing

This is a huge task but will re-establish underwriting as a career.

Perhaps the most important step has been to create underwriting academies within the companies to coordinate and maintain the quality of training.

Tony Tudor, Institute of Financial Services (*ifs*)

13.4.7 Performance management

This has long been a contentious subject in insurance in general and underwriting in particular. How should one reward and incentivize staff in a long-term business? The standard method, of rewarding the achievement of annual targets, can prove to be highly counterproductive. The return on a single year can be misleading, because it may take several years before the impact of current underwriting decisions is translated into claims. The industry is full of stories of underwriters being given large bonuses for adding volume only for the company to make enormous losses on the new business acquired in the succeeding years. (This is discussed in Chapter 16.)

13.4.8 Audit

Finally there needs to be a commitment to having underwriting audits to check that the laid-down underwriting policies and procedures are being followed, both in-house and through the intermediaries. When used properly these can be of great help in training and development, as well as being an essential method of control.

Select bibliography

R Kiln, S Kiln, *Reinsurance in Practice 4th Ed*, Witherby & Co 2001

G Dionne, *Handbook of Insurance,* Kluwer 2000, Chapter 20.

Sigma 2003 No 2, *Natural Catastrophes and Man-made Disasters in 2002.*

L Lucas, J McLean, P Green, *Reinsurance Management,* LLP 1996.

S Diacon (Ed), *A Guide to Insurance Management,* Macmillan 1990.

J Outreville, *Theory and Practice of Insurance,* Kluwer 1998, Chapter 12

Climate Change and Insurance, Executive Summary, Insurance Research and Practice Vol 16 part 1,CII.

G Carlo, *Mobile Telephone Health Risks,* Environmental Claims Journal Vol 14 No 3, 2000.

B Silfer, *Mold: The Next Asbestos?,* Environmental Claims Journal Vol 14 No 3, 2000.

G Flanigan, *A perspective on General Liability Insurance and the Pollution Hazard,* Journal of Insurance Regulation Vol 20, No 3, 2002.

R Harvey, *The Debate on Global Warming,* Geneva Papers on Risk and Insurance Vol 27, No 1, Jan 2002.

C Parsons, *From Accident to Liability – A brief history of Liability Insurance,* Insurance Research and Practice Vol 17 part 2, July 2002, CII.

Appendix to Chapter 13

Figure 13.4

The Underwriting Wheel

Royal & Sun Alliance's model for driving towards world class underwriting shows the interrelationship of the necessary initiatives. Common standards are set and underwriters empowered within a disciplined framework.

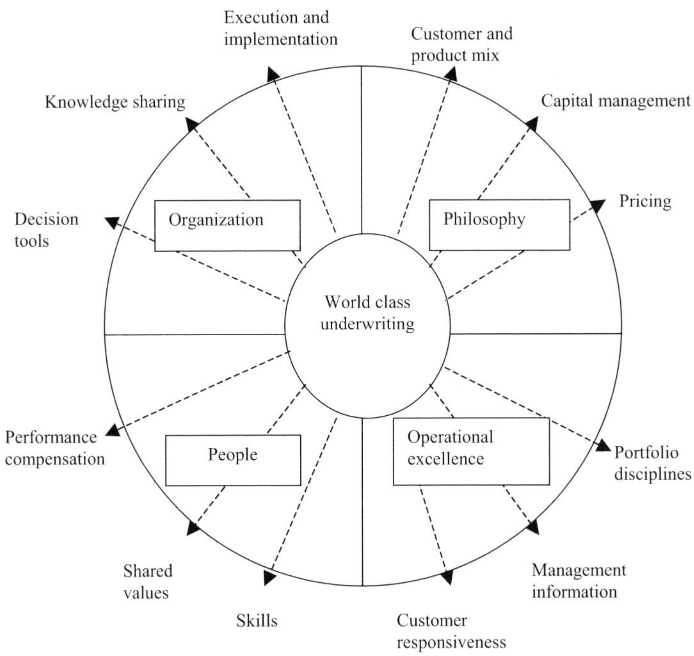

Practical underwriting

The following, deceptively simple, rules were set by Derek Archer of Sun Alliance, who was one of the most successful underwriting managers in the UK market over a period of 20 years. Although they were written some time ago they remain totally valid today.

To achieve and maintain profitable development of an underwriting account:

1. Keep the rates and terms applicable to the existing portfolio under systematic review to ensure that maximum profitability is achieved, quality business not unnecessarily lost and poor quality business is suitably dealt with.

2. Develop new products/product extensions which can be successfully marketed to existing customers, thus building on existing relationships and achieving maximum premium growth from the established portfolio.
3. Maintain programmes of risk inspection/survey for the existing portfolio to ensure that the portfolio quality is maintained and policy terms are closely related to the quality of the risk. Provide risk-improvement advice to customers where applicable.
4. Obtain quality new business at terms that are designed to contribute to profit.
5. Identify target segments of the market that will contribute to the building of a profitable, quality portfolio.
6. Obtain intelligence from customers, intermediaries and the market in general to ensure that products, terms, development and profitability are maintained at optimum levels.
7. Develop streamlined systems at minimum expense, to achieve the maximum degree of account control and service to customers.
8. Maintain tight control of expenses to ensure that optimum competitiveness and profitability are achieved.

Underwriting 'own goals'

From their experience in the analysis of insurance operations' performance, the authors have found that the following are the most common causes of 'self-inflicted' major losses on underwriting accounts:

- underwriters driven by growth/volume rather than profit
- lack of management control over underwriting
- egos at the point of sale 'knowing best' (compared with the Head Office experts)
- moving into areas beyond the core expertise
- no control of exposures
- not understanding the long-term impact of risks
- introducing new underwriting initiatives without:
  - substantial R & D
  - detailed and thorough cost benefit analysis
  - piloting.

Fourteen

The management of claims

Objectives

On completion of this chapter, and wider personal research, the reader should be able to:

- explain how claims are managed by P+C insurers, including: assessment, handling and settlement;
- understand the importance to insurers of fraud and arson;
- appreciate the importance of IT systems and management information in claims management;
- appreciate the issues facing loss adjusters.

14.1 Introduction

As a general rule claims incurred are the largest cost of an insurer, typically accounting for greater than 65% (and often much more) of earned premium. This assumes 'normal' levels of acquisition and management expenses.

A claim is one of the key times that the insurer can make a favourable impression on the policyholder (probably the moment of greatest expectation, referred to by marketeers as the moment of truth). The insurer is thus in a conflict position between offering the best quality service to the customer (to enhance its reputation, increase customer retention, etc) and indemnifying the customer fully within the policy wording at the lowest possible cost.

The insurer's principal interest when notified of a claim is therefore to take control of the claim in its entirety. In this way it can ensure that:

- damage/loss is minimized by early action (eg emergency repairs to buildings to prevent further damage).
- the most cost-effective solutions are provided (eg preferred repairer/ supplier arrangements, replacement goods rather than monetary value).
- the overall claim and time taken to settle is managed in the most efficient way possible.

Thus total claims management (TCM) capability is a key competence of a successful insurer (TCM being an integrated process through which the insurer takes control over every element of the incident/claim, from the moment that it is notified, through to the coordinated delivery of a 'solution' to the policyholder's problem, rather than just a cheque).

In practice, however, an insurer may not be able to establish complete (direct) control over a claim, eg when a third party is involved, such as a policyholder's at-fault car accident with another vehicle. In such a case the other insurer/party can take control of that element of the claim relating to them, and then seek to recover from the policyholder's insurer. The insurer can then only challenge the quantum of the claim submitted by/on behalf of the third party if it is clearly overstated, and has little opportunity to manage the total cost. Some insurers will offer to provide full claims solution services to third parties where their insured is at fault to enable full control over the claim to be established.

14.2 Key steps in the control and management of claims

Notification	the insurer ideally wants as early a notification of a claim/incident as possible, so that a) control can be established, and b) claim reserves can be set up.
Acceptance	not every claim/incident notified by a policyholder is necessarily a valid claim under the policy. The insurer needs to assess the validity of the claim against the policy wording and terms, and decide whether to accept the claim. Refusal/declinature will have a significant impact on relations with the policyholder.
Management and quantification	this involves taking control of the resolution of the problem, identifying and delivering the most cost-effective solution within the terms of the policy, accurately identifying the total cost of the solution.

	This phase may involve significant input from third party suppliers to mitigate the damage, assess and evaluate solutions, and deliver the agreed solution.
Settlement and closure	finalizing the claim, making payments to suppliers, third parties and/or the policyholder and closing the claim once all amounts are settled and any recoveries from third parties obtained.

14.3 Issues and problems

14.3.1 Gradually developing claims causes

Claims events are not always simple incidents that happen over a short space of time such as a car accident, a fire, etc. Some claims events can occur over a protracted period, eg:

- pollution of groundwater from long-term leaks, spills or other day-to-day activities.
- damage to employees' health (cancer, pneumoconiosis, deafness, etc) due to poor work practices, safety standards, use of machinery over time, or pollutants/hazardous chemicals.

As a result, notification of a claim can occur some time after the primary cause operated. In the case of employee health issues, such as those related to asbestos, this can be 20-30 years after initial exposure.

The question then becomes one of 'what was the date of the 'incident' that led to the claim?' and, 'which insurer is liable if the insurer has subsequently changed?' The insurer at the incident date, or the insurer at the date of notification?

In most liability policies this will be clearly defined within the policy wording, but can lead to litigation to clarify in some policies where it is less clear (see example of Claims Incurred v Claims Made in Chapter 11).

This poses a challenge to those responsible for pricing policies and reserving for incurred but not reported claims. Pricing must allow for claims incidents either in the past (if the insurer at date of notification is liable), or any future, gradually developing claim, potentially from a cause that is not known about/fully understood at the date of the policy commencement (if the insurer at incident date is liable). Reserving must take into account any gradually developing claims, whether known about/fully understood or not at the period end.

The problem the insurance industry faces is that new, gradually developing claims types are surfacing all the time. Asbestos-related illnesses have been known about for many years, but the full extent and cost of all asbestos-related claims will remain uncertain for many years. Other, newer causes include: work-place stress, toxic mould and, in the future, potentially, mobile phone radiation, genetically modified organisms, etc.

14.3.2 Determining liability/acceptance of the claim

The first question the insurer needs to determine is whether the claim is valid under the terms of the policy, and if there is any other party who should share or take full liability for the loss being claimed for.

In a motor car accident involving damage to a policyholder's and a third party's vehicle the questions are essentially:

- What was the policy cover? – Did it include damage to the policyholder's own vehicle, or any other amounts being claimed on behalf of the insurer's customer?
- Who was at fault? If the other party was shown to be responsible for the accident, all costs of the claim are then potentially recoverable from the third party or its insurers.

Problems can arise in assessing the eventual cost to the insurer if either, fault cannot be clearly determined or, the other party is uninsured and held to be at fault.

In more complex cases, the extent of cover and whether a particular event was covered by the policy can be much more complex. The exact wording of the policy as issued will be used, in a court of law if necessary, to resolve the issue. The onus is thus on the underwriter to specify the coverage of the policy as clearly as possible at outset, with any ambiguity likely to benefit the policyholder.

14.3.3 Quantification – under-insurance

Most insurance policies will specify a 'sum insured' or other limit on the value insured under the policy. It is the policyholders' responsibility to determine whether this is adequate for their needs. Should the 'value at risk' be greater than the sum insured, the insurer has the right to apply average to the claim, even if the total claim is for less than the sum insured under the policy.

Example

	£	
Sum insured	100	
Value at risk at incident date	120	
Claim submitted	60	
Pro rata (average) settlement	50	$(^{60}/_{120}) \times 100$

Under-insurance can arise for a variety of reasons, although is usually a result of the policyholder incorrectly assessing the value at risk, or specifying a sum insured limit that was inadequate for his or her needs.

14.3.4 Quantification – complex claims

Many complex claims can take a long time to fully quantify the total cost. In the case of liability/injury claims this can be a period of years after the date of the incident, and often result in legal cases where the final award is determined by the courts.

Even complex property damage claims can take a long time to quantify fully where the cost of rectification/rebuilding and the time required to complete the work can be difficult to assess, and may take months or even years in very complex cases such as historic buildings or sophisticated engineering or chemical plants.

The issue becomes one of assessing the most accurate reserves to establish at any point in time and keeping them up to date.

14.3.5 Reinstatement

The object of insurance, and specified in most policies, is to reinstate policyholders to the position they were in prior to the claim event occurring. Thus, if a policyholder suffers loss or damage to a five-year-old item such as a car, piece of manufacturing plant, item of clothing, etc the insurer is responsible for compensation up to the level of a five-year-old item, not a brand-new one.

In addition, the insurer can insist on repair rather than replacement where this is economically valid and the repaired item is fit for purpose/has the same economic value as a replacement item of similar age/wear, even where the insured would prefer replacement. Or, the insurer can insist on writing-off an item (such as a car) where the cost of repair is greater than the economic value of the item, even where the insured would prefer for it to be repaired.

The issues presented concern how the insurer can deliver the most effective and economic form of **reinstatement** from the insurer's perspective, in a way that is acceptable to the insured, and is consistent with the policy terms and conditions and the insurer's desired customer service objectives.

In certain types of policy, however, eg many UK household contents policies, the insurance policy specifically allows for the replacement of items lost or damaged on a 'new for old' basis, ie all items that are to be replaced will be replaced by brand-new goods, even if the original items were not new. This is partly:

- consumer driven – the value of a three-year-old video recorder or TV would only be a small fraction of the new price, and the policyholder would be unhappy having to pay the difference in order to replace it with a new one himself; and partly
- insurer driven – it would cost the insurer a lot of time and effort to calculate the current value of a wide range of damaged articles, identical replacement goods would not be readily available, and policyholders are much more likely to inflate the size of the claim if they think that they will receive only a fraction of the total replacement value claimed, requiring much more investigation and argument. In addition, insurers are able to negotiate bulk-purchasing agreements with replacement goods suppliers and so drive down the cost of replacement.

14.4 Management of the claims process

The basic objective has to be to provide an efficient and effective customer service, to meet the needs of the customer (or third-party claimant) in accordance with the terms and conditions of the policy, at the lowest total cost (claims administration expenses + claim settlement costs). The process differs with the size of the claim.

a) Small claims

For small claims, say less than £200, there is a strong possibility that the cost of trying to manage them tightly will be far greater than the net saving achievable from that management activity. Most retail commodity lines (home, motor, etc) insurers set up some form of fast-track processing for claims below a certain value. Most such claims will be settled with little or no checking, and only samples highlighted by the computer system will be reviewed in detail. With modern computer systems, programs can be established to highlight either random claims for checking, or suspicious ones (ones that meet certain criteria that are typical of a fraudulent claim). The claims handlers also use fraud indicators such as previous experience and 'believability' to separate out those to be investigated.

Any losses incurred by reduced management of these claims should in theory be made up by reduced expenses and premium increases at the renewal following the claim.

Some insurers even delegate the handling of small claims to the introducing broker. In such cases regular audits by the insurer are required to ensure that the claims being settled are valid and are being handled in accordance with the insurer's own standards, rules, etc.

b) Large claims

While being much more complicated in practical terms to manage, large claims typically involve a large number of professionals (loss adjusters, lawyers, experts from other fields). The key risks remain those of mitigating the loss by taking as early action as possible, establishing management control over the loss where possible, and determining and delivering the least-cost solution that is consistent with the policy terms and conditions. Each large claim by its very nature is unique and has to be managed and the solution delivered differently from any other claim. Large insurers will normally establish internal 'best practices' to follow for specific types of cases and encourage knowledge-sharing internally to try to maximize efficiency and minimize cost.

c) The remainder (not small and not large)

In the past, the approach from the insurer was to get the policyholder to arrange for the loss or damage to be rectified, with the insurer paying either the policyholder or supplier of the goods or services when the rectification/replacement was complete. This placed a substantial level of control over the claim into the hands of the policyholder and/or the supplier.

It is now accepted best practice that, as far as possible, it is of benefit to the insurer to take control of the claim as early as possible, and to seek to manage the solution using preferred suppliers/solutions if possible.

Preferred suppliers/solutions can include: retained loss adjusters, approved repairer networks (garages, builders, etc), replacement goods suppliers for household and personal effects, etc. The use of suppliers controlled/managed by the insurer allows:

- volume discounts to be obtained by the insurer
- control of the quality of work performed or service delivered
- greater certainty that the policyholder is receiving reinstatement of his position rather than betterment (being put into a position that is better than that existing at the time immediately prior to the claim event).

This is achieved through formal contracts with agreed service standards and levels with the suppliers. As a result, professional purchasing management is now a core competence of large personal lines insurers, particularly the use of tendering processes, contracts, service level agreements and performance metrics.

Preferred suppliers

A large household insurer might have replacement goods or repair service contracts with each of a:

- Household appliances supplier
- Home entertainment/PC supplier
- Carpet supplier
- Furniture supplier
- Jewellery supplier
- Photographic equipment supplier
- Glazing company
- Roofing company
- General builder

On the basis that, by delivering a replacement item known to be the current equivalent of the damaged item, or controlling the repair process, it saves the policyholder substantial time and effort and gives the insurer control over cost and service levels. The policyholder is presented with a 'solution', not just a cheque, and all arrangements to acquire/deliver/install the replacement items or manage the repair work are made for him.

The policyholder would have to negotiate with the insurer to use any other supplier, or to incur any cost greater than that which would have been incurred through the use of a preferred supplier.

14.5 Claims recoveries (amounts due to the insurer in respect of claims paid)

Separate from managing and settling the claim on behalf of a policyholder, the insurer may be entitled to recover some or all of the cost from others. The main areas for recovery typically are:

1) Deductibles

Most insurance policies have stated deductibles or excesses – the amount the policyholder must contribute towards a claim before the insurer starts to pay. This may be relatively low for a household policy, eg £50-100, or could be hundreds of thousands of pounds for a large liability policy where the customer seeks to self-insure for small claims and only transfer risk to the insurer for large claims.

2) *Recoveries from third parties/their insurers*

Where a third party can be shown to be at fault in causing the loss/claim the insurer can seek to recover the cost of meeting its policyholder's claim from that third party and/or its insurers.

The commonest example of this is a non-fault car accident claim, where the insurer can seek recovery from the at-fault driver/his or her insurer.

The key issue here is establishing fault and getting the other party to accept liability. Fault can often be difficult to prove categorically, and many court cases result from attempts to ascertain liability for incidents leading to a claim.

Some motor insurers, to avoid the cost and effort of continually trying to establish fault in car accidents involving another vehicle, come to arrangements with other insurers to operate a 'knock for knock' arrangement. In an accident where both insurance company's involved are party to such an arrangement, each picks up the cost of its policyholder's claim, and no detailed attempt to apportion fault is made, nor recovery sought from the at-fault policyholder's insurer. This dramatically reduces claims handling and recovery costs and theoretically should even out in terms of claims cost over time.

3) *Contribution/duplicate insurance recovery*

Where a policy is co-insured or duplicate insurance is held (the same loss is covered by more than one policy – a typical example is a camera, lost or damaged while on holiday which may be covered by both a home contents and a separate travel policy) the insurer who handles the claim can recover a proportion of the cost from the other insurer.

4) *Reinsurance recoveries*

Where a policy is facultatively reinsured, a recovery can be made from the reinsurer in accordance with the terms of the policy.

In each case, the insurer needs to operate systems that identify and record recoveries due as early as possible, and facilitates their collection in the most efficient manner.

> Experience shows that it is far harder and more costly to obtain a £50 excess from a policyholder once the claim has been settled, than to deduct the excess due from the final settlement.

14.6 IT systems

The IT systems supporting the claims process are critical. They must:

- help to deliver the service expected by the policyholder and promised by the insurer;
- facilitate the optimal claims management approach;
- capture claims data accurately, on a timely basis to feed the reserving and management information (MI)/pricing processes elsewhere in the operation (includes MI on external suppliers, process performance, etc);
- assist in the identification of potential fraud or error;
- facilitate recovery of all amounts due to the insurer in respect of claims paid, eg excesses or deductibles, recoveries from other insurers or third parties, reinsurance recoveries, etc.

14.7 Management information/claims coding

With the complex, packaged type of product now commonly sold (ie a single contract covers a range of risks, both property and liability) it is important to record not just the cause of the claim, but the segment of the cover to which the claim relates.

In this way, a detailed history can be built up of claims costs, cause and the segment of the policy cover. This history can then be analysed to assess profitability not just at product level, but also at separate cover level within the product, assuming that the premium has been built up by element of cover, so that the relative profitability of each segment can be determined.

In theory, a good understanding of profitability combined with a good knowledge of future developments in claims impact and frequency should enable more accurate (profitable) pricing of products in the future.

14.8 Claims fraud and fraud prevention

Fraud is a major problem to insurers.

Insurance fraud (i)

Insurance fraud is widespread and continues to deteriorate. For example:

- In the UK, ABI research suggests that 40% of consumers think it acceptable to exaggerate a claim, and 29% think it acceptable to invent one.
- In the USA, the Insurance Services Office estimates that the cost of fraud to the property and casualty sector is $24 bn p.a., representing 10% of total claim payments.

Fraud ranges from mild overstatement of the value of items lost or damaged through to organized criminal activity designed to obtain large sums of money.

Insurance fraud (ii)

More theft claims have been received for Nikon cameras by UK insurers than the total number of these cameras imported into the country.

ABI

Every insurer therefore faces a constant challenge: to minimize the cost of fraudulent claims while also providing the desired level of service and claims solution delivery for all valid claimants. Insurers will use a range of techniques to seek to identify fraud which vary depending on the insurance cover/product offered; these include:

- fraud-awareness training for all claims staff to enable potential fraud to be detected as the claim is handled;
- computer programs that highlight potential fraud, based on defined criteria identified from previous fraud experience;
- the establishment of specialist internal fraud investigation departments;
- the employment of external fraud investigation services;
- sharing of claims data with other companies via shared databases, eg CUE the Claims and Underwriting Exchange database in the UK, where the majority of UK insurers share data on all home and motor claims made;
- cooperation with police, government, industry, etc anti-fraud initiatives;
- using contracted replacement goods and services supplier to minimize betterment fraud (the claimant seeking to be put into a better position than he was in before the event) and supplier overcharging/fraud (the local supplier, appointed by the claimant, either overcharging ('because its an insurance claim') or charging for work not done.

Arson: The largest cause of fire insurance loss

- Arson in the UK accounts for about one-fifth of all fires, half of the large fires, and almost half of the total insured loss.
- This disturbing situation is not dissimilar to that of other Western countries.
- No property is immune, but schools and public buildings are especially at risk.
- The main methods of protection against arson are surveillance, prevention of access and fire protection.
- Arson is not restricted to buildings. Each year thousands of cars are deliberately destroyed by fire.
- Motives include:

High frequency	–	Vandalism
	–	Crime concealment
Medium frequency	–	Revenge
	–	Fraud
Low frequency	–	Political
	–	Mental illness

- The majority of arsonists are male and the peak age range is 14-16.

UK Home Office Report on Arson, 1989

(NB It should be noted that damage caused by arson committed by a third party is a valid claim under a fire policy. Arson committed by the insured constitutes an attempt to defraud the insurer, and is not covered.)

14.9 Leakage

Leakage is the term for any additional costs incurred by the insurer beyond those necessary to fulfil its obligations under the insurance contract, but excluding fraud. Thus it covers any inefficiencies or errors in the handling or settling of the claim, failures of service or replacement goods suppliers to act efficiently or according to their service contract, or any other unnecessary cost.

Examples of leakage include:

- failure to recover excesses/deductibles from policyholders;
- failure to recover amounts reclaimable from third parties, other insurers, reinsurers, etc;
- unintentional overpayment of the claim (eg payment in excess of limits of cover or amount claimed);
- excessive claims administration costs, inefficiency, etc;
- failure to decline claims that are not covered by the policy.

Leakage is largely preventable through effective management.

Most insurers will establish some form of audit or benchmarking process to assess regularly the effectiveness of their claims handling service and the level of leakage experienced (based on 20:20 hindsight). From this, action plans and targets can be established to seek to improve efficiency and reduce leakage.

14.10 Industry-wide compensation schemes

Most developed insurance markets will operate some form of safety net or compensation schemes to protect, in particular, the general public from loss or damage resulting from either insurance company failures, or where damage is caused by an individual who is either uninsured or untraceable.

Typical examples of such insurance industry schemes in the UK are:

- The FSCS (Financial Services Compensation Scheme) previously the Policyholders Protection Board. This scheme protects personal lines policyholders of failed/insolvent authorized insurers, by meeting specified types of claim from specified types of customer up to specified limits. The funds to deliver this compensation are raised by means of a levy imposed on the industry at a certain percentage of the premiums written for the particular lines of insurance covered by the scheme. The size of the levy varies depending on the size and impact of recent insurance company failures.
- The MIB (Motor Insurers Bureau). This scheme compensates people who suffer loss, damage or injury from being involved in a motor vehicle accident involving an uninsured driver (not in possession of the minimum legally required insurance cover) or from untraceable drivers, hit-and-run incidents, etc. Again the funds to run the scheme are raised via a compulsory levy on motor premiums written.

It is estimated that, in the UK, up to one in ten cars on the road is uninsured.

All such schemes, by their very nature, represent an additional cost to be borne by the relevant insurers.

14.11 Ex gratia payments

An ex gratia payment is a payment made by the insurer to the claimant without legal obligation under the insurance contract, ie a goodwill gesture. Such payments are totally within the gift of the insurer as there is no legal obligation under the contract. Typical examples of when an insurer might consider such a payment include:

- A very long-standing personal customer with no previous claims finds that, due to inflation over many years, he is underinsured when a claim event

occurs. As a goodwill gesture for the loyalty and past profitability of the customer the insurer might consider an ex gratia payment to cover the underinsured element of the claim.
- Where a commercial client who is advised by a major broker who provides significant, profitable business to the insurer finds that, due to a misunderstanding or administrative error, they had intended to be but are not covered for a particular claim event, the insurer (perhaps with a contribution from the broker) may offer an ex gratia payment for some or all of the loss incurred.

Needless to say, ex gratia payments need to be carefully controlled and managed, and only made where it is clearly in the insurer's interest to maintain goodwill, retain profitable business, etc.

It should also be noted that a decision by the insurer to make an ex gratia payment does not bind any coinsurers of the risk, and there are no rights of recovery from reinsurers or, via subrogation, from third parties in respect of any such payments.

14.12 The role of loss adjusters

Loss adjusters specialize in assessing the cause and extent of insurance claims. They work with their insurance company clients to assist in the delivery of the claims service and manage a complex balance of claims validation and customer service.

Loss adjusters are dedicated to claims handling and are there to facilitate and coordinate the insured's recovery from the trauma of a claim. The benefits can be assessed in terms of the delivery of a professional claims service that adds value to the overall insurance product. Loss adjusters work independently of the insurance companies and provide a site-based claims-handling capability. It is the job of the loss adjuster to ensure that the claim is covered by the policy and to agree with the policyholder the final settlement.

Challenges for loss adjusters

There are a number of strategic challenges facing loss adjusters. Perhaps the most challenging is regulation, where the demands of integrating a regulated service with each insurance company customer is a significant one. In terms of more general strategic issues, there is a need to improve speed of service and support of specific insurer brand values.

Crawfords

There is also an increasing challenge to loss adjusters to show their relevance to insurance company clients. The last few years have seen a lot of debate around insourcing, outsourcing and right-sourcing strategies for insurers. A core element of this is the debate around whether claims management and handling are core skills of insurers. While it cannot be disputed that **claims management** is a core skill for insurers, it must be debated whether **claims handling** should be a core skill, or whether this can be more usefully addressed by a skilled, independent service provider, whose sole business is claims. This will remain a live issue over the next few years. One response, from the larger insurers, is to acquire their own firms of loss adjusters, ie insource something that was previously outsourced. In several countries, specialist companies are already providing outsourced claims management services for insurers. These include: Crawford (UK), Dekra (Germany) and PRISM (USA).

Select bibliography

B Webb, C Harrison, J Markam, *Insurance Operations and Regulation,* Insurance Institute of America 2002, Chapters 13–15.

J Outreville, *Theory and Practice of Insurance,* Kluwer 1997, Chapter 12.

J Lightcap, *Managing Claim Department Operations,* International Claim Association 1991.

J Jones, *Liability Claim Practices,* Insurance Institute of America 2001.

A Newman, *Customer Power Shows it Muscle,* CII Journal March 2001.

Fifteen

The management of reserves

Objectives

On completion of this chapter, and wider personal research, the reader should be able to:

- understand reserving methodology and its impact on the viability of the operation;
- describe the various types of reserve;
- explain the treatment of incurred but not reported claims;
- outline how a book of business is run off.

> **Poor reserving**
>
> 'There is no acceptable excuse for poor reserving. Unless we are accurate with our reserves they will threaten our very existence.'
>
> Tony Lancaster, CEO, Groupama UK

15.1 Introduction

A recurring theme of this book is that insurance differs from most other industries in so far as the majority of its costs are both delayed and uncertain. It is therefore necessary for an insurer to estimate this future liability and put aside money to meet it. The amount can be enormous. For example, in a mature P+C operation these technical (or specifically allocated) reserves may be larger than the annual premium income and can be up to 2 or 3 times annual premium in liability classes.

The approach taken by an insurer in setting its technical reserves has a critical impact on its profitability and solvency. A company that under-reserves will artificially boost profits in the short term, but will eventually have to call upon the shareholders' funds (sometimes known as free reserves) and so reduce its solvency. Conversely, a company that is overprudent in its reserving will understate profits.

15.2 Interested parties' perspectives

The various stakeholder groups have a close interest in the reported reserves but from slightly different perspectives include:

Shareholders

The shareholders will be told about the company's reserves through the annual Report and Accounts. Additionally, if significant reserve strengthening is required during the year, this may be the subject of a stock exchange announcement. Shareholders will obviously wish for the company to be adequately reserved to ensure its future prosperity and avoid nasty shocks. On the other hand, overprudent reserving will reduce the money available for distribution as dividend or available for new investment and therefore will not be welcomed.

Government

A government may consider a company's reserving from two distinct standpoints. As a regulator it would like to see prudent reserving in order to protect the customers from company failure and to protect the insurance market from instability and the burden of funding corporate failure. It does not want solvency threatened by future calls on the company's capital. Conversely, as a **collector of taxes**, the government would prefer that taxable profit is not delayed or avoided by being placed in reserves. For these reasons some governments have set down rules about making a 'best estimate' of reserves and their observance has to be confirmed in the annual audit.

Underwriters

The importance of claims experience in the pricing process was mentioned in Chapter 11. Underwriters study the pattern of reserves development to understand the true cost of claims for whole classes of business to determine the appropriate pure risk premiums going forward. In addition, they will use specific claims histories on cases that are individually underwritten. Accurate reserving is therefore essential, although in reality it is impossible to predict fully the economic, legal and regulatory impacts on claims that may not be settled for years.

Insurance company management

Reserving is also of great importance to company senior management in so far as it indicates the relative profitability of various parts of the portfolio, highlights trends and provides an early warning of future problems.

15.3 Types of technical reserves

There are two basic types of technical reserves: those relating to *premiums* and those relating to *claims*. Although the actual terminology may vary, the following would be recognized in most companies.

15.3.1 Premium reserves

a) Unearned premium reserve

This reserve is necessary because not all premium is earned in the financial year in which the business was written. For example, if a policy is put on the books early in month 10 of the financial year, by the end of the year, when reserving is undertaken, only three months' of cover would have been completed. The other nine months' of premium is still at risk and is said to be 'unearned'. The unexpired proportion of all premiums is held until expiry in an unearned premium reserve. In practice, expenses are deducted from written premiums and the resulting net figure is used to calculate reserves on a monthly or even daily pro rata basis.

b) Unexpired risk reserve

This is a reserve that is no longer commonly used. If an insurer wrote premiums during a year which, in retrospect, are considered to be inadequate because of, say, a soft market, a reserve may be set up for the shortfall. This is called an unexpired risk reserve. If an insurer has to set up such a reserve, questions really ought to be asked as to why it has changed its mind about rates so soon after underwriting the business.

15.3.2 Claims reserves

a) Outstanding claims reserve

This represents the money put aside for paying claims on business that has been written whether or not these claims have been reported to the insurer. There are two separate parts:

Open claims reserve

This is the reserve for claims that have been reported, but have yet to be settled, ie the claims that the insurer actually knows about.

IBNR reserve

IBNR is the term for claims that have been **I**ncurred **B**ut **N**ot **R**eported, ie claims that have occurred but the insurer does not know about. This is one of the main problem areas for general insurers. It is relatively easy to make a reasonable assessment of claims that have been reported. At the very minimum an insurer can apply an average cost for the class of business for any claims arising. The real difficulty arises when the insurer has to speculate what might happen in the future. Typical reasons for an insurer to set up IBNR reserves are detailed below.

Examples of IBNR

1. A property insurer with a December year end will need to reserve for a spate of claims after a December storm. The claims would not have come through the system in time for the end-of-year reserving exercise but the insurer is confident that they will do so in due course.
2. After a dry summer, a property insurer might reserve for future subsidence claims. Buildings will have begun to crack but claims will not be reported until the damage becomes very obvious or the buildings are surveyed by a prospective purchaser.
3. An employers' liability insurer may know that some of the workers in a textile factory have been exposed to excessive noise levels. Ear damage will have been incurred, but because deafness has not fully developed, no claims may yet have been reported. A substantial reserve will be necessary to deal with the claims that undoubtedly will be made in future years.

Another claims factor which may be included in the IBNR reserve is the provision made for any increase on the original estimate for open claims. Some insurers separate this out into a separate reserve entitled IBNER: 'Incurred But Not Enough Reserved'.

Reserving for asbestos

Asbestos is a naturally occurring mineral with remarkable properties which led to it being used in a wide range of industries. It is fire and chemical resistant, an excellent insulator, a reinforcing additive for cement and motor vehicle brake linings, and it can be woven into textiles. Its disadvantage, which eventually resulted in its abandonment, is that it forms extremely fine fibrous dust particles which may cause the degenerative lung disease asbestosis or possibly the rare cancer, mesothelioma, up to 40 years after the exposure.

Asbestos-related diseases have given rise to many claims on employers', public and product liability policies for producers, distributors and users of asbestos products. Recently, the frequency and volume of claims have been increasing rapidly, particularly in the USA where more than an element of emotion has affected the court awards and the fact that judges do not appear to require the disease to have actually manifested itself. In recent cases, workers have received damages in excess of $1m merely for the emotional distress of having been exposed to asbestos. The awards to actual disease sufferers are even larger, eg one mesothelioma claimant has received $33m. In the UK similar cases are being settled at about £150,000. The effect on the P+C market in the USA has been little short of crippling.

Many companies have had to reserve hundreds of millions of dollars for past exposures, and regular strengthening of these reserves shows no sign of ending. Current reserves for asbestos-related claims already run into the hundreds of billions of dollars.

Claims equalization or catastrophe reserves

In some countries, insurers are permitted to set up a reserve to smooth the overall result. In years when claims experience has been favourable, an amount is put into a reserve from where it can be withdrawn in poor years. In theory it is an in-house method of reducing the impact of catastrophes. In practice, some companies may treat this so called equalization reserve as a tax-management tool.

15.4 The reserving process

The purpose of the reserving process is to make reasonable estimates of the ultimate cost to the company of business written to date.

When a claim is notified to an insurer an estimate will automatically be allocated via a computer program or a claims handler will apply an estimate. In the majority of cases, particularly in personal lines, this will be based on an average figure from past experience, modified for changing environmental factors such as the inflation rate. For larger and more complex claims, the handlers will probably put individual estimates on each claim, based on their own subjective judgment and the information available. The accumulation of all these case estimates forms the basis of what will eventually become the outstanding claims reserves.

The next step is for the claims professionals and actuaries to:

- bring the data together
- break it down into practical sub-classes
- review and refine it
- build in provisions for IBNR
- construct auditable reserves.

The selection of sub-classes is critical if any subsequent analysis is to be meaningful. For this reason, each sub-class:

- as far as possible, should contain relatively **homogeneous risks** so that any inferences made on the data are statistically valid
- should **not be too big**, or it will not really help underwriters to set rates.
- should **not be too small**, or the law of large numbers will not apply, ie statistical variances will be large.

The biggest challenges facing the reserver are how to build in the IBNR and reported claims development into the sub-class reserves. The basic approach is to analyse the pattern of the insurer's past experience of claims in the sub-class, apply this to the refined data on current claims and project this into the future. Obviously this has severe limitations, especially in a changing business environment, in long-tail classes and where there is little relevant applicable claims experience (eg in new and emerging risks). The remedy in such circumstances is to try to develop a deeper understanding of what drives claims, see how these factors are likely to change in the coming years and then make a judgment on how this could affect the reserves. Where possible, the reserver should also seek to identify steps that could be taken to manage down the eventual costs.

To analyse the pattern of claims perhaps the most widely used tool is the chain ladder.

Chain ladder

The chain ladder is the name given to a range of techniques designed to display and compare the claims development of claims from different years using tables, usually in the shape of a triangle. (The simple triangulation in Chapter 11 is a typical example.)

A chain ladder for claims paid on a liability account is shown below. This particular example records the year of reporting and the amount paid out in the successive years – known as the years of development.

Claims paid £'000

Year of Development

	0	1	2	3	4	5	6
1998	938	841	740	605	328	105	88
1999	1,191	906	781	635	461	205	–
2000	1,183	1,038	848	701	564	–	–
2001	1,274	1,177	994	832	–	–	–
2002	1,427	1,260	1,018	–	–	–	–
2003	1,886	1,519	–	–	–	–	–
2004	2,129	–	–	–	–	–	–

The aim of the reserver is to fill in the missing half of the triangle by projecting the pattern of previous years. A surprising amount can be done by an experienced reserver just by using simple arithmetic calculations. However, in many reserving exercises sophisticated statistical modelling is used. There is a wealth of software available, some of which will provide highly precise answers, eg claims paid in 2010 will be £10.9m + or – 0.3m with 95% confidence limits (based on the best assumptions input). However, it must be emphasized that these are only mechanical calculations and do not take into consideration the fundamental changes that might be happening to the drivers of the claims – inflation rate, rebuilding costs, legal framework, court awards, medical costs, etc. Wherever possible the reserver needs to make appropriate adjustments to compensate for these.

Other chain ladders can be created to compare different claims data. For example loss ratios, case reserves or the number of claims may be plotted against the year reported, the year the claim was incurred, or perhaps the year the policy was written. Each type of plot has its own particular advantages and disadvantages and each is likely to produce a different answer. It is the job of the reserver to try various techniques and produce what he or she considers to be a reasonable answer. Claims reserving never has been and is never likely to be an exact science.

The following checklist for claims reservers, compiled by the Faculty and Institute of Actuaries in the UK, clearly sums up the whole essence of this complex but vitally important subject.

Checklist for reservers

a) What historical data are available to the reserver and how far can confidence be placed in its reliability?
b) To what extent is homogeneity of the groups in the risk classification satisfactory?
c) What conclusions have shaped the past experience and what significant changes can be deduced which may effect the future outturn?
d) What methods of projection are proposed, and are these properly suited to the given circumstances?

Faculty and Institute of Actuaries, UK

Case study – The Reliance collapse 2000

Even long-established companies can make the same mistakes as new entrants. The Reliance was a highly respected property and casualty reinsurer that had its origins in 1817. In the 1990s it implemented a strategy of aggressive growth and, by the time of its collapse in 2000, was the eighth largest reinsurer of Lloyd's syndicates. As A M Best stated at the time, 'they were growing pretty rapidly in a soft market in some very speciality business. They probably didn't have a full understanding of what the losses could be and what risks associated with the business were. Therefore it was priced and reserved for inadequately.' The management repeatedly strengthened reserves and sold off parts of the company, but they were unable to maintain solvency and had to close, leaving a deficit of £680m.

Closing down an insurance book: Run-off

(This covers both closing a single product line in a multi-line operation, or an entire business operation.)

Unlike many other industries, deciding to exit a product line in insurance is not a simple process. From the moment that a decision is made to stop writing new business (or renew existing business):

- All existing contracts will continue to run until expiry (requiring continued support for billing/collection of premiums, amendments and routine policy servicing).
- New claims will continue to be notified, in some cases up to several years after the expiry of the last live policy.
- All existing and new claims will need to be assessed, managed and settled.
- Reserves will need to be set aside to meet all existing and future claims liabilities and the administrational expenses for running-off the book.
- Reinsurance recoveries will need to be managed and collected.
- Investments and cash flow will need to be managed to meet the settlement of claims over time.
- Procedures will need to be established to maintain, legal, regulatory, financial, etc. compliance over the run-off period.

The run-off process can take from as little as two years, for a very simple product line with no liability or long-tail claims (eg Travel), up to several decades, for a complex liability or reinsurance book of business.

Having made the decision to close the book and put it into run-off, management then needs to decide whether to perform the run-off internally (issues arise regarding staff motivation and incentivization), or to outsource the run-off to a specialist run-off administration service supplier (issues arise regarding control, but there may be potential cost advantages).

Run-off administration is big business – the worldwide liabilities for P+C insurance books in run-off are estimated to be in the region of £150-200 bn and growing at 10% p.a.

Select bibliography

C Daykin, T Pentikäiken, M Pesonen, *Practical Risk Theory for Actuaries,* Chapman & Hall 1994.

B Webb, C Harrison, J Markam, *Insurance Operations and Regulation*, Insurance Institute of America 2002, Chapter 12.

J Outreville, *Theory and Practice of Insurance,* Kluwer 1998, Chapter 13.

P England, R Verrall, *Stochastic Claims Reserving in General Insurance*, British Actuarial Journal Vol 8, Part III, 2002.

S Diacon (Ed), *A Guide to Insurance Management*, Macmillan 1990, Chapter 15.

Sixteen

The management of business services

Objectives

On completion of this chapter, and wider personal research, the reader should be able to:

- evaluate the opportunities, risks and resource implications associated with differing operational models;
- describe how the departments that support the core business are managed, including: finance, investment, information services, human resources, facilities management, corporate affairs, legal/secretarial, risk management and internal audit;
- appreciate the interaction these services have with the core business.

16.1 Introduction

In an insurance operation, *Business Services* is the name usually given to the various departments that support the core business. They are essential to the effective running of the company because they:

- give advice to the line management
- provide an infrastructure in which the business works
- undertake specialist tasks.

Because they are not usually revenue earning in their own right they come under continuous pressure both to reduce their costs and improve the quality of the service they provide to the core business.

Some of the more important Business Services in an insurance operation are listed below:

Business services

Finance	Legal/Secretarial/Compliance
Human Resources (HR)	Internal Audit
Information Services (IS)	Facilities Management (FM)
Investment Management	Risk Management
Marketing Services	Corporate Affairs

16.2 The structure of Business Services

The way that Business Services are structured varies substantially between companies. In some companies the services are mostly *centralized*, shared service departments serving the needs of all the business units. The advantage of this approach is optimizing the benefits of scale, ie lower expenses, concentration of expertise, greater control and uniformity of practice. In other companies, Business Services are *decentralized*, each business unit having its own dedicated service departments. This provides greater focus on the business's needs but the benefits of scale may be sacrificed.

Case study – The cost of moving from a centralized to a decentralized Business Services structure

Shortly after successfully completing a merger with a competitor, a large subsidiary of a major insurance company decided to change from a highly centralized organization to one with essentially independent customer-focused business units. As part of this new organizational strategy the shared Business Services departments were broken up and each business unit set up and managed its own. Costs rapidly increased as a result of replication. In HR, for example, the total number of specialists employed grew from 12 to over 100 within a year as each unit began to develop its own unique pay and reward system. This pattern was repeated in IS and other service areas. Three years later the strategy was reversed, management having calculated that the decentralization had destroyed all the cost savings of the merger.

An alternative, *hybrid* approach to Business Services is now becoming more common. It aims to combine the scale benefits of sharing with the benefits of business focus. The principles are as follows:

(i) activities that are essentially unique to a specific business are decentralized and placed close to the internal customer, eg high added value aspects such as advice.

(ii) activities that are common to most businesses are centralized into shared service units, eg treasury/cash control, facilities management. (This is discussed in Chapter 17.)

(iii) where practicable, activities are outsourced to 'business partners', possibly in lower-cost territories such as China, India and Mexico.

This is, of course, the application of value chain analysis to Business Services. It should be emphasized that there is a considerable amount of intellectual capital residing in business services. However, as it is not core to the business, it does not necessarily need to be retained in-house, and others may be able to do it better.

Transforming an existing Business Services organization into a hybrid structure may prove to be a very painful process. There are likely to be many redundancies and considerable disruption to the business. The business units themselves may need to be convinced of the value of using standardized systems rather than their own bespoke versions.

16.3 Clarity of roles

Confusion may occur between the Business Services and the business unit management unless great care is taken when defining roles. The head of a business unit should be responsible for anything that happens in the business. However, the head of a Business Service will also have responsibilities. These service responsibilities will be especially onerous where the business service is a regulated activity such as finance and is headed by an approved person. The questions may arise: Who is actually making the decision? Who is leading and who is following? Who is responsible for delivery?

16.4 Issues and challenges in Business Services

Business Services become closely involved with many of the important decisions that contribute to the success of an insurance operation. Obviously, it is well beyond the scope of this book to deal with them all. However, anyone studying the management of insurance operations would benefit from an understanding of the following short selection of issues that frequently have to be addressed in Business Services.

16.4.1 Finance

The finance function in an insurance operation plays a pivotal role. Not only does it provide financial advice to management and carry out specific tasks such as reporting, cash collection and credit control, but also the overall finance policy lays out the financial targets and financial control objectives of the company. This policy might lay down objectives and guidelines for the following:

- Overall return
- Trading objectives
- Levels of capital
- Solvency
- Liquidity
- Expense management
- Management information
- Reserving policy
- Cash flow
- Credit
- Currency
- Taxation
- Budgeting and planning
- Reporting

Some of the key issues are described below.

Return and trading objectives

The starting point for a finance policy is deciding the target for the *overall return*, usually described in terms of average net real return on capital (ROC) over the cycle. This will of course depend on the current cost of capital and the exact target needed to enable the company to:

- provide dividends and share appreciation commensurate with shareholder expectations/what they receive elsewhere in the sector;
- maintain an acceptable solvency margin.

In practice, management has little control over share appreciation so will instead aim to grow the net worth of the company and trust that this will be reflected in the share price.

Once the overall return objective has been set, it needs to be translated into individual trading objectives for the business units. These might be expressed as ROC or the equivalent combined ratio. These targets may vary according to the potential volatility of each business – the more volatile, the greater should be the required return: uncertainty has a cost.

Capital and solvency

Capital is required to write business, respond to catastrophes and under-reserving, and also to finance major corporate developments such as acquisitions. Capital comes from the shareholders, borrowings and retained profits. (Mutual insurance companies are unable to raise cheap capital from shareholders and this was one of the reasons for the late 1990s trend towards de-mutualization.)

The optimum level of capital is a key decision for an insurance company. Too high a level opens the company to the criticism of underutilization of assets, whereas too low a level makes the company vulnerable to the unexpected. If it is then unable to raise new capital quickly it may not have the capacity to fund new business. This is known as the *capacity trap*.

The *solvency ratio* is the ratio of shareholders' funds to net premium income. It is the basic measure of capital adequacy and is an indication of the security of the insurance company. Major brokers, large commercial insurance buyers and the rating agencies (Standard & Poors, Moodys, etc) maintain a close watch on insurers' solvency ratios.

(NB Solvency margin is also often used by industry commentators when discussing capital adequacy; it is merely another name for shareholders' funds or free assets.)

In most countries the regulator will specify a minimum acceptable solvency ratio in order to protect policyholders. This could be as low as 17% before the regulator actually closes the company but in practice the regulator may well begin to have informal discussions with an insurer as soon as the solvency ratio drops to around 30%.

Some companies consider a solvency ratio of 40% to be the minimum desirable level. This would enable them to fund growth and retain a buffer against catastrophe. Other companies have historically attempted to maintain a significantly higher ratio, so they are able to keep a mix of investments that is high in equities (and therefore higher risk), and so hope to maximize investment income in the long run.

Any insurer with a solvency ratio below 30% will almost certainly need to consider one or more of the following options (if for no other reason than being required to do so by the regulator):

- suspend or reduce dividends
- undertake a rights issue
- reduce net premium
- sell assets above book value.

In order to overcome the capacity trap, and reduce net premium income while continuing to write similar levels of gross premium, it may choose to arrange quota share reinsurance whereby a reinsurer is effectively providing capital support.

The management of capital is discussed in more detail in Chapter 17.

Dividend

Dividends need to be large enough to satisfy the shareholders' expectations yet not so large as to result in inadequate retained profits that should be ploughed back into the business. Companies usually try to give an increasing dividend that at least keeps pace with inflation. In P+C insurance companies, the dividends may not be covered by the trading returns at the bottom of the cycle but the capital strength of the company is usually adequate. Dividends are reduced only in times of severe problems or capital scarcity and this is, potentially, a warning signal to the market.

The underlying logic of the *composite model* of the insurance company is that the steady profits from Life business compensate for the volatility of P+C business and thereby underpin the dividend. Unfortunately, the recent fall in the profitability of Life companies has cast serious doubts on the long-term validity of this model.

It should be noted that P+C insurance companies have historically been regarded as risky stocks, due to the volatility of the trading results. This has resulted in many of them trading at a discount to net asset value.

16.4.2 Investment management

The responsibility for setting the investment policy of an insurance company will usually lie with the Investment Director, possibly in conjunction with the Finance Director. The policy is carried out by the Investment Department, although there is a growing trend to outsource the activity to an external fund management company.

The main objective of investment activity is to optimize the asset appreciation and income from the funds under management, both the capital of the operation and the insurance funds (claims reserves, unearned premium reserves, etc). Within this broad framework the Investment Department needs to ensure that the funds are:

- Secure
- Liquid enough for the company's requirements
- Spread by investment type and market
- Matched against potential liabilities in terms of both timing and currency of payment.

A different way of looking at these objectives by the Institute and Faculty of Actuaries:

> **P+C investment objectives**
>
> 1. The liabilities of the fund, as far as they can be specified, must be met as and when they arise.
> 2. Liabilities must be met leaving as much surplus as possible.
> 3. The risk involved in managing the return must not be so great as to imperil the fulfilment of liabilities.
>
> Institute and Faculty of Actuaries

The main choices of investments that go into the mix and their relative liquidity include:

Highly liquid	**Relatively illiquid**
Cash	Loans
Government stocks	Property
Other-fixed interest	
Equities	

Highly liquid

Cash – the most liquid form of holding. Interest rates are variable and relatively low. In times of high inflation, interest rates can be less than the rate of inflation.

Government stocks – all governments have a credit rating for their stock issues based on the likelihood of default. Most Western government stocks are deemed to be extremely low-risk investments and, as a result, interest rates are relatively low. The interest rate is fixed at the date of issue and, as a result, the capital value of bonds can vary substantially due to changes in the underlying bank base rate up until the last few years prior to redemption, after which it will trend to the redemption value.

Government stocks are generally freely tradable.

Example:

£100 of UK Government 8% stock, redeemable in 18 years, has a market price of £145 when the base rate is currently 3.75% (but expected to increase in the future).

With the same base rate and expectations, £100 of UK Government 8% stock redeemable in 2 years has a market price of £113, but this will move to £100 by the redemption date because this is the amount that will be repaid by the Government.

But if the base rate was 10% (ie higher than the coupon rate) and expected to remain at this rate, the current market price for both stocks would be below £100.

Other fixed-interest shares and bonds – these are issued by corporations or other non-government entities and, as a result, have less certainty of repayment, and therefore have higher yields to reflect the risk. The market price will fluctuate as the bank base rate changes and if there is any doubt as to the ability of the issuing organization to repay them. Most major Western economies have large and liquid markets for this kind of security.

Equities – these investments have no certainty of income (eg coupon rate) or value (eg redemption value); as a result, they are higher risk than other forms of investment. If all goes well, the returns can be very large; if things go badly others (bond holders, etc) will have priority access to the company's assets.

The main return on equity investments has been through share price appreciation rather than via dividends over the last 40 years. All countries operate some form of stock market for equities and sometimes have several different markets for different types of company (eg technology stocks, small capitalization, etc). The liquidity of such markets varies, but the major markets (London, New York, Tokyo main stock exchanges) are extremely liquid.

Illiquid investments

Loans and property are relatively illiquid (ie they cannot be bought or sold quickly or easily) and there is no high-volume market within which to trade them, as there is for government stocks, corporate bonds and equities. As a rule, they tend to be higher risk than government stocks but lower risk than equities. A balanced investment portfolio will probably include some of these investment assets for balance, but generally they will not be a major proportion.

The optimum investment mix will vary depending on the purpose of the investment fund. Investments supporting claims reserves, for example, will need to match the future pattern of claims: long-tail claims permitting longer-term, potentially higher return, less liquid investments. Shareholders' funds are also suitable for longer-term/higher-risk investments, eg a higher proportion of equities.

The fund management skills built up in an Investment Department may become a marketable commodity in their own right. For this reason some insurance companies have set up their own retail fund management operations to provide investment products to retail customers. Some of these have been successful but others have failed, usually as a result of having an insufficiently strong retail brand to ensure rapid growth to critical mass.

16.4.3 Information Services

The effectiveness and efficiency of an insurance operation's IT systems, and the timeliness and accuracy of its data, will have a significant impact on the cost base of the operation, the quality of the customer service that can be provided, and the quality and appropriateness of the information used in key decisions. Obviously, the larger and more complex an insurance operation is, the greater the impact of any inefficiency or lack of effectiveness. The greater the volume of real-time customer or intermediary interfaces (call centres, EDI, Internet, etc), the more likely that any inadequacies will become apparent to third parties.

It goes without saying that the targets for any company's IT systems should incorporate:

- systems that are fit for purpose
- systems that are easy to use
- systems that are simple to maintain
- data is held and processed accurately and completely
- systems that are easy to upgrade/develop
- systems and data that are secure
- all interfaces between systems, both internal and external, are effectively controlled.

Because of the nature of the business they write, most insurance operation's systems are extremely complex and highly integrated. This in itself makes them more difficult to maintain and develop. An additional complicating factor is that insurance was one of the earliest users of computer systems back in the 1960s (when they were principally designed to replace ledger-based record keeping systems and for managing receipts and payments) and has constantly increased their use, and their complexity, ever since. What this can mean therefore is that current systems are in fact based on extremely old systems that have constantly been improved, had new functionality added on to them, etc over decades. As a result of this continuous development approach, it can become extremely difficult to replace the old systems that underlie all the more modern additions, even if they are relatively inefficient, costly to maintain, or are no longer 100% fit for purpose.

There is a tendency, because of the complexity of existing systems, where new IT functionality is required, to introduce a new system to perform the new activity. Yet such new systems, frequently duplicate some activity already performed by existing systems, but the duplicate activity in the old systems is not removed as part of the new system introduction. You then end up with several different systems performing similar activities.

Justifying closing down old, but working systems

- It is relatively easy to cost justify the introduction of a new IT system.
- It is nearly impossible to cost justify the expense and effort of migrating data off, and switching off, an old IT system that still functions without serious problems.

Mergers and acquisitions just compound the problem of multiple systems and increasing complexity unless very rigorously managed.

Because of the complexity of systems operated and the high cost of maintaining existing systems and developing new systems, some insurers are considering outsourcing some or all of their:

- IT infrastructure (hardware, computer centre operations, etc); and/or
- System maintenance activity; and/or
- System development activity

to specialist IT service suppliers, having decided that such IT skills are not a core competence required to be possessed by the insurance operation itself, and that others can perform these functions more efficiently and cost effectively. Also, increasingly, entire functions are being outsourced in totality (ie processes, systems and people, not just the IT part), where it is judged that external partners can manage and invest in these activities as their primary business.

16.4.4 Human Resources

Personnel management becomes directly involved as implementer or adviser in:

- Recruitment
- Remuneration
- Training and development
- Organizational design
- Change management
- Industrial relations
- Pensions provision.

In recent years however, there has been a concerted move to align these activities more closely with business strategy. This has often been reflected in the renaming of the function as human resources management.

HR

Human Resources Management 'combines human relations thinking with strategic thinking.'

Michael Armstrong

Some of the key HR issues affecting insurance operations are discussed below.

Recruitment

At a time when industries are having to compete for talent, insurance is not attracting the best graduates and school leavers. This is partly due to rewards being lower than those in, say, accountancy, law, management consultancy and investment banking. Even more significant perhaps is its poor public image. Like mainstream banking, it is at best considered to be boring and, at worst, an exploitative industry that tries to avoid its obligations. Those who join insurance companies take a very different view, but negative image has become a major challenge for HR.

Remuneration

As has been emphasized throughout this book, insurance is a long-term business where the result of today's decisions may not become evident for months, years or even decades. This does not sit easily with the current management emphasis on performance-related pay. Extreme care must be taken to ensure that:

(i) Staff are not incentivized to act against the interest of the company, eg underwriting for short-term premium growth rather than for profit, or under-reserving to boost the short-term insurance result.

(ii) Rewards are not based on the apparent result rather than the real result that is likely to materialize in the future.

In one company, the management team dealing with multinational business received a bonus of 50% of salary for the high level of short-term growth and profitability of the account that had been delivered. But, over the following few years, losses of several times net premium were recorded.

There is an old saying in insurance that many people have had highly remunerative careers because they always managed to move job every two or three years before the results caught up with them.

Training and development

In 1999 the UK National Training Organizations sponsored a major study of the skills required in financial services (insurance, banking and building societies), which was undertaken by the research institute CREATE. Although the surveys were carried out in the UK, the conclusions are probably applicable to many other markets. The main skill sets identified are shown schematically in Figure 16.1.

Figure 16.1

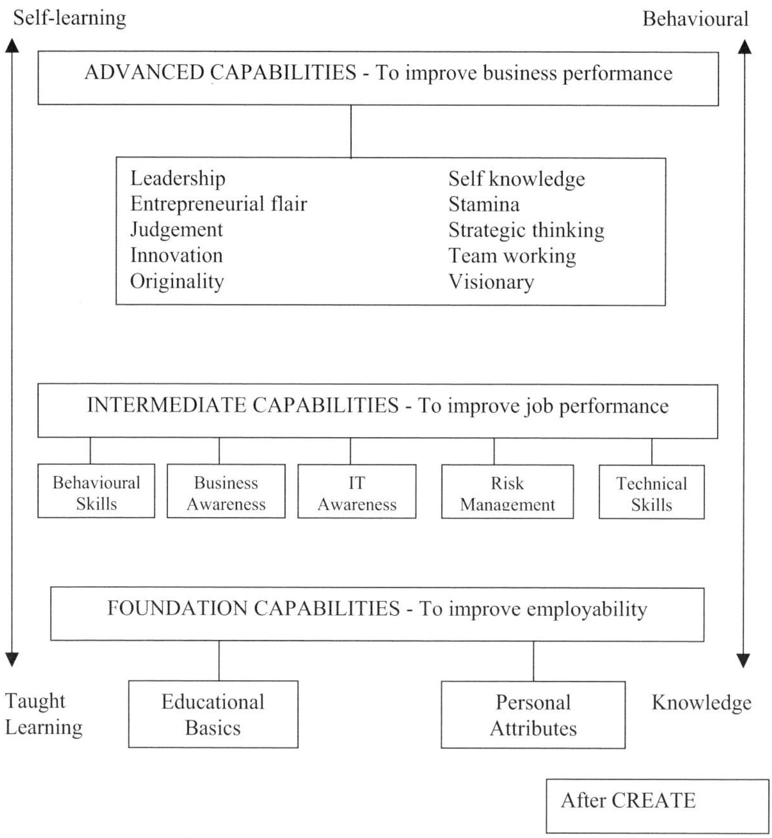

Ref: *Competing Through Skills*: Amin Rajan, Penny Van Eupen and Kirsty Chapple CREATE 1999 – ISBN 1.898879.22.2

The *foundation capabilities* of Educational Basics and Personal Attributes are acquired starting in school. In the next stage, the employee develops the *intermediate capabilities*. This involves skills, values and behaviours consistent with a high level of job performance in the five key areas Behavioural Skills, Business Awareness, IT Awareness, Risk Management and Technical Skills. The final stage of an individual's progression is to acquire *advanced capabilities* which are described as the 'holistic attributes that maximize the overall organizational effectiveness'.

As the stages are worked through the emphasis moves from taught learning to self-learning and from knowledge to behaviours.

The survey identified the main skill gaps in financial services as:

1. Leadership skills
2. Business awareness
3. IT skills
4. Behavioural skills

To overcome these gaps companies have been changing the *staffing profile* and adopting new approaches that promote *self-learning.*

The staffing profile is being changed by targeting younger age groups with high-level qualifications with greater gender and racial diversity. The aim is to replicate wider society and produce a workforce with more affinity to the emerging business culture.

The structure of jobs is also changing.

- ♦ low-skilled → high-skilled
- ♦ technical → knowledge-based
- ♦ single-skilled → multi-skilled

The new approaches that promote self-learning include:

- ♦ mentoral learning – coaching, etc
- ♦ experimental learning – assignments, job transfers, etc
- ♦ distance learning – computer-based learning, case studies

Since this highly influential report was commissioned, the insurance market has experienced a serious downturn, highlighting a lack of technical skills in the core areas of underwriting and claims management. One of the largest insurers in Europe has publicly stated that this is now their greatest internal challenge. It will be interesting to see if companies will focus more of their training effort on the traditional technical areas. In the UK this is especially likely because the FSA is imposing a commitment on employers in respect of training and competence such that each authorized business has a requirement to ensure that:

1. Its employees are competent;
2. Its employees remain competent for the work that they do;
3. Its employees are appropriately supervised;
4. Its employees' competence is regularly reviewed; and
5. The level of competence is appropriate to the nature of the business

Charismatic leadership

The academic Steven Bloomfield writing in *The Professional Manager* highlighted a management phenomenon to which insurance has not been totally immune. He described the amount of unhealthy interest in the theories of *charismatic leadership* which focuses on an individual's personality, with management competencies given only secondary attention.

The literature on the subject appears to stress the exceptional qualities of people like Napoleon, Churchill and Henry V and suggest that senior executives should try to emulate them. Unfortunately, as Bloomfield pointed out, these leadership qualities almost certainly cannot be taught, although their flamboyant style might be imitated. Too often a senior executive adopting this approach, and using the language of the most current management fashion, 'inspires to delight with his vision of where the business might be – all at the expense of real substance'. Charismatic leadership usually produces short-lived benefits and may have been a contributory factor in some of the corporate scandals of recent years.

The alternative for executives Bloomfield called *rational leadership* with management at its core. He proposed that it is more likely to generate shareholder value over the medium to long-term by using:

1. Conscious consultation on a course of action
2. Active deliberation
3. Application of logic to the problem.

The benefits of rational leadership are evident in the long list of companies that quietly prosper and develop while others come and go.

Professional Manager, v 12, issue 1, 2003

Pension provision

As implied above, insurance used to be a highly stable career where employees would generally stay for many years with the same company. Pensions therefore tended to be based on final salary and were often subsidized, if not fully non-contributory. However, the increased mobility of the workforce (in particular in relatively new areas such as call centres), mergers, rationalizations, outsourcing and other significant staff-reduction exercises, combined with reduced investment returns, have led many companies to switch to defined contribution/money purchase schemes. These are designed to be more portable and are very much cheaper/lower risk for the company. For employees it represents a significant reduction in benefits that has to be managed.

16.4.5 Facilities Management (FM)

FM deals with a whole raft of activities that are necessary for the day-to-day running of an insurance operation. These may include management of: office premises, security, motor fleet, catering, cleaning, etc. In some companies FM will also include responsibility for purchasing goods on a company-wide basis, in others purchasing may be split between different functions or controlled by experts within claims management.

The current dominant issue in FM is whether the service should be provided internally or whether it should be outsourced. Traditionally, larger insurance operations have maintained large FM organizations, providing the majority of services themselves. They have been able to do this because they have sufficient scale to be reasonably efficient. There is now, however, a growing tendency to outsource such activities. The role of FM then becomes that of a relationship manager for external partners and a procurement manager.

16.4.6 Marketing Services and Corporate Affairs

Marketing Services were discussed in Chapter 9.

Corporate Affairs

Corporate Affairs functions are there to build and manage a broad base of trust and understanding of the company, its business and its plans for the future. Some marketing professionals have described it as maintaining a continued 'licence to trade'. The activities undertaken will vary significantly depending on the exact nature and ownership of the operation. For a quoted company it will probably include the following areas:

Investor Relations

The management of the company's relationship with its shareholders and capital providers; it should involve an active programme of presentations and meetings with investors, analysts and financial commentators. It is important that the 'owners' of the company and the investment markets fully understand and support the management's strategy.

Media Relations

The primary objective is to maintain good relations with the media at all times in order to receive a balanced hearing for the company's activities and views on television, radio, and in the press.

Public Affairs

This covers the management of relationships with elected representatives at local, regional and national level. Major companies will usually wish to contribute to relevant bodies and authorities affecting the insurance industry through representation on legislative and industry forums, input to consultation processes and participation in lobbying and pressure groups.

Corporate Affairs requires people with a deep knowledge of the industry and an ability to build long-term relationships. It is not sufficient to communicate with the shareholders only in difficult times; they might not believe the company if they do not understand how the management thinks, or if they suspect that the company is secretive/withholds information that should be made public.

16.4.7 Legal/Secretarial/Compliance

In addition to the normal requirement for a company to have a formal company secretarial function (to perform statutory duties as laid down in company law), and the need for corporate level legal advice (as opposed to the use of lawyers to handle disputes relating to policy terms, or claims validity or quantum) all UK regulated insurance operations are required to have a nominated executive responsible for compliance with FSA regulations.

Between them, these functions must ensure that all relevant law and regulation is identified and complied with across all operational units of the company.

> **Compliance and outsourcing**
>
> Where elements of the business are outsourced, responsibility for ensuring compliance on behalf of the insurer cannot be transferred and remains with the insurance operation. As a result, all outsourcing agreements have to include full legal and regulatory compliance obligations and a process to demonstrate that these obligations have been met on a consistent basis.

Internally, responsibility for compliance with external requirements may well be delegated to other areas, eg:

- Compliance with accounting rules to the finance function
- Data protection compliance to a special data protection team within IS.

However, the central team must ensure that a formal process is in place to ensure that these delegated tasks are performed effectively.

16.4.8 Risk Management

There is increasing awareness, following recent corporate scandals, that corporate boards require a much better understanding of the risks facing the business and the risk management processes in place to manage/mitigate those risks. The challenges presented in formalizing risk management in an insurance operation are discussed in more detail in the next chapter. The UK regulator, the FSA, requires all regulated P+C insurance businesses to have formal risk management processes in place from 2004.

Whether, like the UK, required by regulation or not, the creation of a formal and effective risk management process, for both corporate and operational risks, is now deemed best practice corporate governance and could be expected to be established in all reputable companies.

The risk management process and its relevance and importance to an insurance operation is discussed in more detail in Chapter 17.

16.4.9 Internal Audit

Internal Audit is part of the corporate and operational risk-monitoring process and independently assesses the adequacy of controls and processes operated. Between them the heads of Compliance, Legal/Secretarial, Risk Management and Internal Audit should operate and manage the insurers risk and compliance processes and report on these to the executive/board.

All UK Stock Exchange listed and UK-regulated insurers would be expected to have an internal audit function, although this service could be outsourced.

Select bibliography

E Turban, K Rainer, R Potter, *Introduction to Information Technology 2nd Ed*, John Wiley & Sons 2003.

P Bocij, D Chaffey, A Greasley, S Hickie, *Business Information Systems 2nd Ed*, F T Prentice Hall 2003.

S Diacon (Ed), *A Guide to Insurance Management*, Chapter 7 and Chapter 16.

J Outreville, *Theory and Practice of Insurance*, Kluwer 1998, Chapter 13.

H Krause, D Bean, R Cawthorn, R Oakley, L Young, *Insurance Information Systems 3rd Ed*, Insurance Institute of America 1999.

M Taylor, *Technological Changes in IT and Their Influence on Insurance*, The Change Ahead Geneva Papers on Risk and Insurance Vol 26, No 1, Jan 2001.

M Carrington, P Langguth, T Steiner, *The Banking Revolution: Salvation or Slaughter?* F T Pitman 1997.

A Rajan, P van Eupen, K Chapple, *Competing Through Skills,* CREATE 1999.

M Armstrong, *Human Resource Management,* Kogan Page 1994.

C Handy, *Understanding Organisations, 4th Ed,* Penguin 1993.

Seventeen

Cross-business challenges

Objectives

On completion of this chapter, and wider personal research, the reader should be able to:

- discuss the impact of current cross-business challenges on P+C insurance;
- explain the application of e-business, change management, outsourcing, risk management and business ethics.

There are a number of issues that challenge the way the entire business, or key elements of both insurance operations and business services together, are managed, some of which have been referred to in earlier chapters. Below we discuss a number that are particularly relevant to insurers at the present time.

17.1 E-business and insurance

> 'The Internet differs from earlier technology ... being suited to swapping unstructured information, allowing multiple parties to view the same documents, yet preserving the integrity of those documents. All of a sudden the rush is on ... in the hope of cutting out costs and improving customer service.'
>
> Derek Austin, *Insurance Technology,* Nov 2000

E-business is the application of Internet technology to business. It is a much wider concept than e-commerce, which relates specifically to the marketing of products and services via the Internet.

The original technology was developed by the US military to link together defence sites so that, if any were destroyed by enemy action, the whole network could continue to function. As such, it was designed to give simultaneous access to vast amounts of data. It proved to be an extremely powerful and flexible communication medium giving rise to the worldwide web and opening up unprecedented opportunities for companies across the full spectrum of industries. As an IBM spokesman said at the time, 'We don't know where it is all leading, if we did we would make a fortune!'

However, it soon became clear that e-business specifically offered the potential to:

- provide round-the-clock access to customers in any location
- drive down costs substantially
- improve flexibility and speed of response
- allow customers to control parts of the transaction
- link in with other suppliers to provide joint propositions
- create new business models, and even enable existing companies to reinvent themselves.

Some sectors, notably online stockbroking (eg Charles Schwab) proved to be particularly adept at exploiting e-business. Existing insurance operations, on the other hand, were much slower in taking it up. This was attributed to a combination of channel conflict and an inherent reluctance to embrace change. In retrospect, this tardiness probably saved the industry hundreds of millions of pounds over that pioneering period, as most initiatives ended in disappointment.

Insurers' caution on e-business

According to a survey by Andersen Consulting, insurers were the 'least enthusiastic backers of the Internet channel during its boom days. Having, as a sector avoided jumping on the Internet bandwagon, they felt vindicated by their caution and remain firmly of the view that the Internet is **a** channel not **the** channel. They described the Internet as primarily for information and service rather than sales.'

They are expecting this channel to develop over time, but for the moment most saw 'the Internet as entering a period of pause, before a younger wave of customers re-energized its growth.'

Andersen Consulting

When e-business did begin to gain momentum in insurance, it followed a similar path to that which had evolved elsewhere (see Figure 17.1).

Figure 17.1

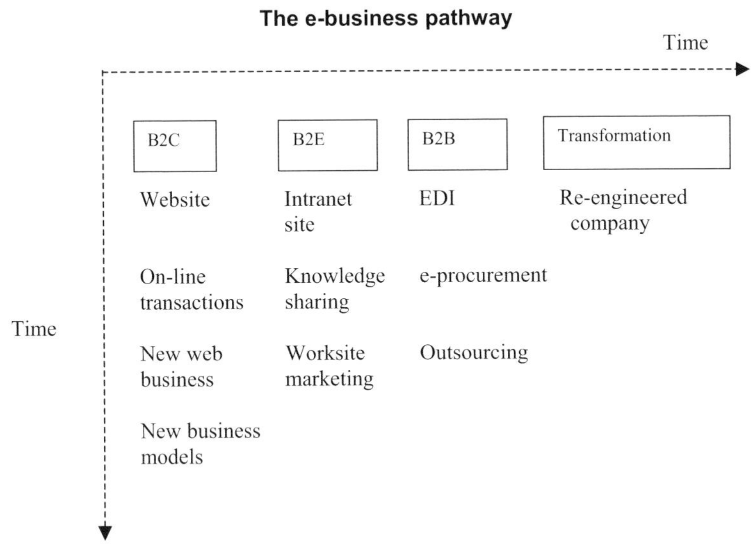

The pathway begins with B2C (Business to Customer) applications, moves on to B2E (Business to Employee) and B2B (Business to Business) applications and culminates in the potential transformation of the companies themselves. Taking these in sequence:

a) B2C

- Almost all insurance operations have set up their own web sites displaying product information and company contact details. This is really just a form of passive advertising (or 'brochureware'), but it has provided management with experience of the new medium.
- Most operations have since moved on to web-enable existing sales channels, to provide some transactions on-line. These may range from a simple quotation to a more comprehensive service of granting cover, collecting premiums, managing claims, mid-term alterations, etc.
- The next stage of B2C is that some operations have created self-contained new web businesses. This enables the operation to start with a blank sheet of paper. Obviously new entrants have been able to move directly to this position; existing insurers have taken a little longer. Examples include:

(i) directline.com, which uses the Direct Line brand to quote and sell motor insurance and provides information on other general, life, loans, savings and pension products.

(ii) The American Association of Retired People, AARP teamed up with the Hartford to create a new web business to quote and sell motor and home insurance.

- The final stage of B2C is to establish a radically new business model that did not exist before the development of the Internet. The following are examples of models that have been introduced:

i) Portal

This is a web business that introduces its customers to chosen companies' products. They may be very broad in their scope (eg Yahoo) or focused on a special interest such as cars or weddings. The main attraction for an insurer using a portal to sell its products is that potential customers are more likely to visit a portal than trawl around insurers' individual web sites. A portal is essentially an agent.

ii) Aggregator

One disadvantage of portals is that they do not provide a choice of quotations from a panel of insurers. This is overcome by the aggregator model (also known as a mall, navigator, or supermarket). In effect, the aggregator is an on-line broker, although not necessarily giving the individual advice that a traditional broker has on offer.

Typical examples of aggregators are Quotesmith and Insweb. Many businesses who tried this model struggled because they were:

- unable to deal with the complexities that arise in the sale of insurance; and
- not paid for renewals, and so generated insufficient income.

iii) Reverse auctions

In this model an on-line auction company invites large commercial risks to advertise on its web site. Insurers visiting the site are able to tender for the business. An example is insureXL.de.

Insurers have two major concerns about the Internet:

a) It is unsatisfactory when it comes to risk selection.

b) It cannot provide the human touch which is necessary because insurance has to be **sold** rather than being **bought**. Most customers appear to want to talk to a person before purchase.

Andersen Consulting

It is interesting to note that even the most successful B2C insurance operations have found that a substantial proportion of customers are happy to use the web to compare products and prices, but prefer to speak to someone from the company before completing the purchase. The telephone is far from obsolete in insurance.

b) B2E

- Most large insurance operations have set up intranet sites. These internal networks are accessed by their employees, via their desktop computers. Intranets are ideal for company communications and training, and may include feedback capabilities, so that employees can respond to the information.
- Intranets can be used for knowledge-sharing by providing technical manuals, chat rooms and access to in-house specialists. This arrangement is particularly useful for companies that operate globally or where expertise is thinly spread.
- Some insurers have extended the use of intranet sites to worksite marketing, ie selling products, their own or those of partners, direct to their employees.

c) B2B

- Internet technology lends itself particularly well to electronic data interchange, EDI, such as information transferred between insurers and brokers. In the more sophisticated variations, brokers are able to track the progress of a case through the insurer's system.
- One area where genuine benefits are manifest is *e-procurement*. This is the use of the Internet to facilitate purchasing by a company from preferred suppliers. Two examples are:
  i) Employees use their desktop computers to create an order for office equipment; this is automatically referred to an authorizing manager, then passed to the supplier. This is much cheaper than traditional manual purchasing systems and is very easy to control and audit.
  ii) The linking-in of replacement goods suppliers to an insurance operation's claims system has the capability of speeding up the post-loss service, and substantially reducing costs.
- Although e-business is not a pre-requisite of outsourcing it certainly enables work to be relocated thousands of miles away in different time zones. AXA, Standard Life and Willis Faber are among many prominent companies that have outsourced processing activities to India using Internet technology. Outsourcing is discussed in more detail later in this chapter.

d) Transformation

> **The long-term impact of e-business**
>
> 'E-business is likely to be as important for financial services as the rise of the supermarket was for retailing. But I must emphasize it is *not* just about distribution. It is about applying an entire technology to our core business processes. I believe that it will completely transform many aspects of our industry over the next decade: how we operate, how we share knowledge, how we are structured, the products and services we offer and, of course, the competencies we will require.'
>
> Paul Spencer, UK CEO, RSA

The availability of Internet technology is an important catalyst to changes in the way insurance operations structure themselves. Obviously, it can be used to streamline internal processes, improve communication with partners and suppliers, and greatly improve the handling of customer data. However, beyond this, some of the really big transformation opportunities become more feasible. Examples include:

- Companies could begin to operate as genuinely global entities, having shared processing in one country, the underwriting expertise in another and customer service units spread between many markets.
- Concentration on selected parts of the value chain becomes easier. For instance, the Zurich's decision to split business between manufacturing and distribution units would have been impractical without Internet technology to link the different units together.
- Cross-industry propositions will undoubtedly become more common. The main motor manufacturers, for example, are using alliances and acquisitions to develop networks of product propositions to surround the customer (sales, loans, services, insurance, breakdown, etc). As these become linked together by e-technology, radical new propositions will begin to emerge.

An overview

Undoubtedly e-business was oversold when it was introduced in the 1990s. Investors believed the extravagant claims and dubious extrapolations that were made at the time. B2C demonstrated all the characteristics of an economic bubble: rapid rise in public sentiment followed by equally rapid collapse (see Figure 17.2).

Figure 17.2

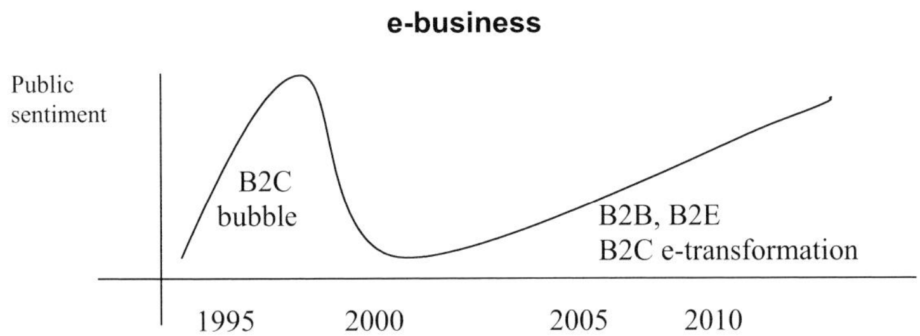

Few early e-business models succeeded in having a demonstrably superior customer value proposition, a strong brand and above all the ability to convert web site hits into profitable sales. As one insurance company director has said, 'The laws of economics were not suspended for the convenience of e-business'.

However, there is always a danger with any new technology to overestimate the effects in the short term, but underestimate those of the long-term. Behind the scenes there is slower, but sustainable, growth in B2B, B2E and the better thought-through B2C models. These, and the major transformations that e-business makes possible, will have profound implications for the future of the insurance industry.

Strategy not technology

'Too often, the hype that is e-business has led to technology investments being made before their business value has been assessed. Like any business decision, it must start with clarity around how the organization is choosing to differentiate in the marketplace. The opportunities presented by e-business can then be applied to that strategy.'

Joining the E-Business Revolution,
Executive Briefings, Bywater 2000

17.2 Change Management

It's not new

'There is nothing more difficult to plan, more doubtful of success, nor more dangerous to manage than the creation of a new system. For the initiator has the enmity of all who would profit by the preservation of the old institutions, and merely lukewarm defenders in those who should gain by the new ones.'

Niccolo Machiavelli (1469-1527)

In insurance, like all other businesses, significant change is now the norm rather than the exception. A company's ability to manage and deliver major change programmes will have a significant influence on its future success. There are many ways of managing change. IBM, for example, made a study of a large number of successful programmes and found that the following factors were usually present:

Critical success factors for change programmes

- A compelling reason to change
- A committed leadership willing to drive change from the top down
- A collective will to make change happen
- A commitment to radical change and a resistance to reducing its scope
- Concrete, measurable goals for the desired end state
- Measures, rewards and compensation aligned with the goals
- A methodical and structured approach

IBM

Key change challenges faced by many insurance operations include:

- Compliance with new regulations
- Simplification and rationalization of legacy products, processes and IT systems
- Introduction of new IT systems
- Implementation of e-business and other technology and communications developments
- Outsourcing/insourcing/creation of shared service functions
- Offshore relocation of processes and functions.

Business process re-engineering

Change of course is by no means a new phenomenon in business but the current wave of change programmes seem to be both more radical and frequent. All this dates back to the introduction of business process re-engineering (BPR) a decade ago. This was not so much a methodology, but a mind set that gave companies the courage to make fundamental changes to their business processes.

BPR

Business Process Re-engineering is a dramatic change initiative that contains five major components:

- Refocusing company values on customer needs;
- Re-designing core processes, often using technology to enable improvements;
- Re-organizing into cross-functional teams with end-to-end responsibility for a process;
- Re-thinking basic people/organizational issues;
- Improving business processes across the organization.

Management Tools and Techniques, Bain & Co 1998

BPR was based on the assumption that, because most large companies have been established for many years, they inherit an infrastructure that originated in a business environment that no longer exists. Processes were designed for different customers, competitors and a previous generation of technology. As a result of this legacy, such companies often find themselves at a disadvantage to new entrants who are free to design their processes and systems from scratch. In their famous book, *Re-engineering the Organization,* Michael Hammer and James Champy challenged CEOs to start from the premise that, if they were creating their companies today, what would they look like. They advocated re-engineering companies which they defined as the 'fundamental re-thinking and radical re-design of business processes to achieve dramatic improvements in critical, contemporary measures of performance such as cost, quality, service and speed.'

The concept was enthusiastically adopted by large companies in many industries across the world. The results have been mixed, but in some cases the competitive position of those using BPR-inspired change programmes have undoubtedly been transformed.

The need for business process re-engineering in insurance

In 1996 Peter Taylor, MD of a composite insurer, succinctly explained the need for re-engineering to the Insurance Institute of London in the following way:

'The insurance industry is mature with far too much capacity. Competition is intense from existing players, from new entrants and through the breakdown of barriers with other financial services. We are having to compete on a more international stage. We have all the challenges of new technology and above all there has been a revolution in customer expectations in terms of price, service and the transparency of our operations. As a result, our industry is rationalizing and it is predicted that many existing players will not survive. Those companies that wish to remain in business are having to renew themselves.'

Reasons for the failure of business process re-engineering programmes

Hammer and Champy, who introduced the BPR concept, have been among the first to admit that at least half of such programmes fail to deliver the promised benefits. The most common reasons cited include:

a) Re-engineering is often undertaken without any strategic context – there is little consistency in views as to how the re-engineered unit is going to fit into and operate within the company in the future;
b) Analysis is inadequate, so the programme begins without a proper understanding of the core processes;
c) The human factor is ignored – there is no thought given to the different skills and culture necessary to make the re-engineered unit work effectively;
d) Scope creeps and programme management lose sight of the original objectives.

The process of managing change

For most organizations, delivering change is a regular challenge. It may be new IT applications, major cost-reduction programmes or outsourcing activities – all of which need to be aligned because they involve finite resources and interrelated activities. To manage change effectively there must be clear accountabilities and processes set up to manage the change environment as a whole, and within it individual projects and programmes. You should be able to answer all of these questions with an unhesitating yes!

- Are all new projects prioritized against the business strategy before resources are allocated?
- Do all projects have agreed business cases?
- Are all projects assessed against a target operational model and target systems infrastructure?
- Are all projects and programmes run using a defined management process, eg Prince2 or SPM?

Kieran Flynn

Change, reorganization or transformation?

Management theory is full of jargon, and there is always a danger that, if something is given a new name, people will believe that it is a radically new or different concept. Change is a typical example.

At one time the usual word for what we now call a change programme was *reorganization.* In the 1980s, under the influence of leading academics such as Rosbeth Moss Kantor of Harvard, the expressions *change management* and *change programme* became more usual. This was probably because they implied initiatives that involved more than changing the structure of the organization.

After Hammer and Champy's work *re-engineering* was frequently applied to any change programme. In recent years, however, the term has become less popular because it sounds hard and mechanistic, and does not reflect the softer cultural and people issues necessary for successful change. The current fashionable term is *transformation.*

The reader can quite safely treat all these names as broadly interchangeable and include the application of a wide range of techniques and branded toolsets (TQM, BPR, Business Excellence, etc). Whatever you call it, and however you do it, the challenges are the same. As Neil Russell-Jones says in his extremely useful *Managing Change Pocketbook:*

> 'It is very difficult, the further you go the harder it becomes, and the less the change has in common with the organization's culture, the less likely you are to succeed.'

> **The impact of an organization's 'culture' to an insurer**
>
> 'Strategic Change needs to take into account *what is possible* in terms of change in the organization, *rather than what is theoretically desirable.*'
>
> Richard Lynch, *Corporate Strategy*

17.3 Outsourcing

Outsourcing is an effective tool for a company to reduce processing and fixed costs and better leverage investment in business support functions. Activities traditionally handled by internal staff are managed by an external service provider while regulatory responsibility remains with the insurer. Control is established through detailed contracts and service level agreements (SLAs) which are closely monitored.

> **The value of outsourcing to an insurer**
>
> To compete successfully, insurers need to constantly improve their efficiency and their effectiveness. Most insurers would find it impossible to invest enough management time, capital and the relevant expertise to improve all aspects of their business simultaneously. The solution has been to outsource 'non-core' activities such as the support for systems infrastructure to partner organizations. Consequently there is an increasing number of specialist outsourcing services firms operating in the financial services industry. Outsourcing taken to its logical conclusion has seen the arrival of the virtual insurer, for whom supplier management has become the core skill.
>
> Kieran Flynn

Any activity outside the core business could be outsourced. IS, Facilities Management and the routine processing for Finance are particularly common. Increasingly functions such as call centres, or routine policy/claims processing are being considered, as value chain analysis challenges companies to assess their strengths and core competencies and focus their energies on those where they have a competitive advantage.

The introduction of Internet technology has helped to overcome the traditional limitations of time and distance, so enabling companies to select low labour cost locations for outsourcing such as Eastern Europe, India, China and Mexico.

Specific advantages of outsourcing include:

- freeing up internal management and resources to focus on core capabilities
- sharing risks with a partner
- gaining access to superior external capabilities
- changing fixed overhead costs to volume-related costs
- service provider is motivated as a profit centre.

The main risks of insurance outsourcing are based around confidentiality, security and above all control. In the UK, the regulator has made it clear that, even if an approved person outsources an activity, he or she will retain personal responsibility for the regulatory compliance of that activity.

The key factors influencing successful outsourcing are:

- the company having clear objectives
- selecting the right service provider who is aligned with the company's objectives and culture
- a robust contract with a workable service level agreement (SLA)
- active senior executive support and involvement
- continuous management of the relationship
- both parties feeling that they benefit from the arrangement
- results being measurable and comparable against pre-established standards
- retention of key personnel by the outsourcing operation.

The potential dangers of outsourcing

'It is false economy to simply move costs to another place on the balance sheet. You also lose expertise and down-skill your workforce by outsourcing. Once that expertise is gone you can't get it back.'

Roy Hebburn, Allianz Cornhill, *Post Magazine*, 8 November 2001

'Although outsourcing can bring significant benefits to insurers and their customers, there is a risk that insurers may have reduced control of the outsourced function.'

FSA Consultation Paper 140, July 2002

17.3.1 Shared service organization (SSO)

A shared service organization is an alternative to outsourcing in order to reduce costs and improve a company's processing and service functions. An internal centre is created to provide common processing services to all/the majority of the company's own business units, and possibly also to those of external companies (insourcing). In the latter case the SSO effectively becomes a separate legal entity.

The main advantages of an SSO are:

- releasing business management to focus on core activities
- achieving cost reductions via economies of scale
- keeping control of all processes within the company
- applying best practice across the company
- generating cash flow from external companies.

The main risks of an SSO could be a lack of credibility with internal customers, inability to compete with specialist service providers and insufficient investment and support. In addition, it may be very difficult for an SSO to make the cultural transition necessary to supply external companies. Successful SSOs often apply the tools and characteristics of an outsourced service provider, eg formal service level agreements.

As with outsourcing, the location of an SSO can be offshore, but this potentially increases the management challenges involved if expertise in managing offshore processing units is not currently possessed by the company.

The advantages/disadvantages of shared service organizations

Many organizations containing several businesses have moulded their support functions (IT, finance, HR, procurement) into shared service organizations (SSOs) with advantages seen as standard processes and lower costs, as well as the opportunity to move to outsourcing as a next step. It is essential, however, that the objectives of such SSOs are closely aligned with the strategic priorities of the businesses they support. For instance if the performance management process of the SSO is not geared to rewarding the behaviours required to deliver business targets of the businesses it supports, the fact that the process itself is clearly defined, well executed and low cost will be of little benefit to the business overall.

Kieran Flynn

17.4 Risk management and insurance operations

17.4.1 Introduction

Top 10 risks to companies

In a survey of commercial enterprises across many industries in 2000, the multinational broker Aon identified the following as the most important risks as perceived by company management:

1. Loss of reputation
2. Failure to change
3. Business interruption
4. Product liability
5. Computer crime
6. General liability
7. Physical damage
8. Employee recruitment/retention
9. D & O liabilities
10. Employee accident

Risk management is the name given to the broad group of disciplines by which risks are analysed and handled by businesses. A company needs to consider the various pure risks that it faces, eg:

- health and safety
- natural disasters
- fire
- political and social risks
- liability
- crime
- business interruption

and decide what needs to be done about them. A similar approach can also be taken with speculative risks such as trading risks. An inadequate response to any of these risks could result in serious damage to the viability of the company.

Risk management is especially important to an insurer because it must not only manage its own corporate and operational risks, but must also be actively concerned and involved with the risk management processes of its customers.

Traditionally, the management of risk within business has been rather fragmented and, in many cases, treated almost as an add-on to the business. The exception was in the high-hazard industries, such as chemicals, and in larger, more progressive, organizations where companies have employed professional risk managers to coordinate the activities.

The need for risk management to become a more integrated part of the business has been emphasized in the UK Government sponsored Turnbull Report on internal controls and risk management, published in 1999. This made it clear that it is the responsibility of the board to determine its policy towards risk and ensure that line management implements it. In the UK Turnbull and the various high-profile company failures in recent years has strongly influenced the regulators and the FSA's draft *Prudential Source Book* contains detailed requirements for authorized firms to have structured risk management processes in place from 2004. The key elements of the requirements follow.

UK Financial Services Authority risk management requirements

i) High-level risk management

- Clarity of roles for all board members and senior executives.
- A structured process to identify and analyse the impact of risks, including new/emerging risks.
- A formal process to assess the appropriateness and adequacy of management actions in place/planned to manage or reduce the identified risks.
- A formal review of risks and risk management activity by the board, or a sub-committee thereof, on a regular basis.
- Formal processes to manage underwriting, market, credit and other 'trading' risks.

ii) Operational risk management

In addition to formal high-level risk management structures, there is also a requirement for a formal operational risk management process to be in place, to monitor, manage and report on the risks encountered in the day-to-day operational activities of the insurer. These include both normal, day-to-day risks, which can be managed by standard processes and procedures, as well as more complex risks that are not as susceptible to proceduralized controls. Such complex risks include external events, eg:

- changes in the economic environment (interest rates, stock market, etc);
- changes in law or regulation;
- catastrophe incidents (earthquakes, floods, terrorism);
- competitor activity; and so on

and also internal issues, eg:

- lack of capabilities in core areas such as underwriting, claims management, change management, etc;
- outsourcing of key elements of the business, (such as IT).

Financial Services Authority, Draft Prudential Source Book

17.4.2 The risk management process

> 'Risk management is key to the running of all insurers ... and should be integral to the day-to-day operation of the business.'
>
> FSA Consultation Paper 140, July 2002

The generic risk management process is shown in Figure 17.3.

Figure 17.3

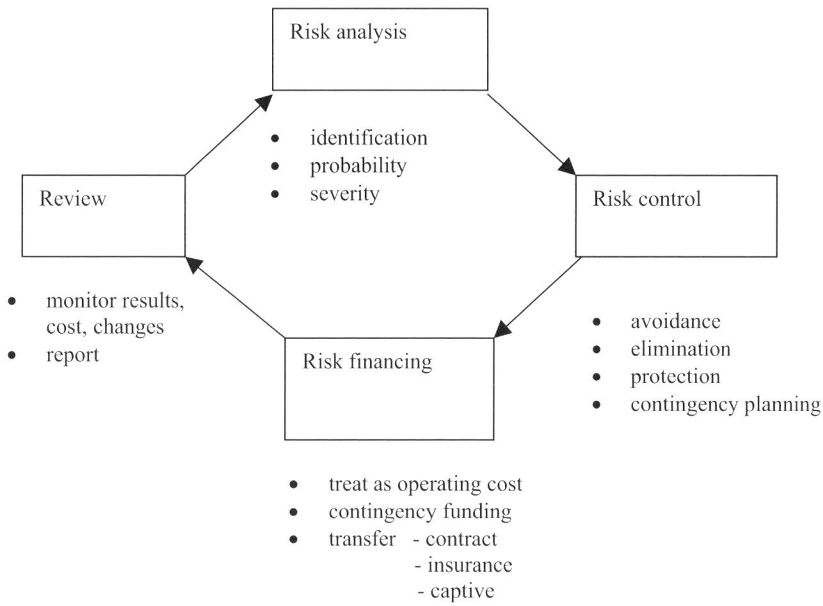

a) Risk analysis

The process starts with the **identification** of risks using check lists, flow charts, surveys and audits, and then making some estimate of the **probability** of an event occurring and its **severity**. Consideration then needs to be given to its acceptability, its priority and who should be responsible for its management.

Decisions then need to be made as to how identified risks should be handled, the two main stages of this being risk control and risk financing.

b) Risk control

The company must ask itself, can the risk be **avoided** or **eliminated** in some way? Could **protective measures** be taken to reduce the probability or severity of the event, eg fire protection, improved security, guarding of machinery? **Contingency planning** should also take place to minimize the impact on the business should the event occur. For example, alternative suppliers, duplicate records, recovery procedures must be organized.

It is perhaps because of the wide range of skills necessary to control all the risks faced by a company that risk management has tended to be fragmented.

Once the risks have been controlled as far as is reasonably practicable, the company must decide how the consequences of those risks should be financed.

c) Risk financing

The simplest way of financing a loss is by treating it as an **operating cost**. In fact, most minor risks and most speculative risks are handled in this way. It has the advantage that, if the event does not occur, no money has been expended. Obviously, if the event does occur it has an immediate impact on the bottom-line results.

The next level of sophistication is to have a **contingency fund** to cover the loss. Theoretically, this should not be so cost-effective as insurance.

Alternatively, the company may decide to **transfer** the cost of the risk away from the day-to-day business. This could be done by **contract**, eg disclaimers or contract terms. Such an approach is excellent if it works, but unfortunately it is extremely difficult to transfer all of a risk and any contract is only as good as the financial resources of the other party.

By far the most common risk transfer mechanism is **insurance**, although it is generally available only for pure risks. As mentioned previously, large companies may decide to set up their own insurance company or **captive** to carry their risks. In this case, risks are transferred away from the business but the financial consequences are retained by the holding company through their ownership of the captive.

d) Review

The final stage of the risk management process is to monitor the adequacy and effectiveness of risk management activity, the incidence of risk events (including near misses), costs and changes in the risk environment, and report back to the board. The cycle then begins again.

Risk management will generally be operated at two levels:

- **corporate and complex risks:** looking at the major risks and issues that challenge the very existence/ viability of the entire company, and how these are identified assessed and managed at the highest level, and
- **day-to-day operating and procedural risks:** looking at the more routine risks encountered in the day to day operations conducted by the business, where controls tend to be proceduralized.

In practice, because of the different level and nature of these risks and the potentially different way they need to be managed, there may need to be two separate but linked processes to effectively manage all risks facing the business.

By the very nature of an insurer accepting others' risks as part of its normal trading activity, and the influence of many external factors on the likely out-turn of its business, the analysis and assessment of all risks within an insurance operation can be extremely complex.

17.5 Business ethics

> 'Not all commercial organizations believe that they have a role beyond their own business; they take the view that society is perfectly capable of looking after itself, and the prime responsibility of the enterprise is to care for its shareholders. There are other companies who take the view that it is in the long-term benefit of both the company and its shareholders to play a role in society beyond the minimum described by law. Sponsorship, welfare provisions, strong ethical beliefs and standards may all follow on from this view.'
>
> Richard Lynch, *Corporate Strategy*

17.5.1 Introduction

Ethics is the branch of philosophy concerned with moral judgments: right and wrong, good and bad. It has exercised some of the greatest secular and religious minds over the millennia. In this book all we are able to do is to explore a few of the ways in which this huge and complex subject affects an insurance operation.

> **Can ethics be taught?**
>
> 'Can ethics be taught? Unethical conduct continues despite the fact that over 500 Business Ethics courses are currently taught on American campuses.'
>
> John Naisbitt, Harvard University

17.5.2 The low public opinion of insurance

Big business is often identified by the public at large as being self-seeking and even dishonest. This position has been reinforced by the media, with their focus primarily on the bad, and also by the many, high-profile, corporate scandals in recent years.

Insurance itself is particularly low in the public esteem, probably due to the following:

- It is an intangible, usually unwilling purchase, that appears to be expensive with little immediate benefit.
- Many buyers do not understand the nature of an insurance contract and are extremely angry when they find they are not covered in the event of a claim.
- It is not a transparent industry, and many people are highly suspicious of commissions paid to intermediaries.

Despite this apparent view, as seen from the newspapers and comments from the Government, regulators, etc, customer surveys by insurers generally show high levels of trust and customer satisfaction. Unfortunately, it is the few bad news stories that make the newspapers, not the 99.99% of things that go right. This image has not been helped by the industry as a whole, which has not sought to communicate its 'value to society' in a positive way over the years, or engage positively in addressing important issues, such as red-lining (avoiding risks in vulnerable areas, eg flood plains, and so depriving whole communities of cover), liability, etc, in an open and constructive way with Government, etc.

This image has also been compounded by the behaviour of some insurers who have knowingly miss-sold products, quibbled over small print when paying claims, or engaged in red-lining. It has not been helped by the tone of much industry advertising, which implies that competitors are overcharging and are unwilling to pay claims.

In reality, business in general is no more moral or immoral than any other section of society. It has a normal spectrum of people working in it. Moreover, business is of fundamental value to society because it creates:

- the goods and services people need to live their lives
- the wealth which the caring professions or the State 'gives away'.

Insurance is of special value because it provides positive assistance in difficult times and gives peace of mind.

17.5.3 Setting an ethical framework

Against this background, it is clear that companies should be setting down a common ethical framework within which decisions can be made. This may sound fairly straightforward but it is not at all easy in a modern company. A typical insurance operation may transact business in many countries, have a number of business partners, and thousands of employees drawn from a wide range of cultures. Ethical differences across cultures, and even within cultures, are real and need to be thought through if everyone involved with the company is to behave in the same way when faced with decisions. Nevertheless, the best companies are able to achieve an acceptable compromise.

a) Corporate ethics

One way of approaching this is to use value statements or charters which explain the company's relationship with each of the stakeholder groups: shareholders, customers, employees, society, etc.

The principle behind this is valid in almost every traditional system of ethics, that an organization's wealth is something that has to be looked after as a trustee and should not be misused. The management are the trustees of the company's assets and it is their duty to balance the use of resources between the conflicting demands of the stakeholders, as discussed in Chapter 5. When management lose sight of this basic principle companies can get themselves into serious problems. Focusing on the needs of one stakeholder or, worse still, the management themselves, at the expense of the others, is the root cause of most corporate scandals – Maxwell, Fire, Auto & Marine, Enron and the rest. An example of a corporate charter used by one major insurer is shown below.

Case study – Corporate charter

1. **Shareholders** (institutional and other): In return for their investment we will:
   - Outperform our peer group and provide a well above-average dividend growth;
   - Protect the interests of long-term shareholders;
   - Communicate effectively with shareholders to discover and rapidly satisfy their needs;
   - Not diversify beyond our core competences.
2. **Customers**: In return for their premiums and utmost good faith we will:
   - Provide quality, value for money products which meet their needs;
   - Maintain competitive service standards;
   - Communicate with them in an adult-to-adult manner in plain language;
   - Conduct our business with fairness and integrity;
   - Provide effective procedures to resolve complaints and disputes.

3. **Intermediaries:** In return for the introduction of new business and effective customer management we will:
    - Pay a fair rate of commission;
    - Communicate effectively with intermediaries to identify their needs and meet their reasonable expectations;
    - Maintain competitive service standards;
    - Provide effective procedures to resolve complaints and disputes.
4. **Employees:** In return for their service and professional skills we will:
    - Provide training and job opportunities which seek to match individual career aspirations with abilities, skills and business requirements;
    - Fairly reward individuals with regard to local salary practice, ensuring that such rewards recognize individual performance;
    - Ensure equality of opportunity for all, regardless of sex, race, colour, nationality, religious belief, or political opinion;
    - Provide working conditions that are safe, healthy and conducive to high standards of work;
    - Encourage staff at all levels to take personal responsibility for their own self-development while providing support and encouragement.
5. **Communities and environment:** We will:
    - Make a fitting contribution to the communities in which we operate;
    - Discharge our social responsibility through a community investment programme, creating a culture of caring and community service by our employees and providing a focus outside work;
    - Conduct our business according to environmentally sound principles.
6. **Governments and regulators:** In each territory in which we operate we will:
    - Conduct our business within the legal framework;
    - Deal with regulatory authorities in an open and cooperative manner;
    - Communicate openly on issues of importance to our business;
    - Support bodies that promote professional standards in our industry.

It is also becoming increasingly common, under pressure from government and environmental pressure groups, for companies to research the environmental impact of their activities and express their findings and relevant policies, actions, etc in an **environmental report**, which is made available to any interested party. This might include issues such as:

- Energy usage and conservation
- Water usage and conservation
- Pollution and pollution management
- Greenhouse gases produced and targets for reduction
- Recycling
- Sourcing of environmentally sound supplies.

From the environmental reports published by insurance operations it is clear that the industry is directly affected by such issues, but the industry's greatest opportunity to improve the environment may be indirectly, as an underwriter, claims manager and as an investor. Clearly, underwriters cannot be environmental policemen, but they can promote risk-reducing behaviours in their customers. Claims managers can actively seek to reduce the impact of environmentally-damaging incidents, promote recycling of damaged articles and support environmentally friendly repair/replacement solutions. As major investors, insurers can establish their own 'ethical investment' policy and choose to invest in companies that take their environmental responsibilities seriously.

Environmental issues

'We consider our environmental impacts to fall into three main categories: operational (waste, energy, etc), insurance and investment related. For insurance and investment activities, it is our potential to influence the behaviour of others that is significant.'

Environmental Report 2000-2001
UK Insurance Company

b) Individual ethics

Standards of behaviour may be set by the operation for individual employees. The reason for this was succinctly put by the Institute of Business Ethics (IBE) in its contribution to a UK Government investigation into standards in public life.

> **Code of business ethics**
>
> At a time when it is no longer possible to rely on the home, school or church to have taught the ability to make a moral judgment, then it is in the company's interest to introduce a code of business ethics as a guide to best behaviour. Such a code:
>
> - Tells employees what is expected of them;
> - Tells employees what standard to expect from their employers;
> - Protects newcomers from exploitation;
> - Helps to preserve the reputation of the company.
>
> IBE

Such codes tend to be illustrative rather than prescriptive, should be made part of the contract of employment, and should be regularly updated. Typical subjects covered include:

- Financial inducements
- Conflicts of interest
- Appropriate behaviour in the workplace (eg guidance on bullying, discrimination, inappropriate language, appearance, etc)
- Insider dealing
- Fraud
- Pornography/inappropriate use of the Internet.

It may also deal with procedures for 'whistleblowing' (ie allowing employees to report breaches without fear of reprisal).

Select bibliography

G Dickson, *Risk Analysis,* Inst. Risk Management, Witherby & Sons 1991.

Croner's Management of Business Risk, Croner, CCH Group 2003, Chapter 3.

B Poutney (Ed), *Handbook of Risk Management,* Kluwer 1999.

T Reischl, *Ethics and Customer Service,* The National Underwriter Co 1999.

N Baglini, *Ethical Behaviour, Corporate Culture and Financial Services,* Geneva Papers on Risk and Insurance, Vol 16, No 3, 2001.

T Johns, S Connock, *Ethical Leadership, Institute of Personnel & Development* 1995.

S Webley, *Applying Codes of Business Ethics – A Report on Best Practice,* Institute of Business Ethics 1995.

First Report of the Committee on Standards in Public Life, Chairman, Lord Nolan HMSO, London 1995.

L Drennan, M Beck, *Managing E-Risk: Between Opportunity and Certainty,* Insurance Trends, ABI Jan 2003.

D Fanning, *E Commerce – Driven by Quality*, CII Journal, March 2001.

H Jones, *Outsourcing: Have insurers learned when the time is right to simply let go?,* CII Journal Nov 2001.

E Clemans, M Thatcher, B Webber, *Impact of* e *Commerce and Enhanced Information Endowments on Financial Services :A Quantitative Analysis of Transparency, Differential Pricing and Disintermediation,* Journal of Financial Services Research, Vol 22, No 1/2 2002.

M Foot, *Operational risk management for financial institutions,* Journal of Financial Regulation and Compliance, Vol 10, No 4, Nov 2002.

M Hammer, J Champy, *Re-engineering the corporation,* Nicholas Brearly 1993.

Richard Lynch, *Corporate Strategy,* Pitman 1997, Chapter 21.

N Russell-Jones, *Change Management Pocketbook,* Management Pocketbooks 1995.

T Grundy, *Managing Strategic Change*, Kogan Page 1993.

V Grover, M Manuj, *Business Process Re-engineering – A Tutorial on the Concept,* Evolution, Method, Technology and Application, Journal of Operations Management, Aug 1997.

Eighteen

Assessing the profitability and management effectiveness of an insurance operation

Objectives

On completion of this chapter, and wider personal research, the reader should be able to:

- understand and apply methods that can be used to assess the performance of an insurance operation;
- understand how comparisons can be made with similar operations;
- explain and apply key metrics used in the industry;
- appreciate some of the lessons of the past in respect of insurance operation performance and failure.

18.1 Profitability

What is profit? In very basic terms profit can be defined as:

Revenue earned – costs incurred = Profit

However, for insurance business the components of this apparently very simple equation are more than normally complicated. Even in very simple terms, the components of each element for the overall insurance operation potentially consist of the following:

Revenue earned

Gross premium earned: premiums written in the period proportioned between the current period and future periods, plus that premium written in earlier periods that relates to the current period

plus

Investment income earned (dividends, interest, etc plus capital gains) on premium and claims reserves

plus

Investment income earned on 'capital'

Less

Costs incurred

Claims incurred on premiums earned in the period, net of reinsurance recoveries

plus

Changes to claims reserves for claims relating to premiums earned in earlier periods, net of reinsurance recoveries.

plus

Commission/acquisition costs relating to written premiums

plus

Reinsurance outwards premiums relating to premiums earned in the period

plus

Administration costs incurred (including investment management costs)

plus

Costs of capital (eg bank and loan interest, etc)

This calculation produces the overall profit for the entire operation. To understand individual product line profitability there are further complications concerned with allocating costs, capital, investment income, etc between products, which will be discussed later in this chapter.

18.2 Issues to be addressed when assessing the performance of an insurance operation

18.2.1 Written v Earned

If the operation has a financial year the same as the calendar year (ie from 1 January to 31 December) and writes 12-month insurance contracts, and if a policy is written (ie comes into force/the premium is due) on 1 January, then all that premium will be earned in the financial year.

However, for any contract written on any other date in the year, some proportion of the premium will relate to a future financial period, eg:

Contract starts	Earned in current year	Following year
1 April	75%	25%
1 July	50%	50%
1 October	25%	75%

12-month contract, financial period = calendar year

But also the current financial period will *earn* those elements of premiums *written* in prior periods that relate to the current period (see Figure 18.1).

Figure 18.1

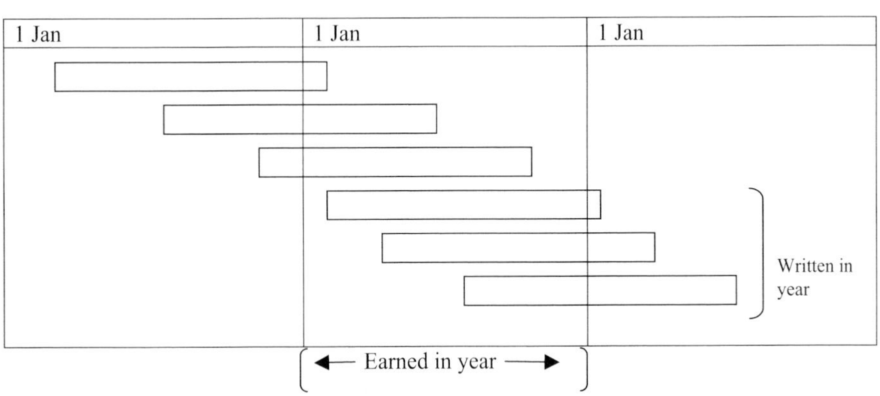

These calculations become more complicated if contracts covering more than one year are written.

The 'unearned' portion of premiums written is carried forward on the balance sheet (unearned premiums) to the period when they are earned.

18.2.2 Gross v Net

Where the operation utilizes reinsurance outwards to transfer elements of the risk accepted, both premiums and claims can be shown as 'gross' – the total written, earned or incurred before transfer of the reinsurers' share, or 'net' – the total written, earned or incurred reduced by the amounts due to/from reinsurers.

Unless there is doubt over the recoverability from reinsurers, accounting and performance measurement is normally based on net figures, the income/cost retained by the organization.

18.2.3 Expense allocation

Typically, in an insurance organization, costs will be incurred in a range of areas:

Potentially recordable by product/channel

- Marketing/distribution
- Risk acceptance/front-line underwriting
- Commission
- Background processing of policy data (premium collection, policy amendments, etc)
- Claims processing and management
- Technical underwriting and pricing

Services supporting the entire insurance activities

- HR
- Finance/tax
- Banking/treasury
- Compliance/legal/audit
- IT
- Facilities/property services
- Executive management

Other

- Investment management
- Capital (loan & bank interest, etc)

To determine the overall profitability of an operation is not that complex because, once adjusted for earned/unearned elements, all costs can be allocated against net earned premiums and net incurred claims.

However, if you wish to assess profitability at product or segment level within an operation you need to determine which expenses to allocate to the different segments, and how to allocate them between segments.

Segmental reporting is common for regulatory returns, market/analyst presentations and for internal assessment of relative performance. However, to enable effective comparisons, the allocation basis has to be consistent.

It is common for some companies, when reporting segmental results (underwriting profit, COR, etc by major product line), to not allocate certain corporate costs to the segments, but hold these separately. In some cases this can be several hundred million pounds not allocated. Comparisons with companies that allocate all costs down to segment level then become much more complex.

The same problem arises with investment income,

- should it all be allocated to segment level? If so,
- how between segments? (based on capital allocated + claims reserves – segmental working capital?) – but on what basis is working capital allocated between segments?
- but what about investment income on any excess capital held by the company?

Taking a simple example of two companies that write just Motor and Home accounts but differ in the way they allocate costs to the segments for reporting:

Company A (only partly allocated)

	Motor	**Home**	**Corporate expenses**	**Total**
Premiums earned	100	200	–	300
Claims incurred	(70)	(120)	–	(190)
Expenses	(30)	(40)	(50)	(120)
U/W result	–	40		
Net investment income	15	10	5	30
Insurance result	15	50	(45)	20
COR	100%	80%		

Company B (fully allocated)

	Motor	Home	Corporate	Total
Premiums earned	100	200		300
Claims incurred	(70)	(120)		190
Expenses	(40)	(80)		120
U/W Result	(10)	–		(10)
Net Investment Income	15	15		30
Insurance Result	5	15		20
COR	110%	100%		

Which is the better managed company? Which has the better Motor or Home account results? Could this change depending on whether you look at underwriting result or insurance result?

Regulatory returns will frequently establish a certain degree of commonality and consistency, but differences in what is allocated and how it is allocated will still remain.

And is a low expense ratio automatically good?

A low expense ratio implies that the insurance operation is efficient in the way that it processes business. But in an area such as underwriting, where the primary objective is to assess and price the risk, and only accept appropriate risks at an appropriate price, pure efficiency is not the only driver.

By spending a bit more time/cost on underwriting, risk selection, risk control surveys, etc in non-commodity lines, it should be possible to improve the quality of the book/reduce the subsequent claims cost by a far greater amount than the cost of the additional underwriting activity at risk acceptance.

For commodity lines there is usually little opportunity to influence individual cases in a similar way; the onus therefore falls on the appropriateness of the risk-assessment and pricing models built into the IT systems used for taking on such business.

On its own, therefore, the expense ratio is not the most useful of measures, and as can be seen in the example above, can be influenced heavily at product level by cost allocation differences.

18.2.4 Investment income/total investment return

The total investment return of an insurance operation comprises both investment income (interest, dividends, rents, etc received) plus any capital gains or losses on the investment portfolio. Exactly how this total return is credited to the insurer's results can vary widely between individual operations and between different accounting regimes. Issues that arise regarding investment returns include:

- It has been the accounting practice in certain countries to retain all investments at 'cost' in the balance sheet until the investment is disposed of, and only then take the gain or loss on disposal through revenue (although the increasing adoption of international accounting standards mean that this is becoming less common). This means that, if investments are held for long periods, an insurer could have large, 'hidden' gains on its investment portfolio or, more worryingly, and more possible given the poor stock market performance in the late 1990s and early 2000s, could have large, hidden losses. Regulators and rating agencies will require some assessment and reporting of any such matters, but this information may not be available publicly.
- The allocation of investment returns, both income and capital, and how such returns are disclosed in the operation's figures can vary tremendously depending on the allocation bases used, the accounting policies adopted by the insurer (which can be different between published/statutory data and internal data/management information), and the generally accepted accounting principles applied.
- Different companies will, almost certainly, apply different criteria/bases for allocating returns to and between different classes of business, and retaining a proportion relating to the investment return on the operation's capital 'centrally' (ie not allocating certain elements).
- Some companies may allocate the total investment return, others only the investment income, either taking the capital return separately through the revenue account centrally, or sometimes taking it straight to capital without it passing through the revenue account.
- Some companies, in an attempt to smooth investment returns over time, calculate a 'long-term investment return' figure based on average returns for different types of investment over a number (eg 5-10) years, which they then allocate to the business classes. They then have to adjust for any variation between this theoretical return and that actually achieved in the year through an adjusting entry, either in the central revenue account, or directly against capital. In times of volatile markets this adjusting entry can be very large, meaning that there is a significant discrepancy between actual investment returns and that credited to the individual class of business revenue accounts.

18.2.5 Movements on claims reserves brought forward

In addition to claims incurred in the financial period, the company will also be impacted by any adjustments to the claims reserves brought forward at the start of the year.

Claims reserves can often be greater than total premium earned, particularly where liability/long-tail business is written. As a result, any adjustments to existing reserves can have a significant effect on current year profitability.

Most regulators would expect that claims reserves are established prudently, with the expectation that, if anything, they will run off with a small surplus (releasing a modest profit on final settlement and closure) across the book. However, claims reserving is not an exact science and adjustments to reserves are required for:

- Changes to average claims costs
- Claims moving from average to actual reserves as more information is obtained
- IBNR estimates at the previous period end being replaced by actual data
- Changes in the external environment (eg economy, statute, case law, consumer activity) that require existing reserves to be re-assessed because the currently expected out-turn is now different from that previously anticipated.

18.2.6 Large, one-off or other unusual events

Insurance, by its nature, is there to cover both 'normal' accidents/incidents/etc that lead to claims and which affect relatively few policyholders at a time, plus very large or abnormal events which affect very many people, eg major storms, earthquakes, terrorist incidents such as September 11.

Very large/abnormal events occur relatively infrequently, and certainly not every year, and are difficult if not impossible to predict accurately in advance in terms of either frequency or impact. 'Normal' events, on the other hand, occur on a regular basis and are reasonably predictable within an expected range of frequency and impact.

In trying to assess the profitability of insurance operations, the challenge is – should you look at the results with large/abnormal events recorded in the year they occur, or should they be 'smoothed' in some way, and spread over a number of years?

Logic says, that if the pricing of the business properly takes into account these large events, then every premium includes a provision for such claims when they occur, and thus reserves should be set up from these premium elements (called equalization or catastrophe reserves – see Chapter 15) which accumulate over time until a large/abnormal event occurs. The costs of the event are then (hopefully) largely covered by the accumulated reserves (see Figure 18.2).

Figure 18.2

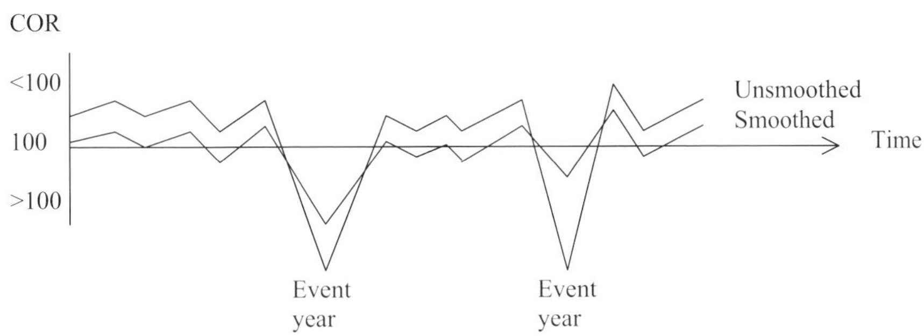

Unsmoothed = claims charged to the year of incidence, no catastrophe reserves held.

Smoothed = catastrophe reserves built up in non-event years and depleted when events occur.

Matters to note

- Given the uncertainty over frequency and impact of large/abnormal events there is no certainty that equalization reserves established over time will be sufficient to meet the full extent of any major event.
- The tax authorities in some countries allow Equalization Reserves to be established as a charge against taxable profits – normally general reserves of this nature are not allowable against tax.

18.2.7 The impact of a premium increase

How long does it take to fully earn an across-the-board price rise in premiums?

As an example, using a simplified model of 12-month contracts renewing evenly across the year on the first of the month only, with a price rise implemented 1 January, we have something like the model shown in Figure 18.3.

In this model only approx. 56% of the price rise flows through to the bottom line in the first 12 months after the increase. Thus, the full extent of any price rise will not be earned until the second full year after it is implemented.

Figure 18.3

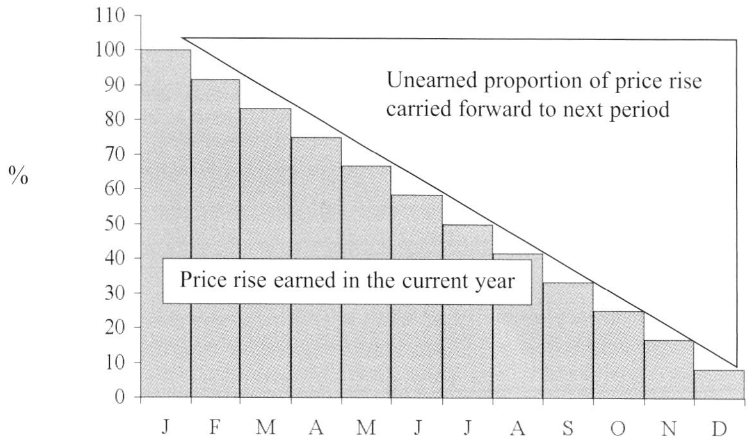

18.2.8 The impact of 'going for growth'

In P+C insurance it is relatively easy to acquire new business if you are prepared to quote a lower price than the rest of the market. The question is: What impact will this have on profitability?

In commodity lines (eg Home and Motor), where there are millions of similar risks, the likelihood of a normal claim occurring and its cost are reasonably predictable if you have sufficient data (although major claims events (storm, flood) are less predictable) and a company can, to some extent, model the impact of price adjustments, both upwards and downwards, on profitability.

However, once you move away from commodity lines you tend to encounter a noticeably longer time-lag effect between the writing of the premium and the development of the associated claims – an hysteresis effect (see Figure 18.4).

Figure 18.4

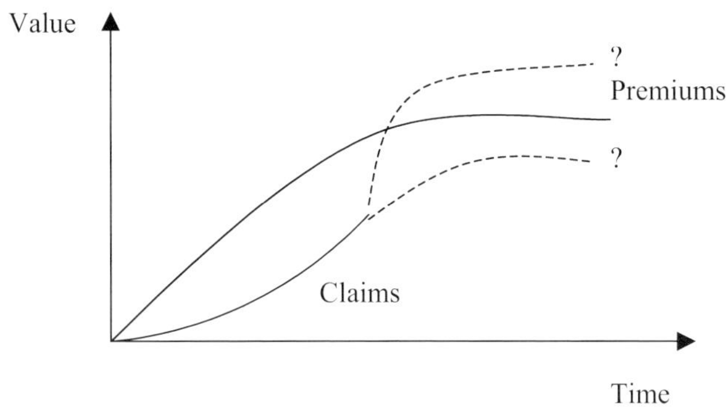

This delay in claims development is particularly noticeable in new areas of insurance because of two factors:

- claims do not tend to be notified within the first few months of a new policy being written (if they were, the underwriter might reject them as pre-existing at the date of the contract).
- the exact quantum of the claim frequently takes some time (sometimes years) to finalize. In new areas of activity this may result in underestimating the eventual cost in the early stages and subsequently having to increase the loss reserves as more information is acquired over time.

If adding new business in a known area of insurance, allowances can be made for this period of apparent 'super profitability' through IBNR reserving, etc.

However, when going for growth in new areas it may not be possible to forecast exactly how and when claims will stabilize and therefore what the long-term profitability of the account is likely to be.

The insurance market is littered with examples of companies entering new product areas, writing significant volumes of business, and appearing to make super profits in the first few years, and then making very substantial losses (in some cases many times the value of the premium written) as the hysteresis unwinds (see Figure 18.5).

Figure 18.5

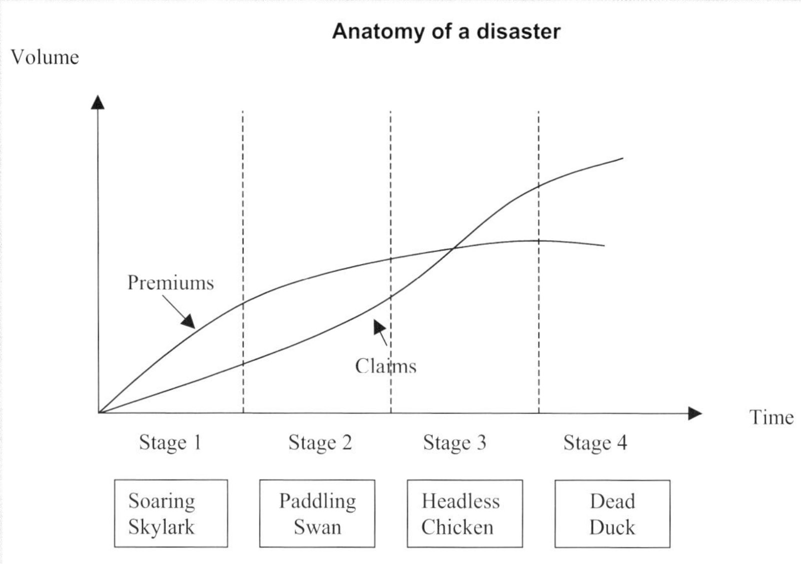

This scenario applies to either an entire company or just a business segment of a larger entity.

Stage 1

- Management either, enter a completely new area or, aggressively attack an area, that they believe is overpriced by the competition, and where they have not had a significant presence previously.
- Year-on-year compound growth exceeding 20% is achieved in premiums, as business is stripped away from the competition.
- The hysteresis effect on claims means that claims growth lags premium growth, with very high levels of premium growth the gap between the two lines grows, appearing to demonstrate super profitability.
- Management basks in glory at the success it has achieved.

Stage 2

- As the premium growth rate starts to fade, as inevitably it must, the claims curve heads towards the premium line, as claims come through on previously written business.
- Management will start to look at ways to reinvigorate premium growth, through diversification, acquisition, further price reductions, or other means. Only by maintaining high premium growth can it stay ahead of the hysteresis curve.

- At this point existing management might seek to sell the business (based on past super profits), or collect its management incentives and move on before things get worse.

Stage 3

- The movement of the claims line can no longer be ignored and is becoming apparent to outsiders.
- Management may become pressurized to under-reserve or in some other way seek to minimize the trend in claims.
- Management may seek 'growth at any cost', or take other high-risk actions.

Stage 4

- Claims growth can no longer be denied or hidden, it now becomes an issue of crisis management.
- Reserves have to be set up for the full value of claims on existing business. As a result, the solvency/viability of the business is called into question. Regulators may become involved.
- Additional capital to fund the emerging losses is required.
- All policies must be re-priced on renewal at an acceptable level to cover expected claims, or not renewed. Policy count drops, though total premiums may not.
- The management that initiated the growth plan would no longer be involved in running the business.

The key to long-term success remains one of fully understanding the risk being transferred (and therefore how claims will develop in terms of both time and cost). If you do not understand this you risk making some very expensive mistakes.

Case study – The Independent collapse 2001

The Independent was the investment analyst's favourite P+C insurer in the 1990s. With its strategy of selective underwriting, special deals with brokers and low premiums it grew rapidly to take a significant share of the liability market and show high profitability. Inevitably claims caught up and the company ceased trading in 2001. Tony Lancaster, the CEO of Groupama, observed at that year's CII conference: 'The Independent failed because it did not get the basics right. Growing when they should have been slowing, reserving inadequately against exposures they were writing – while management it its broadest meaning – seemed to have got it very wrong.'

Case study – The Vehicle & General crash

The V & G story is a classic example of what can happen when a company grows faster than the managerial competence of its directors. The company was set up in 1961 to write motor business at a time when the UK market was still dominated by tariff underwriters. The business model was both novel and simple:

- High rate of no claims discounts to attract accident-free drivers
- High basic premiums to discourage bad-risk drivers
- Selective underwriting to exclude certain categories of risk
- A policy of fair and speedy settlement of claims together with a strict system of checking garages.

The directors aimed for rapid growth and within a few years they had captured 10% of the UK motor market.

The success of V & G prompted its competitors to react strongly. The motor tariff was abandoned, the business model copied and V & G was put under immense pressure to maintain its performance. As a result, serious mistakes were made, including:

- Inadequate outstanding claims reserves and unexpired risks provision at a time of high inflation
- A continued refusal to increase premiums to sufficient levels because the directors did not believe the underwriting results
- A disorganized computer department
- Ill-judged acquisitions in an attempt to diversify and grow. It eventually had interests in life, commercial insurance, brokers and travel agents, and in total had 41 subsidiary companies.

V & G's collapse was even more rapid than its growth. It was declared insolvent in 1971 and its millions of customers were taken over by its competitors.

18.2.9 Short term v long-term (full cycle) management

Because of the significant levels of judgment involved in determining key values, particularly in the area of claim reserving, it is possible to manipulate any one period's reported results by slight variations in reserving, etc. Continuous under-reserving will eventually require putting right, but can sometimes be sustained for a number of years.

Ideally, an insurance company should be performance-managed across the entire insurance cycle, including the impact of one-off/large events which are part of the normal claims environment. In this way management should be judged on long-term profitability, shareholder return and effectiveness of management in good times as well as bad. However, insurance companies can end up being run on a short-term view (single year/next 2-3 years basis). This can be either in response to market pressures (analysts, etc) to deliver better results, or as a result of short-term management incentivization.

Where an insurance operation is being managed on a short-term basis, there is a significantly greater risk regarding long-term performance and the adequacy of claims reserves, particularly if significant growth is being achieved.

18.2.10 Effective capital management

As emphasized earlier in this book, an insurer's capital is the core to its existence. It defines how much business it can write, it indicates strength and ability to withstand 'shocks', and is a key measure used by both regulators and other external analysts to assess the company. As a result it should be actively managed by the company.

Capital

'There are contradictions between financial analysts and rating agencies. It appears that a high rating from a rating agency has a positive effect on the share price. To get a high rating requires a large amount of excess capital, while financial analysts, representing investors, would like excess capital to be got rid of as soon as possible. There is therefore a continuous conflict in the way you conduct your business.'

Andersen Research Papers, Issue No. 6 2001

A company needs to have a clear understanding of (and be able to clearly explain to third parties):

- how much capital it has at any point in time
- how much capital it needs to write its targeted volumes and types of business (using techniques such as risk-based capital – see below)
- what it plans to do in the event of having:
  - too much capital for its planned business volumes
  - too little capital for its plans.

Risk-based capital

Risk-based Capital (RBC) is the name given to a number of modelling techniques for calculating the capital that an insurer requires to support each of its component businesses. (Note. The same term is also used by the National Association of Insurance Commissioners in the USA to describe the formula-based calculation of the minimum capital an insurer requires to support its operations, given its specific risk characteristics.) These individual allocations help the insurer to understand the return each business should be making if it is to contribute fairly to the overall result, taking into consideration the cost of volatility.

In a typical RBC exercise, the performance of each business is modelled using historical data and future assumptions. The capital required to prevent the minimum statutory solvency margin being breached more than once in 100 years is estimated. For a highly volatile account, such as liability, the allocated capital might well represent a current solvency ratio of more than 100%, whereas in a stable account like PA it might be 25% – the inference being that much higher returns are needed from volatile accounts.

RBC is a theoretically elegant approach to capital management. In practice, however, it may be difficult to persuade business managers to accept different rates of return objectives for different classes of business that are based on complex modelling and speculative assumptions about future volatility and out-turns over many years.

The problems of too much capital

As noted above, investment analysts become concerned if they believe an insurer has excess capital. Their premise is that, unless management can clearly demonstrate what they plan to do with the excess capital, that will generate a return on that capital greater than investors can gain themselves, independently, then that capital should be returned to investors for them to choose how they invest it. Companies with excess capital have been known to 'waste' it on over-priced or ill-judged acquisitions, or unprofitable growth initiatives. Returning capital to investors via share buy-backs can have a positive impact on the short-term share price of a company (and therefore be of personal benefit to the management of the company, through its ownership of shares and share options in the company).

The problems of too little capital

Too little capital will restrict the volume of business that can be retained by the company so, either less business is written, or more reinsurance is required to maintain a net retention consistent with the capital base. In times of hardening, profitable markets, too little capital will restrict the growth and profitability of an insurer. Instead of taking out more reinsurance or restricting volume, a listed company could also seek additional capital in the marketplace by issuing more shares. A rights issue or other significant capital raising will, in general, depress the share price of the company, at least in the short term, until the new capital demonstrably generates significant additional profits.

The problems of active capital management

In theory, active capital management, using Risk-based Capital models, where excess capital is returned to investors and capital shortages are solved by issuing more shares when needed, should be an efficient method of operating a company. In practice though it seldom works that way. While it may be relatively easy to return capital to investors, it is often the case that, where a company is known to be short of capital, this will damage its share price and make the raising of new capital more difficult/expensive or even impossible.

The other problem is determining what is 'enough' capital and what is 'excess'. All capital modelling uses estimates, assumptions and judgments on what will happen in the future, but the only thing we can be sure of is that things are going to change in ways we cannot fully predict, particularly in insurance (liability, regulation, emerging risks, consumerism, etc). This is why the credit rating agencies like to see a significant surplus of capital over that deemed the minimum necessary to run the business, to allow for the inherently uncertain future. The tighter that capital is managed, the greater the risk that unforeseen events will damage the ability of the company to grow and prosper in a changing marketplace and environment.

18.2.11 The importance of management information/the operation's core data

By the very nature of its business, an insurance operation's data (on risks, policies, claims, etc) is vital to the successful management of the business. Some would say that an insurance operation's core data is the second most valuable asset it possesses after its core intellectual capital (and the use of its intellectual capital is severely constrained without adequate data). Such data is required to support effective decision making in:

- product pricing,
- risk acceptance
- claims reserving
- capital management

and to support a wide range of other functions and decisions within the business.

As a result, the quality (timely, accurate), depth (volume, length of history) and relevance of the data held by an insurance operation, and the management information available from that data, is something that should be monitored and managed closely. In essence, the better the management information possessed, the greater the chance of making correct decisions based on it.

- Legacy IT systems pose a challenge to the older, larger insurance operations because data may be stored in different ways on different systems and 'joining up' information across multiple systems may be complex.
- Care is required because management information systems and the primary financial records of the operation often use different underlying definitions, timing criteria, etc, and therefore do not produce the same answer to the same question. At any point, management needs to be clear which base data is being used (in reports, presentations, comparisons, etc) and not unwittingly mix/compare data from the two different sources. Given the significant analysis now produced as a norm as part of annual reporting and the statistical and other returns produced for regulators, rating agencies, reinsurers, etc, this is a significant issue.

18.2.12 Internal control

At several points in the book so far, the importance of maintaining 'control' has been emphasized. As with any company, management of an insurance operation should establish a system of controls and processes across the business that ensures that things happen in the way expected/required, and any failures are detected and corrected as soon as possible. How this is done in any company will depend, among other things, on its: size, structure, culture, complexity, chosen management style, strategy, etc; but could include:

- Defined organizational structures, hierarchies and responsibilities
- Standard policies and procedures
- Authorization processes (approving payments, unusual transactions, etc)
- Security processes (restricted/controlled access to buildings, IT systems, valuable items, etc)
- Procedure manuals/prescribed ways of working (call centre scripts, IT systems that have to be used in standard ways)
- Management checks and balances (reconciliations, etc)
- Independent audit and review processes.

It is part of management's overall responsibility under most corporate governance rules to ensure that an appropriate and effective system of internal control is established and operated within its business and to report thereon as part of its annual financial reporting.

In addition to the areas common to all types of company, an insurance operation must have effective controls over:

- Risk acceptance (front-line underwriting)
- Claims reserving

- Investment management
- Outsourcing
- Data security/integrity
- Regulatory compliance.

Significant failure in any one of these areas could significantly damage the viability of the entire operation.

18.3 Insurance company failures

It is a sad fact that many insurance companies fail, and even more are taken over, as a consequence of their deteriorating performance prior to them actually failing.

William McDonnell of the FSA has provided useful insight into the common causes of insurance failures. His study arose out of the discussions of a working group of regulators with collective experience of many years supervision of insurers in 15 countries. Those relating to P+C insurers were as follows:

The causes of insurance company failures

a) **Parent company investment policy**
The parent company's investment policy had other objectives than the prudent management of the insurance subsidiary. This might result in illiquid or procyclical investments that were not suitable to support an insurance firm.

b) **Parent company had poor understanding of insurance**
This might lead to poor underwriting strategy, under-pricing or inadequate asset/liability matching.

c) **Mutual insurer facing conflicting objectives**
A mutual insurer must look after the interests of its members, as well as manage the insurance business prudently. This might lead them to invest in its own group companies or, in some cases, keep rates low for its members.

d) **Diseconomies of scale**
Large firms built up by mergers can be difficult to manage effectively and may have multiple legacy systems, diverse types of business and poor management information. Central control may be difficult, leading to a lack of financial and underwriting discipline.

e) **Stagnating insurer diversifies**
Stagnating firms tried to grow by diversifying into non-core business. This was particularly true of niche firms where the management moved outside their area of expertise.

f) **Firms have inappropriate distribution strategies**
An inappropriate strategy could result in high costs, poor risk selection, poor customer service, or poor pricing control. The case was generally one of a lack of desire for change among senior management, so that there were few attempts to improve distribution or rationalize channels.

g) **Catastrophe/inadequate reinsurance planning**
Companies failed to assess the risks and their exposures adequately and so, when a catastrophic loss occurred, they found they had insufficient reinsurance.

(h) **Outsourcing of key functions**
Firms outsourced an activity and failed to maintain control, so that it was not performed in line with supervisory or commercial needs.

Managing Risks: Practical lessons from recent 'failures' of EU Insurers
William McDonnell, FSA Occasional Paper Series no. 20, December 2002

So what are the early warning signs that an insurer might be heading for trouble? The following list was prepared by UNCTAD in 1995. In the light of some of the difficulties experienced by P+C insurers since then, the list appears to be as relevant as ever.

Management practices that may spell doom for an insurer

- Cash flow underwriting
- Rapid premium growth
- Deteriorating reserves
- Poor asset management
- Exposure to volatile investments
- Sale and lease back of office buildings
- Significant change of business
- Poor product diversification
- High operating expenses
- Poor control over agents
- Poor accounting and reporting

UNCTAD 1995

18.4 Some key challenges when looking at an insurance operation

Based on the various matters noted above, here is a brief, high-level list of some key challenges an independent observer, non-executive director or senior member of an insurer's management team might seek to raise when presented with data about an insurance operation:

- Are all figures, including comparatives, prepared on a consistent basis (earned/written, gross/net, etc)?
- On what bases are expenses, capital and investment return/income allocated and is this consistent?
- Do management, and the underwriters setting prices, fully understand every line of business written and the likely impact and frequency of both normal claims and large events?
- What evidence is there to suggest that claims reserves, both known and IBNR, are adequate?
- Are there any market-wide developments, particularly in liability areas, that might suggest that current claims reserves might need to be increased in the future (ie are they potentially understated at present)?
- Is there any evidence of 'going for growth'? If so, is the claims development that lags volume growth clearly understood and reserved for?
- Is the account susceptible to 'large events'? If so, do premiums adequately provide for such events, and have adequate equalization catastrophe reserves been built up in non-event years to cover the expected frequency and impact of large events?
- Is management taking a short-term or full underwriting cycle approach to managing the business?
- Can management effectively and coherently explain how they manage the operation's capital, including how much is needed, how much they have, and what they plan to do about any 'excess' or 'shortfall' that results?
- Are management managing the capital base for the benefit of the short-term investor (eg looking to influence the share price under pressure from investment analysts), or for the long-term benefit of all the stakeholders of the company?
- What information is available to confirm the accuracy and validity of the core data of the operation and the management information produced therefrom?
- When analysis is provided, is it clear whether it is based on management information or the primary financial records of the operation? And is it clear to all recipients whether there are any significant differences, in terms of accounting policies or principles, allocation bases, etc, between primary financial record data and management information data?
- What information is available to confirm the adequacy and effectiveness of the operation's risk management, regulatory compliance and internal control processes?

Select bibliography

K Palepu, P Healy, V Bernard, *Business Analysis and Valuation using Financial Statements 2nd Ed*, South Western College Publishing 2000.

Diacon (Ed), *A Guide to Insurance Management,* Macmillan 1990, Chapter 9.

B Webb, C Harrison, J Markam, *Insurance Operations and Regulation,* Insurance Institute of Am Erica, Chapter 12.

G Dionne, *Handbook of Insurance,* Kluwer 2000, Chapter 24.

J Bannister, *Insurance Solvency Analysis 2nd Ed*, LLP 1997.

J Outreville, *Theory and Practice of Insurance,* Kluwer 1998, Chapter 15.

Best's Insurance Reports, Property & Casualty, A M Best (Annual).

D Marshall, W McManus, K Scoles, *Accounting and Finance for Insurance Professionals 2nd Ed,* American Institute for CPCU 2001.

S Pottier, D Sommer, *The Effectiveness of Public and Private Sector Summary, Risk Measures in Predicting Insurer Insolvencies, Journal of Financial Services Research,* Vol 21, Nos 1/2 2002.

S Myres, J Read, *Capital Allocation for Insurance Companies,* Journal of Risk and Insurance, Vol 68, No 4, Dec 2001.

Nineteen

Conclusion

Objectives

On completion of this chapter, and wider personal research, the reader should be able to:

- consolidate his or her understanding of previous chapters;
- form a view on potential scenarios for the future of insurance;
- explain the importance of these scenarios for the management of insurance operations.

19.1 Where lies the future of P+C insurance?

Here are some thoughts from McKinseys:

> 'The era of the traditional European multi-line insurer is over. These players have become lumbering conglomerates, with clients ranging from individuals to large corporations, and products from life insurance through property and casualty to asset management and banking. This breadth could increasingly be a handicap. Different product/market segments enjoy very different prospects for growth and profitability, and the skills and business models needed to succeed will vary from one to another.'
>
> *McKinsey Quarterly* 1998 No. 3

> 'The (insurance) industry has already started on a transformational journey. We see more mergers, both domestic and cross-border, divestment of P+C businesses by savings-focused institutions, and a disaggregation of the industry with the entry of new niche players.'
>
> McKinsey 2002

19.2 Increasing challenges

As noted earlier in this book, insurance has been around for hundreds of years, but the challenges faced by the managers of insurance operations have increased enormously over the last decade or so, including (but not limited to):

- Changes in socio-economic behaviours and expectations – increasing wealth, consumerism, changing lifestyles, the growth of direct business, brandassurers, etc.
- Changes in the economic environment – the end of the bull market in general, and the bubble in IT and telecoms shares in particular, lower expected levels of inflation, interest rates and investment returns in the future.
- A spate of corporate scandals and collapses, damaging trust in corporate management in general, and leading to yet more regulation and law.
- Changes in the approach to regulation and law in relation to insurance – greater emphasis on protection of the consumer/fairness.
- Changes in the frequency and impact of major claims events:
  - impact of climate change: more floods, storms, droughts, etc
  - increased impact of man-made disasters, September 11, oil spillages, etc
- The increasing impact of known, long-tail claims for previously written business – asbestos, pollution, tobacco, etc.
- The essentially unknown impact of new long-tail claims causes (potentially: electro-magnetic radiation, genetically modified organisms, etc).
- The changes in society's attitude to liability and the size of liability claims awards granted by the courts.
- Consolidation and globalization in business in general, and in the insurance market in particular.
- The significant developments in technology, in particular in communications and e-business.

19.3 Proposed areas for management focus going forward

One thing that is certain is that things will continue to change, including in ways and at speeds that we cannot predict today. So what potentially are the core attributes, or areas of focus, of a successful and well managed primary P+C insurance operation going forward? The authors would propose the following (non-prioritized) list of 'C's:

1) **Capital** – Companies must maintain adequate capital to withstand both predictable and unpredictable 'shocks'. This could imply carrying more capital than the investment analysts are happy with in an increasingly volatile, changing and litigious environment.

2) **Control/corporate governance** – Management must be able to show that it has control over every aspect of its business functions, whether operated in-house or outsourced. This will need to be demonstrated through structured risk management and internal control policies and processes.

3) **Clarity of focus** – Is it logical to continue operating in the way the organization has in the past? The business must be very clear about not only which product lines, customers, etc it is targeting, and which elements and functions of the value chain it will perform itself (and which it will outsource/delegate), but also be able to clearly demonstrate *why* it will succeed by focusing on these parts of the market, value chain, etc.

4) **Combined operating ratio** (the need to underwrite for profit) – This requires a detailed understanding of the risks accepted and the ability to calculate and charge an adequate premium. The quality of technical underwriting and pricing skills will be fundamental to the future performance of the business, and tight control must be maintained over front-line underwriting to ensure that only appropriate risks are accepted at an appropriate price.

5) **Claims management** – The ability to manage the cost of claims effectively will remain core. Managed 'claims solutions' where the insurer (or its agent) manages the entire process including replacement of goods, rather than simply paying a cheque to the insured, are likely to become more common. This requires significant supplier management skills from the insurer.

6) **Claims reserves** – Increasing scrutiny on the adequacy of claims reserves will require that reserves may well need to be disclosed in more detail than previously, and therefore require greater justification as to their adequacy. Comparisons between companies' reserves are likely to become more common. Adequate reserving at all times will become a demonstrable requirement, as compared to previously where it was not unusual for companies to have to periodically strengthen prior-year claims reserves.

7) **Compliance** – Regulation and law are likely to increase in both complexity and volume. Compliance is not optional, and must therefore be fully integrated into the core business processes, rather than looked on as an unnecessary and costly overhead.

8) **Change capability** – Is the organization capable of changing to meet the new challenges/ways of operating? Change will not stop, if anything it is likely to increase. An organization's ability to implement change effectively, and deliver the anticipated benefits of that change promptly, will be a core determinant in the future success of the business.

9) **Clairvoyance** (a clear view of the future) – The more accurately and effectively an insurer can foresee future developments whether in society, the economy, the market, product structure, pricing, demand, supply, technology, etc, the more likely it is that it can develop a strategy and set of plans that will bring success. Effective research, strategy development and planning for future changes will be essential to success.

10) **Conflicting demands** – Insurers face increasing conflicts of interest with governments, regulators and their customers, whether from the current liability/blame/compensation culture, or through issues such as insurers' unwillingness to offer cover for houses on flood plains, high-crime inner city risks or terrorism risks. These must be addressed positively with government/society as a whole, and not simply resisted. This requires the insurance industry to approach such issues in an open and positive manner that, perhaps, has not been seen from it in the past.

11) **Communications technology** (and technology as a whole) – As major users of IT, making the most effective use of developments in technology, particularly communications technology, will be a key requirement for providing access to customers and intermediaries and delivering cost-effective processing solutions.

12) **Consolidation and globalization** – There are likely to be more take-overs and mergers in the future worldwide, both in insurance and in other industries. Each company needs to determine its response, both to the actions of others and in determining its own strategic objectives and targets.

13) **Communication** – Insurance companies and the insurance industry as a body do not tend to be the most effective communicators with society as a whole – explaining the role and value of the industry, dealing with problems openly and positively, producing easily understandable and reliable financial results, etc. For the industry as a whole to prosper in the future this must change. In the UK, the insurance industry is far better known for its failures and mistakes, and price rises (whether justified or not), than for the value of the services it provides.

14) **Core skills** – Insurers must fully understand what their core skills are (and how to assess/measure them) and then put in place processes to acquire, develop, retain, share those skills across their business. It is an often repeated (but rarely backed up by action) statement in many companies' Report and Accounts that the staff are the major asset of the business. In insurance this is particularly true, and successful companies will have to 'walk the talk' not just 'talk the talk', and manage intellectual capital and skills just as strongly as they manage their other assets.

19.4 Some reminders:

- The underwriting cycle is not dead (despite what some commentators say).
- Aggressive growth frequently ends in large underwriting losses (despite what some analysts say).
- As a rule, insurers should not accept others' trading risks, or risks that the other party understands better than the insurer (despite what some customers or brokers say).
- Technology is a tool, not an end in itself (despite what some IT consultants say), and finally
- The full implications of your recent and current decisions will not be evident for some years to come (despite what this year's performance assessment might say).

In the constant search for new markets/products/solutions it is easy to forget these basic truths.

19.5 The views of others

The following are a range of observations and opinions from insurance industry observers regarding the future of insurance.

Future winners in insurance will:

- Know what business they want to be in
- Focus on long-term profitable revenue growth
- Be cost effective
- Organize around the needs of the customer
- Attract and retain the right people
- Develop alternative distribution channels
- Invest appropriately in technology

The Centre for Future Studies

The future of insurance will see:

1. Mergers and acquisitions among insurers and between brokers.
2. A move towards increased specialization by insurers and brokers.
3. Underwriting results become more critical as low inflation and low interest rates reduce the scope for capital growth.
4. Concentration on reduction of the cost base assumes greater importance and organizational/process reviews become more common.
5. Higher consumer expectations in terms of product benefit, product relevance and standards of service.
6. Innovation in product design and delivery mechanisms. Personal lines products become integrated with other product offerings. Commercial lines undergo a major transformation with insurance being one of a number of risk-transfer options and risk management becoming part of the service.
7. Changing distribution channels with a reduction in the number of provincial brokers.
8. E-commerce to increase.
9. Virtual insurance companies to be established and challenge the cost-laden, traditional players.
10. A shortage of skills in the insurance industry will mean that having the right people to manage change will become a critical success factor.

The Centre for Future Studies

Emerging UK insurance market trends

1. Massive consolidation and restructuring in P+C – both personal and commercial, widening the split between P+C and Life insurance.
2. Acceleration of value chain disaggregation, leading to the rise of new niche providers.

IBM

Financial Services, personal lines – an assessment

1. The largest financial services providers have diversified but are finding it extremely difficult to cross-sell – customers dislike it.
2. It is difficult to link up asset management, banking, brokerage and insurance silos with the different channels.
3. It is proving too expensive to be in every channel – you must choose.
4. Some players are choosing to concentrate on manufacturing and have sold their distribution.
5. New technology is being used, but most transactions are still face-to-face.
6. Mobile phone access will grow, but only to drive other channels.
7. Few web sales strategies have been successful.
8. Few web-based aggregators will survive
   - customers won't buy enough
   - lower prices come from direct sources.
9. 'Wealth Management' strategies have failed.

The expected revolution in personal lines financial services is taking much longer than expected, but will come by 2010.

Gartner 2000

Future developments

Personal lines	Economies of scale will prevail and continue to drive consolidation. New distribution alternatives will keep on squeezing margins, even if not always stealing share from traditional distribution channels.
Commercial lines	Large corporate clients will require insurers to upgrade their risk skills. Small corporate clients, on the other hand, will evolve towards standardization … and even direct distribution.

McKinsey 2002

Winning back trust

'So what can management do to start winning back trust? Key steps include:

- Building robust risk and compliance management and control structures in our companies.
- Getting back to basics in our core skills.
- Focusing on robust pricing models that will give customers more confidence through the cycle as well as reassuring shareholders and regulators that we are getting it right.
- Simplifying our business models so we can genuinely modernize the way we do business.'

Duncan Boyle, CEO, RSA UK

19.6 Some fashionable solutions that failed to deliver

And finally, a reminder of some of the 'bright ideas' that, as a rule, have failed to deliver the promised improvements in results/new/paradigm/other substantial benefits:

Dogs that failed to bark

- Larger-than-life celebrity leaders
- Executive compensation schemes
- Technology as a solution in its own right
- Mergers and acquisitions
- Big transformation programmes

Dr Jules Goddard, London Business School

19.7 Authors' conclusion

In the authors' opinion, management is as much an art as a science. In this book we have provided an insight into the nature of P+C insurance and the issues and challenges that need to be managed. We have also provided some insights, tools and examples of how these issues could be managed. As stated at the beginning, by its very nature and the restrictions of time and space, this book has only skimmed the surface of such a large and complex subject, and many of the individual chapters in this book could each be expanded to become entire books in their own right, detailing the theory and practice in each area. The select bibliography will, hopefully, have been supported by further reading, including journals and press and investment analysts reports, etc, which will have put more substance around the issues raised. The art is in how you put this knowledge and information into practice, in a complex and fast-changing industry and in the unique situation presented by each situation/challenge/company.

Management of an insurance operation must address the challenges of today and tomorrow, while at the same time remaining fully mindful of the lessons of the past.

Twenty

Glossary of terms

ABI
Association of British Insurers. Trade association for insurers authorized to transact insurance in the UK.

Accident year
The financial year in which a loss or accident occurs.

Accident insurance
A class of insurance including personal accident, credit, fidelity and contingency covers.

Accumulation
A concentration of risk whereby an insurer may cover many properties or liabilities that could produce losses at the same time.

Act of God
A legal term – something that occurs in the course of nature, which was beyond human foresight, and against which human prudence could not have been expected to provide.

Actuary
An insurance mathematician involved in setting rates and reserves. The role differs between countries and may be defined by law.

Additional Perils
See *Fire insurance.*

Adjuster
A person acting for an insurer in assessing and settling claims. Also *Loss Adjuster.* The term *Assessor* may be used but this is increasingly reserved for a person appointed by the insured to negotiate a claim on their behalf.

Adverse selection
Receiving more business from those with a higher risk of loss than would be expected from a purely random sample.

Agent
A person who introduces customers to an insurer in return for commission. The role may differ with the agency agreement and could include holding cover and assisting with administration and claims handling.

Allfinanz
See *Bancassurance.*

All Risks
Insurance against loss by any fortuitous cause except those specifically excluded.

Alternative Risk Transfer (ART)
An imprecise term for a range of non-conventional risk transfer techniques including finite reinsurance and captives.

Apportionment
Dividing the payment of a claim between insurers who share the risk.

Arbitration
The use of an independent person to settle a dispute between an insurer and an insured.

Arson
A deliberately caused fire. This is normally covered by a Fire insurance policy unless caused by the insured.

Assistance Services
Additional, non-insurance services provided by an insurer to support its insurance products, eg legal or medical advice helplines, repatriation following illness abroad.

Assurance
See *Insurance*.

Automatic reinstatement
A clause in a reinsurance contract guaranteeing further cover after a claim.

Average

(1) The proportionate amount an insurer will pay on a loss if the sum insured is less than the value of the property at risk.

$$\text{Average} = \text{Loss} \times \frac{\text{Sum insured}}{\text{Value at risk}}$$

(2) In Marine insurance:

- Particular Average is damage to a ship caused by a marine peril.
- General Average is cargo jettisoned to save a ship.

This loss is shared by all the parties benefiting from the ship not sinking.

Awayday
The practice of taking a management team off site, to undertake intense team working, free from the distractions of the office.

Bail Bond
A bond to pay for the release of an insured person, eg a motorist imprisoned following a road accident.

Bailee
One in legal possession of another's property, eg jeweller, garage, warehouseman. A bailee may have an insurable interest in the property.

Balanced Scorecard
A tool for assessing performance of an organization using a comprehensive range of measures, both financial and non-financial, which reflect all the key objectives of the business.

Bancassurance

(1) Joint marketing of banking and insurance products.

(2) Joint ownership of bank and insurance operations. Also *Allfinanz*.

Betterment
Any improvement in the insured property to a condition better than before the loss occurred.

Binder
An agreement by an insurer that an agent may grant cover.

Binding Authority
The authority given to a broker to grant cover in the name of the insurer.

Blanket policy
A policy where a single sum insured covers a number of items at risk, eg buildings.

Bordereau
List of insured risks, premiums and losses maintained by a broker or bank for an insurer.

Boston Matrix
A portfolio matrix model created by Boston Consulting Group. Introduced concepts such as Cash Cow, Dog, Star and Question Mark.

Broker
A person who places insurance business. The title is controlled by legislation in some countries. A broker differs from a simple insurance agent in so far as being full-time, having specialist expertise and maintaining agency agreements with a number of insurers.

Brokerage
A commission received by a broker.

Burning cost
A method of calculating a premium using the insured's recent claims experience.

Business Interruption
Insurance to indemnify a business for those costs that cannot be stopped or reduced in proportion to the reduction of sales caused by fire, machinery breakdown, or other insured peril. Same as *Loss of Profits* or *Consequential Loss*.

Business Process Re-engineering (BPR)
Re-design of the core business processes to achieve dramatic improvements in efficiency, quality, etc. See also *Transformation*.

Business strategy
The strategy for the product lines and supporting service functions within a single business.

B2B
Business-to-business transactions.

B2C
Business-to-customer transactions.

B2E
Business-to-employee transactions.

Call Centre
Advisers, supported by smart technology, who deliver propositions and service to customers over the phone. Also called a Contact Centre.

Cancellation
Termination of a policy by an insurer on the instruction of the insured.

Capacity
The total amount of insurance an insurer or market is able to accept.

Capital Employed
Same as *Free Reserves.*

Cargo insurance
Insurance of goods carried by sea or air.

Casualty
Liability and *Accident* insurance, as opposed to *Property* insurance.

Catastrophe
A severe disaster causing a large loss.

Catastrophe Reserve
Same as *Equalization Reserve.*

Cede
To purchase reinsurance cover.

Chain Ladder
A range of techniques to display and compare the development of claims from different years using tables usually in the shape of a triangle. Same as *Triangulation.*

CII
Chartered Insurance Institute, UK.

Claim
A demand for payment as provided by an insurance policy. Also *Loss*.

Claims Incurred

(1) In insurance accounting: the claims paid in the year plus the changes in claims reserves brought forward at the start of the year.

(2) In policy wording: *Claims Incurred* are claims that have their cause in the period of the policy. This is distinct from *Claims Made*, ie claims that are reported to the insurer in the period, but may have been caused in an earlier period.

Claims Made
See *Claims Incurred.*

Claims Ratio
The ratio of claims incurred to earned premium. Same as *Loss Ratio*.

$$\text{Claims Ratio} = \frac{\text{Net incurred claims (NIC)}}{\text{Net earned premium (NEP)}}\ \%$$

Clause
A particular stipulation in an insurance policy.

Coinsurance
Sharing of a risk by a number of insurers. Effectively separate contracts apply, so that, if one coinsurer becomes insolvent, the insured, rather than the other coinsurers, is liable for the uncollected portion of a loss.

Collapse
In engineering insurance: the sudden and dangerous distortion of a vessel or boiler.

Combined Ratio/Combined Operating Ratio/COR
The main measure of an insurer's underwriting performance. It is the sum of the claims ratio and the expense ratio. An insurer having a combined ratio of less than 100% has made an underwriting profit. Same as *Underwriting Ratio* or *Operating Ratio.*

Commission
The payment to an agent for the introduction or renewal of business. It is usually a set percentage of the premium.

Commoditization
The pressure to create high-volume, low-cost, low-complexity products for the mass consumer market. Differentiation being almost solely on price and brand.

Competence
A skill, knowledge or process that creates customer value.

Composite insurer
An insurer transacting both Life and P+C insurance.

Comprehensive policy
A policy covering a range of insured perils, eg comprehensive motor policies cover loss or damage to the vehicle as well as liability to third parties.

Concealment
Deliberate non-disclosure of a material fact by a proposer.

Conditions
Provisions in an insurance policy specifying some important fact. The non-observance of a condition may make a claim avoidable by the insurer. If the condition is written into the policy it is known as an *express condition*. In addition, there are *implied conditions*, which do not have to be written, eg *insurable interest*, *utmost good faith*, and *contribution*.

Consequential Loss
See *Business interruption*.

Contact Centre
See *Call Centre*.

Constructive total loss
This occurs when the cost of repair exceeds the value of the property insured.

Contingency insurance
Bespoke insurance against remote possibilities, eg reappearance of missing beneficiaries to a will.

Contribution
If another insurance contract exists that covers the same interest, subject matter and peril, it is an implied condition that any claim must be apportioned between the insurers.

Corporate governance
The internal structures and processes by which companies are controlled and managed at the highest level.

Corporate strategy
The strategy through which a holding company adds value to its component businesses.

Cover
The protection provided by a policy.

Cover Note
An interim document giving proof of cover prior to the issue of full policy documentation.

Creditor insurance
Insurance of loan repayments in the event of unemployment, sickness or death.

Cross-selling
Selling additional products to existing customers, saving acquisition/administration costs and 'deepening' the customer relationship.

Customer Relationship Management (CRM)
A company-wide set of activities designed to maximize the delivery of service and value to customers and the value of those customers to the business.

Declaration policy
A policy that requires the insured to regularly declare a rating factor (eg the value of inventory) so that the premium can be adjusted.

Deductible
The amount to be borne by the insured prior to the payment of the remainder of the claim. Same as *Excess*. It differs from *Franchise*, where nothing is payable until the franchise amount is reached; then the claim is paid in full.

Deposit premium
An advance payment by the insured prior to the calculation of the full premium.

DIC policy
Where an insured has policies covering its operations in a number of countries it may take out a difference in conditions (DIC) policy to compensate for any gaps in cover resulting from differences in market practice between countries.

Differentiation
Creating a product or service offering that is considered in some way to be unique.

Direct marketing
The use of newspaper, radio and TV advertising, and unsolicited bulk-mailings to potential customers, to stimulate a direct response to an insurer.

Direct writer
An insurer dealing directly with the customer, ie not via an intermediary.

Disclosure
The duty of a proposer to reveal all material facts that might affect the insurance.

E & O
Errors and Omissions. An alternative name for *Professional Indemnity insurance*.

e-business
The application of Internet technology to business.

e-commerce
The completion of transactions and the distribution of products via the Internet.

Earned Premium
The proportion of premium relating to the period for which cover has already expired. For example, 50% of the premium for a 12-month duration insurance policy taken out at the beginning of January will have been 'earned' by the end of June.

Employers' Liability insurance
Insurance for the liability of an employer for accidents or disease relating to its employees. It is a legal requirement in some countries. *Workers' compensation* is a wider cover that is offered in certain markets.

Emerging risk
A new risk that may create potential claims in the future, eg the electromagnetic radiation from mobile phones.

Endorsement
A note added to a policy, altering particular details of the policy.

Engineering insurance
The insurance of plant and machinery.

Environmental Report
A report to shareholders and the public in general setting out a company's approach to energy conservation, pollution control, recycling, etc.

Equalization Reserve
A reserve permitted in some countries to smooth the overall result of an insurance company. In years when claims experience has been favourable, an amount is put into a reserve from where it can be withdrawn in poor years. Also *Catastrophe Reserve.*

Equitas
A reinsurance company set up to run-off all pre-1992 liabilities of Lloyd's.

Ethics
The branch of philosophy concerned with moral judgments:, eg right or wrong, good or bad.

Ex gratia payment
A payment made by an insurer by way of goodwill where a claim has been rejected.

Excess
Same as Deductible.

Excess of Loss
A reinsurance contract that provides cover for all claims amounts in excess of an agreed level per claim.

Exclusion
A restriction in the scope of a policy.

Expense Ratio
A measure of an insurer's operational efficiency.

$$\text{Expense Ratio} = \frac{\text{Management expenses (excluding claims handling costs)}}{\text{Net written premium (NWP)}} \%$$

NB Claims handling costs are included in the claims ratio.

Experience
The claims record for an individual risk or a class of risks.

Exposure
(1) The amount of risk (as measured by cumulative sums insured or limits of indemnity).
(2) The state of being exposed to a possibility of loss.

Express Conditions
See *Conditions*.

Extranet
The extension of a company's intranet to business partners in order to share information.

Facilities Management (FM)
The management of the day-to-day activities connected with the provision of office premises and associated services (light, heat, phones, security, catering, etc).

Facultative reinsurance
Reinsurance of individual risks. From the French *facultatif* meaning optional. The primary insurer is not obliged to cede, nor the reinsurer to accept. Compare: *Treaty reinsurance*.

Financial Services Authority (FSA)
The unitary regulator for the majority of financial services businesses in the UK.

Financial Services Compensation Scheme (FSCS)
A scheme, funded by levy, to protect UK retail customers of failed insurance companies. Formerly known as the Policyholders' Protection Board (PPB).

Finite reinsurance
Financial or non-traditional reinsurance. It tends to be cheaper than traditional reinsurance with less risk transfer.

Fire insurance
Insurance against fire, lightning and explosion. The standard policy may be extended to include *additional perils*: storm, tempest, flood, hail, earthquake, subterranean fire, subsidence, riot, civil commotion, locked-out workers, burst pipes, aircraft, sonic booms, etc.

First loss insurance
Property insurance where the insurer accepts that the sum insured is less than the full value of the property at risk but contracts to pay claims in full up to the sum insured, ie no average is applied.

Force majeure
An uncontrollable circumstance that prevents a contract from being carried out.

Fortuitous
Random, as opposed to fortunate.

Franchise
See *Deductible*.

Free Assets
Same as *Free Reserves*.

Free Reserves
Excess of assets over liabilities. Also: *Free Assets, Solvency Margin, Surplus, Shareholders' funds* or *Capital Employed.*

Freight
Money paid for transporting cargo.

GAAP
Generally Accepted Accounting Principles.

Gap analysis
Comparing the current position of an organization with the planned/desired position. Associated with John Argenti.

General insurance
Insurance other than life or permanent health. Also called P+C insurance.

Goodwill
In accounting, the value of future benefits from intangible assets, eg a brand, or the existing customer base of an acquired business.

Green Card
An international certificate providing evidence of third party motor insurance.

GWP
Gross written premium. The total premiums before deduction of outwards reinsurance.

Hazard
A circumstance that promotes the probability of a loss, eg faulty electrical wiring in a building.

Heave
Upward motion of the ground causing damage to a building. The opposite of *subsidence.*

Hold Harmless agreement
Agreement relieving one party of liability.

Hospital Cash insurance
Insurance providing a cash payment for periods spent in hospital.

Hothouse
A task force sent into isolation to come up with new ideas to resolve difficulties or change the business fundamentally, using people fresh to the problem/situation, such as graduate trainees

IBNER
A reserve for Incurred But Not Enough Reserved claims.

IBNR
A reserve for Incurred But Not Reported claims.

IFA
Independent Financial Adviser, a widely used term for a broker specializing in life, pensions and savings. The role may be defined by legislation.

IFS
Institute of Financial Services (brand name of The Chartered Institute of Bankers, UK professional institute).

ILU
Institute of London Underwriters. An association of companies writing Marine and Aviation insurance in the London Market.

Implied Conditions
See *Conditions.*

Incurred claims
See *Claims incurred.*

Indemnity
Unless otherwise stated, insurance policies are contracts of indemnity. The purpose is to put the insured back into the same monetary position as before the loss. The insured is not entitled to anything more than the amount of the loss. This has given rise to the insured having to contribute towards any *betterment* after a claim. To overcome this problem in Home insurance, some insurers offer *reinstatement* or *new for old* policies, for a higher premium, the insurer will replace the lost or damaged goods with new items.

Inland Marine
Insurance transacted by Marine insurers for inland risks, eg canal traffic, goods in transit.

Insurable interest
A principle of insurance whereby the insured is so situated that the happening of the insured evident would involve him or her in loss or diminution of any right recognized by law, or in any legal liability.

Insurance
(1) A contract for the payment of a sum of money (by an insurer to an insured) on the occurrence of a specified event that is contrary to the interest of the insured.

(2) The sharing of risks by a large number of individuals.

Same as Assurance.
NB: the term assurance tends to be used for Life and Marine insurance.

Insured
(1) Covered by insurance.

(2) The policyholder.

Intermediary
A party that distributes insurance products manufactured by another for a fee (commission), eg agent, broker.

Internet
A global network comprising numerous smaller networks, eg world wide web and e-mail.

Intranet
An internal network for employees using Internet technology.

Inwards reinsurance
Reinsurance business accepted by an insurer.

Intellectual capital
The intangible asset associated with the specialist knowledge and skills inherent within an organization.

Knock-for-knock agreement
An arrangement between motor insurers to pay their own costs for accidents regardless of blame. The purpose is to minimize litigation and administrative expenses.

Lapse
Termination of a policy due to non-payment of premium.

Lapse Ratio
Annual percentage of policies that are not renewed.

Layer
A level of an individual risk, or of an excess of loss treaty.

Lead underwriter
The underwriter who determines the rating and terms for a large risk to be shared by a number of insurers.

Leakage
Avoidable loss to an insurer due to non-observance by staff of laid-down underwriting or claims-handling procedures.

Liability insurance
Insurance covering losses resulting from obligations to others arising out of negligence, law or contract.

Light on the hill
A technique used to develop a series of statements describing the key steps in delivering the long-term strategy of an organization. It is written as a retrospective Chairman's statement (typically 5 years hence) and describes the key actions that were taken to deliver the strategy.

Limit of indemnity
The maximum amount payable under a policy.

Line
A share of a risk underwritten by a number of insurers.

Liquidity
The ease with which an item (particularly an investment) can be converted into cash.

Lloyd's
Lloyd's of London. A corporation of individual underwriters.

Lloyds's agent
An agent appointed by Lloyd's to undertake surveys and handle claims.

Lloyd's broker
A broker authorized to place business at Lloyd's.

Lloyd's Syndicate
See *Syndicate*.

LMX spiral
An undesirable practice in the London Excess of Loss reinsurance market whereby multiple layers of cover were provided for the same risk by the same underwriting syndicate.

London Market
The insurance and reinsurance markets in which Lloyd's brokers operate.

Long-tail business
Insurance business where claims may take years to be reported or settled, eg liability.

Long-term agreement
An arrangement for an insured to renew a policy for an agreed number of years in return for a premium reduction.

Loss
(1) A claim.

(2) The event giving rise to a claim.

Loss Adjuster
See *Adjuster*.

Loss Control
The process of reducing the severity and frequency of losses. Same as *risk control*.

Loss of Profits
Same as Business Interruption Insurance.

Loss Ratio
Same as *Claims Ratio*.

Malus
A penalty premium loading applied for poor claims experience. The opposite of a bonus or *no claims discount*.

Managing Agent
An agent running the affairs of a Lloyd's syndicate.

Marketing mix
The way in which the various elements of marketing are combined: proposition, place, price, people and promotion.

Material fact
A fact that would influence a prudent underwriter on whether to accept a risk, under what terms and at what premium.

Mission Statement
A statement defining the future direction of an organization. May also be called a 'vision statement'; if so it may be more inspirational in nature.

Moral Hazard
An intangible human aspect of a risk, eg dishonesty, carelessness.

Motor insurance
The insurance of motor accident damage and liability.

Mutual
A company owned by its customers/members for mutual benefit.

Name
An underwriting member of Lloyd's.

NEP
Net earned premium. Earned premium after deduction of reinsurance outwards premiums.

Net Asset Value
Total of all assets less liabilities.

New for old
Payment of a claim without deduction for wear and tear.

NIC
Net incurred claims. Incurred claims after deducting amounts recoverable from reinsurers.

Niche marketing
Focusing on a narrow range of products or customers.

No claims discount
An agreement to reduce premium following a claims-free period.

NWP
Net written premium. Total premium after deduction of outwards reinsurance premiums.

Ombudsman
An independent official appointed to investigate customer complaints.

Operating Ratio
Same as *Combined Ratio*.

Operative clause
The clause in a policy that sets out the perils which are insured.

Outwards reinsurance
An insurer buying reinsurance cover from a reinsurer.

Overinsurance
A sum insured that is in excess of the value at risk.

Particular Average
See *Average*.

Peril
A potential cause of loss, eg fire, earthquake.

PEST
An acronym used in the analysis of the business environment to classify external influences: **P**olitical, **E**conomic, **S**ocial and **T**echnological.

Pluvious insurance
Insurance against cancellation of outdoor events due to adverse weather.

Policy
A document containing a contract of insurance.

Policyholder
Same as *Insured*.

Pool
An arrangement whereby a group of insurers agree to share, on an agreed basis, all risks of a particular type, eg nuclear risks, non-standard motor risks.

Pool Re
A pool set up to write reinsurance for terrorism in the UK market in excess of members' retentions.

Porter's 5 Forces
A model used for analysing the business environment, developed by Michael Porter.

Premium
The payment for an insurance.

Premium income
Total premiums received by an insurer in a year.

Premium tax
Tax levied in some countries on insurance premiums.

Product Liability
Insurance covering liability for damage or injury caused by an insured's products.

Professional Indemnity insurance
Insurance covering professional negligence, eg accountants, solicitors, civil engineers. Same as *E&O*.

Profit commission
Additional commission paid to a broker based on the insurer's profit on the account. This is intended to provide an incentive to the broker to supply good-quality business.

Property insurance
Insurance of physical property against perils such as fire, theft, accidental damage.

Proportional reinsurance
An arrangement where the insurer and reinsurer share premiums and claims proportionately, eg *quota share*.

Proposal
Application to an insurer for the provision of insurance.

Provision
In general insurance a provision is synonymous with a *reserve*.

Proximate cause
Legally this is 'the active, efficient cause that sets in motion a trail of events which brings about a result, without the intervention of any force started and working actively from a new and independent source'. Policy liability arises where the insured peril is the proximate cause of the loss.

Quota share
See *Proportional reinsurance*.

Quotation
A written or verbal statement made by an insurer to indicate to an enquirer how much premium would be charged for a risk.

Rate
The sum charged for each unit by which premium is calculated, eg £0.75 for each £100 of sum insured is referred to as a rate of 0.75%.

Reassurance
Reinsurance of Life business.

Red-lining
Exclusion of a group of customers due to their high risk of loss. The expression originated from the concept of an insurer drawing a red line around a problem area on a map, such as a flood plain.

Reinsurance
Acceptance by a reinsurer of a share of an insurer's accepted risks in order to help to spread the insurer's risk or increase its capacity.

Reinstatement
A condition of property insurance whereby the insurer can insist on a building being rebuilt after a loss, rather than pay a sum of money. It may be exercised where fraud is suspected.

Renewal
The continuation of insurance after expiry of the policy period.

Reserve
Money put aside by an insurer to meet future liabilities.

Retail
The provision of products to personal (rather than commercial) customers.

Retention
An amount retained by an insurer after reinsuring the remainder.

Retrocession
Reinsurance of reinsurances, ie a reinsurer passing a share of a risk to another reinsurer.

Risk
(1) The subject matter of the insurance.
(2) Degree of probability of loss.
(3) A factor likely to cause the loss.

Risk-based Capital
The capital an insurer allocates to support each of its businesses on the basis of their underwriting and investment risks.

Risk classification
The separation of risks into 'types' with shared characteristics for study and analysis. The following classifications have been derived by a number of different researchers. They overlap considerably.

Pure risks:	Those that result only in loss, eg theft.
Speculative risks:	Risks where there is a possibility of gain as well as loss, eg investment.
Trading risks:	Risks that may be considered to be core to the purpose of the business, eg lending for a bank.
Fundamental risks:	Risks that affect a broad segment of the population, eg socio-economic risks such as recession, health.
Particular risks:	Risks that arise out of individual events and affect few parties, eg accidents.
Systemic risks:	Those risks in a system or market that could affect all participants at the same time, eg stock market collapse.
Static risks:	Risks that occur irrespective of the state of the economy, eg perils.
Dynamic risks:	Those that result from economic or social change, eg price, consumer tastes, technology.

Risk Control
Same as *Loss Control.*

Risk management
The management process of identifying, evaluating, minimizing and dealing with the consequences of pure risks.

Risk Surveyor
Same as *Surveyor.*

ROC(E) Return on Capital (or Return on Capital Employed)
This is the result of dividing the net earnings of a business by the capital (equity, debt, etc) used to support that business, expressed as a percentage. (NB The calculation of both net earnings and capital employed can vary significantly between businesses/ business units.)

Run-off
Business that is no longer written by an insurer, but where claims remain outstanding.

Salvage
(1) Amount paid to an insurer for the sale of damaged property after a claim has been paid.
(2) In Marine insurance, the amount paid to someone who saves or recovers a ship or its cargo.

Scenario planning
Testing alternative scenarios as part of the planning process.

Schedule
Part of a policy document showing the variable details that apply to that particular insured.

Shareholders' funds
Same as *Free Reserves.*

Silo
A vertical structure within an operation that performs all functions itself internally, duplicating functions also performed in other parts of the operation.

Slip
A broker's document providing details of a risk for presentation to an underwriter.

SME
Acronym: **S**mall/**M**edium **E**nterprises – the smaller-sized commercial customers.

Solvency Margin
Same as *Free Reserves.*

Solvency Ratio
The ratio of free assets to net written premiums. This is a measure of the financial strength of an insurer, and is subject to regulatory control in most countries.

Stakeholder model
A model whereby the company manages a series of mutually beneficial relationships with its various stakeholders: customers, employees, business partners, shareholders, public and government.

Stop Loss treaty
A contract where the reinsurer agrees to pay all losses once the primary insurer's loss ratio exceeds a certain value for a class of business or other group of policies.

Strategic control
A method whereby a holding company controls the performance of its subsidiary businesses through a framework of high-level policies and procedures, within which the subsidiaries are then free to operate as they see fit.

Subrogation
An insurer's right to recover a loss from a third party by taking on the rights of the insured.

Subsidence
The sinking of land causing damage to a building.

Sum insured
The insurer's maximum liability as specified in a policy.

Surplus
See *Free Assets*.

Surplus treaty
Reinsurance on the basis of lines. The primary insurer decides the proportion of the risk (line) it is prepared to retain. The remainder of the risk is divided into lines of equal size and is ceded to the reinsurers for automatic acceptance.

Surveyor
A person able to report on a risk on behalf of an underwriter and make recommendations on loss control. Same as *Risk Surveyor.*

SWOT
An acronym used in analysing the key issues identified in the planning process: Internal **S**trengths and **W**eaknesses, External **O**pportunities and **T**hreats.

Syndicate
An association of Lloyd's names employing underwriters to accept business on their behalf.

Terms
Statements made by an insurer that affect the conditions under which a policy of insurance operates. Insurers often state that a policy is subject to 'normal' or 'standard' terms and these are usually written in the policy wording. Sometimes insurers add further special terms which may restrict or increase cover, increase or decrease rates, or delete or impose an excess.

Third party
A person who is not a party to a particular contract but becomes involved with it.

Tort
Breach of duty in law leading to liability for damages.

Total Claims Management (TCM)
An integrated process by which the insurer takes total control over every element of a claim, from the moment it is notified to the coordinated delivery of the solution.

Total Quality Management (TQM)
A systematic approach to determining the performance requirements of products and services, then meeting them with zero defects.

Transformation
Re-engineering a business. This term is currently more popular than BPR because it implies recognition of the softer cultural and people issues.

Treaty reinsurance
Reinsurance of a class of risks. The primary insurer must cede all risks of the type and the reinsurer must accept them.

Triangulation
See *Chain Ladder*.

Underinsurance
Insurance where the sum insured is inadequate to cover potential losses.

Underwriting
The profession of assessing, accepting and pricing risks.

Underwriting cycle
The periodic behaviour of insurance markets where years of soft (low) premium rates are followed by periods of hard (high) rates.

Underwriting Ratio
Same as *Combined Ratio.*

Underwriting Result
Earned premiums less incurred claims and underwriting expenses.

Unearned premium reserve
A reserve for the proportion of premiums that has not been earned at the time of reserving. See *Earned premium.*

Unexpired Risk Reserve
A reserve for business written during a period of inadequate rates.

Underwriting authority
The limit of freedom granted to individual front-line underwriters based on their competence.

Utmost good faith
Uberrima fides. An *implied condition* of all insurance contracts. The insured, who is deemed to have greater knowledge of the risk than the insurer, has a duty to disclose all material facts.

Value chain
The component activities that link together to create value in an organization or industry.

Virus
A computer program that attaches itself to another program and carries out unwanted operations.

Void
Not valid in law.

War games
A method of stress testing a potential strategy, when managers role-play the behaviour of competitors.

Warranty
A warranty is an undertaking by the insured that:

- something shall be done
- something shall not be done
- some condition is fulfilled.
- eg that the insured premises are alarmed.
- A breach of warranty renders a policy voidable by the insurer.

Workers' Compensation
See *Employers' Liability.*

Written premium
Premium for the whole term of the original policy.

Index

A

Accident insurance
credit, 115
personal, 115, 119
Accounting
three-year, 51
Advertising
managing, 133, 134
Affinity groups
agent, as, 141
Agency
law of, 50, 51
Agent
affinity groups, 141
both parties, for, 141
brandassurers, 141
distribution by, 139-141
legal duties, 140
work of, 140
Alternative risk transfer
captive insurance, 173, 174
example of, 173
Arson
fire insurance loss, as cause of, 202
Audit
internal, 233
underwriting, 186
Average
principle of, 26
Aviation insurance
losses, 119
scope of, 118
war risks, 162

B

Bancassurance
bank, sale of insurance by, 88-90
meaning, 88
problems with, 90
meaning, 141
Brands
management, 124, 125
strong branding, 143
Broker
added value services, 149
challenge facing, 147
commercial lines, 150
commission v consultancy fees, 149
direct business, threat from, 147
distribution by, 140
globalization, 149
original focus, 148
personal lines, 150
regulation, 150
technology, burden of, 150
types of, 148
Business ethics
corporate, 255-257
environmental issues, 257
framework, setting, 254-258
individual, 257, 258
moral judgments, 253
Business process re-engineering
basis of, 243
components, 243
failure, reasons for, 244
need for, 244

Business services
centralized, move from, 218
compliance, 232
corporate affairs, 231, 232
facilities management, 231
finance, 220-222
human resources, 226-230
hybrid approach, 219
importance of, 217
information services, 225, 226
internal audit, 233
investment management, 222-224
issues and challenges, 219
legal, 232
list of, 218
meaning, 217
risk management, 233
roles, clarity of, 219
secretarial, 232
structure, 218, 219

C

Call centres
use of, 95
Capital
maintenance of, 285
management, 275-277
need for, 31, 33
optimum level of, 221
renting out, 32
risk-based, 276
too little, 276, 277
too much, 276
Captive insurance
alternative risk transfer, 173
development of, 173, 174
Catastrophes
effect of, 180, 181
Change management
business process re-engineering, 243, 244
key challenges, 242
process of, 245
reorganization and, 245
success factors, 242
transformation, and, 245
Claims
acceptance of, 194
chain ladder, 212, 213
coding, 200
compensation schemes, 203
complex, 195
control and management, key steps, 192, 193
cost of, 191
ex gratia payments, 203, 204
fraud, 200-202
gradually developing clauses, 193
handling, business of, 108
insurer, position of, 191, 192
IT systems, 200
large, 197
leakage, 202
liability, determining, 194
loss adjusters, role of, 204, 205
management information, 200
management, 285
preferred suppliers/solutions, 197, 198
process, management of, 196-198
quantification, 194, 195
recoveries-
contribution, 199
deductibles, 198
duplicate, 199
reinsurance, 199
third parties, from, 199
reinstatement, 195, 196
small, 196
taking control of, 197
total claims management capability, 192
under-insurance, 194, 195
Class actions
advent of, 11, 12
Coinsurance
meaning, 29
Compensation
culture, growth in, 11
schemes, industry-wide, 203
Computer risks
product development opportunity, 120
Contingency fees
advent of, 11
Contingency insurance
scope of, 116
specialist expertise, 119
Contract
law of, 50
Contribution
principle of, 25

Corporate affairs
functions, 231, 232
Corporate governance
increased focus on, 49
insurers, challenges to, 50
rules, scope of, 49
Cross-selling
steps in, 95
success or failure of, 96
Culture
impact of, 246
organization, of, 56

D

Directors and officers liability
scope of, 117
Distribution of insurance
agent, by, 139-141
brandassurers, 141
broker, by, 140. *See also* BROKER
channel, choosing, 145, 146
development of, 139
direct, 142, 143, 146
intermediation, 139-141, 146
key issues, 147
mix, 137, 138
technology, impact of, 143-145
Distributors
meaning, 29
Diversification
lack of success, 97
Dividends
levels of, 222

E

E-business
aggregator, 238
B2B, 239
B2C, 237-239
B2E, 239
insurers' caution, 236, 238
Internet, nature of, 235
meaning, 236
original technology, 236
overview, 240, 241
pathway, 237
portal, 238
potential, 236
reverse auctions, 238
transformation, 240
Electronic Data Interchange
use of, 143, 144
Employers' liability
renewal, assessment at, 160
scope of, 117
unprofitability, 119
Engineering
insurance, 114

F

Facilities management
scope of, 231
Fidelity insurance
meaning, 116
specialist expertise, 119
Finance
capital, 221
dividend, 222
function, 220
return, 220
solvency, 221
trading objectives, 220
Financial Ombudsman
dispute resolution by, 44
Financial services
convergence, 5-7
sectors, 6
Financial Services Authority
regulation, approach to, 49
risk management requirements, 250
rules and regulations, compliance with, 46
statutory objectives, 48
Financial Services Compensation Scheme
purpose of, 203
Fire insurance
arson as cause of loss, 202
risk control survey, 157
Standard Fire Policy and Additional Perils, 112
Fraud
claims, 200-202
insurance, 200, 201
insurance company, 45, 46

G

Gamblimg
insurance contract, absence of, 24
General insurance
distribution, 137
internal company organization, 110
nature of, 109
statutory classes, 110
Geneva Association
role and activities of, 52, 53
Globalization
degrees of, 7
insurance, of, 7, 8
technology, 8
Glossary of terms, 293-319
Goods in transit insurance
scope of, 118

H

Holding company
value, destroying, 91
Human resources
areas of, 226
pension provision, 230
recruitment, 227
remuneration, 227
training and development, 228-230

I

Indemnity
contracts not being, 25, 26
principle of, 25
provision of, 25
Industrial diseases
large-scale liability claims, 11
Information
management, 277, 278
Information services
function of, 225, 226
targets, 225
Institutional investors
requirements of, 57
Insurable interest
need for, 20, 24
Insurance
barriers to entry, 4
compulsory, 43
convergence, 5-7
fund-
concept of, 20
equilibrium conditions, 23
investment, 22
globalization, 7, 8
government action, 10
low public opinion of, 254
meaning, 17
modern operation, complexity of, 1
multidisciplinary nature of, 1
need for, 15
operation of, 20-23
P+C. *See* P+C INSURANCE
regulatory action, 10
risk transfer, as, 17
specialists, 1
statistics, 18
summary of, 20, 21
supply and demand, 4
value of, 2
Insurance company
capital. *See* CAPITAL
consolidation, 9
crashes, 273, 274
diseconomies of scale, 10
failures, 279, 280
fraud, 45, 46
internal control, 278
investment income, 34
key challenges, 281
limited, 32
maximum loss, 34
mergers and acquisitions, 9
model of, 22
mutuals, 32
operating structures, 31, 32
operation, assessing performance of-
capital management, effective, 275-277
claims reserves brought forward, 268
core data, 277, 278
expense allocation, 264-266
going for growth, impact of, 270-274
gross v net, 264
internal control, 278
investment income/total investment return, 267
large, one-off or unusual events, 268, 269
management information, importance of, 277, 278

premium increase, impact of, 269, 270
short term v long-term management, 274, 275
written v earned, 263
organization types, 31, 32
outstanding, characteristics of, 56
strategic planning. *See* STRATEGIC PLANNING
unlimited liability, with, 32

Insurance contract
utmost good faith, principle of, 23, 24

Insurance cover
regulations, 43

Insurance industry
fashionable solutions, failure of, 290
future of, 287-290
influence on, 43-46
management, art of, 290
mission statements, 68
observations and opinions, 287-290

Insurance market
distributors, 29
domestic, 39
government, interests of, 47
intermediaries, 29
management organizations, 30
multinational, 39
players in, 27, 28
primary insurer, 28, 29
profitability cycles, 37, 38
rating agencies, 30
regulation. *See* INSURANCE REGULATION
reinsurers, 30
representation, 30
service providers, 30
worldwide, 39

Insurance pools
concept of, 20
operation of, 29

Insurance premium tax
charge of, 51

Insurance products
categories of, 109
development opportunity, 120
key elements of, 110, 111
packaging, 111

Insurance regulation
compliance, 46
compulsory insurance, 43
corporate entities, affecting, 42
Financial Services Authority, approach of, 49
influences on, 52
insurers, specific to, 42
international, 44
scope of, 42
types of, 47

Insurance service providers
nature of, 30

Insurer
primary, 28, 29

International Association of Insurance Supervisors (IAIS)
role of, 45

Internet
distribution by, 144
e-business. *See* E-BUSINESS
original technology, 236
outsourcing, effect on, 246

Investment
income, 34, 167, 177
total investment return, 267
interest rates, 37
management-
choice of investments, 223, 224
objective, 222, 223
market, 37

L

Liability
compensation culture, growth in, 11

Liability insurance
difficulty in underwriting, 119
directors and officers, 117
employers', 117
need for, 116
product, 116
professional indemnity, 116
public, 116

Life insurance
nature of, 109

Lloyd's of London
operation of, 32

Loss adjusters
role of, 204, 205

M

Marine insurance
market, 119
scope of, 118
war risks, 162
Marketing
advertising, 133, 134
brand management, 124, 125
communications, 133, 134
concept of, 122
customer relationship management, 134-136
direct, 142
market analysis, 123, 124
mix-
meaning, 130
people, 133
place, 132
price, 132
promotion, 133
proposition, 130-132
process, 122-134
purpose of, 121, 122
segmentation-
attitudinal, 128
commercial customers, 129, 130
life stage, 127, 128
personal customers, 125-129
questions, 125
real world, in, 129
socio-economic groups, 126
value, perception of, 126
techniques, adoption of, 122
Mergers and acquisitions
basic rules, 86
going wrong, factors in, 87
growth by, 85-87
Motor insurance
commoditization, 119
products, 117
Motor Insurers' Bureau
compensation scheme, 203

N

Niche players
collapse. 83
defence of position, 82

O

Outsourcing
advantages of, 247
Internet, effect of, 246
key factors, 247
meaning, 246
potential dangers of, 247
shared service organization, 247, 248
value of, 246

P

P+C insurance
challenges, 3
convergence, 5-7
exposure, 35
future of, 283
increasing challenges, 284
management focus, 285-287
outcome, certainty of, 35
overview, 2, 3
personal products, range of, 36
product, 2
scope of, 2
socio-economic drivers, 35-37
supply and demand, 4
value proposition, 3
Policy
alternative wordings, 162
contract, as, 50
deductible, meaning, 161
exclusions, 161
terms and conditions, 160-162
warranty, 161
Premium
burning cost, 166
equilibrium conditions, 23
flow, 23
gross v net, 264
increase, impact of, 269, 270
investment income, 34, 167
pricing-
book rate, 164-167
effect of, 167
investment income, consideration of, 167
process of, 162-164
pure risk, 165
written v earned, 263

Product liability
scope of, 116
Professional indemnity
scope of, 116
Profit
costs incurred, 262
definition, 261
revenue earned, 262
Property insurances
Business Interruption, 113
Commercial All Risks, 112
Commercial Combined, 113
Contractors All Risks (CAR), 113
engineering, 114
home, 114, 115
stability, 118
Standard Fire Policy and Additional Perils, 112
theft, 112
Public liability
scope of, 116

R

Rating agencies
role of, 30
Regulator
role of, 48
Reinstatement
object of, 195, 196
Reinsurance
excess of loss, 171
facultative, 170
management, 184, 185
mechanism, 169
non-traditional, 173
quota share, 171
reasons for, 169, 170
recoveries, 199
stop loss, 172
surplus, 171
traditional, 170-172
transfer of risk by, 30
treaty, 170-172
Renewal
assessment at, 159, 160
Reserves
approach to, 208
chain ladder, 212, 213
checklist, 214
claims, 210, 211
interested parties, perspectives, 208, 209
movements on, 268
poor reserving, 207
premium, 209
process, 211-215
technical, 209-211
Risk
acceptance, 157-159
assessment, 155
control surveys, 156, 157
dealing with, 16
determinable, 19
emerging, 178, 179
existence of, 15
financial loss following, 18
fortuitous, 19
homogeneity, 20
independence, 20
insurable, 18-20
interest of insured, 20
management, 233
analysis, 251
control, 252
Financial Services Authority requirements, 250
financing, 252
levels of, 253
meaning, 249
need for, 249, 250
process, 251-253
review, 252, 253
physical and moral hazards, 155, 156
protection, desire for, 16
public policy, 20
pure, 19
results of, 16
sharing, 22
small proportion, materialization of, 20, 21
top ten, 249
trading, 19
transfer, 17
uninsurable, 18
Run-off
process, 215

S

Solvency
margin, 221
ratio, 221
Strategic planning
analytical tools-
benchmarking, 63
Boston Matrix, 61, 62
scenario planning, 63, 64
stakeholder model, 65, 66
value chain analysis, 64, 65
5 Forces Model, 62, 63
business environment, analysis of, 60
emphasis, 58
failure, reasons for, 73
generic process, 77
implementation, 72
key issues, identification of, 66, 67
monitoring, 73, 74
need for, 57
objectives, development of, 67-69
options-
determining, 70-72
gap analysis, 70
generation, 71
group strategic direction, 75, 76
selection, 71, 72
organization's culture, recognizing and working with, 56
plan, functions of, 58
process, 59-77
questions, 58, 59
realistic, being, 58
scorecard, 74
SWOT analysis, 66, 67
variances, dealing with, 73, 74
Strategies
business-
aim of, 79
call centres, 95
commoditization, 94
cross-selling, 95, 96
distribution, securing, 94, 95
portfolio, 84
classification, 79
corporate-
geographical spread, 90, 91
knowledge sharing, 93
organizational, 91-93
origin, 79
portfolio, 84-90
size, 80-84
diversification, 97
organizational, 91-93
planning. *See* STRATEGIC PLANNING
portfolio-
acquisition or merger, growth by, 85-87
balance, 84
bancassurance, 88-90
design, 85
organic growth, 85
strategic alliance, growth by, 88
size-
disadvantages of, 83, 84
experience, 80
market power, 81-83
scale economies, 80, 81
Subrogation
principle of, 25

T

Taxation
insurers, areas specific to, 51
Technology
brokers, impact on, 150
challenges of, 10, 11
claims process, supporting, 200
digital communications, 144
distribution of insurance, role in, 143-145
Electronic Data Interchange, 143, 144
globalization, and, 8
information services, 225, 226
Internet, 144
threat, as, 145
value chain, impact on, 107, 108
Theft
insurance, 112
Tort
claims, 52
law of, 52

U

Underwriter
meaning, 154
Underwriting
acceptance, 157-159
adverse selection, 159
assessment, 155
criteria, 183
cycle, 176-178, 287
exposure management, 168
in-house, 154
income and profit, source of, 153
investment income, 177
limitations of, 3
management-
approach to, 175, 176
audit, 186
catastrophes, 180, 181
liability and emerging risks, 178, 179
overview, 181, 182
performance, 186
policy framework, 182-186
prerequisites, 176-181
pricing policy, 183, 184
retention and reinsurance, 184, 185
skills, 185, 186
meaning, 153
own goals, 189
philosophy, 183
physical and moral hazards, assessing, 155, 156
policy terms and conditions, 160-162
practical, rules for, 188, 189
pricing-
book rate, 164-167
effect of, 167
investment income, consideration of, 167
process of, 162-164
process of, 153
proposal, 154
renewal, assessment at, 159, 160
risk control surveys, 156, 157
survey, 183
technical function, as, 175
wheel, 188
Utmost good faith
principle of, 23, 24

V

Value chain
analysis, 100
components, 100, 101
core elements, operation of, 103, 104
diagram of, 100
drivers, 100
challenge of, 105-107
evaluation, 101
logic of maintaining, 102
management, challenges for, 102-107
meaning, 99
multiple silos, starting from, 102, 103
technology, impact of, 107, 108
theoretical construct, issues arising, 106
tool to stimulate thinking, as, 107
vertical organizational structures, 99
world-class activities, maximizing leverage of, 104

W

Warranty
meaning, 161